The Hungry Heart

The Hungry Heart

Jean R. Cane

iUniverse, Inc.
New York Lincoln Shanghai

The Hungry Heart

iUniverse books may be ordered through booksellers or by contacting:

iUniverse
2021 Pine Lake Road, Suite 100
Lincoln, NE 68512
www.iuniverse.com
1-800-Authors (1-800-288-4677)

Because of the dynamic nature of the Internet, any Web addresses
or links contained in this book may have changed
since publication and may no longer be valid.

The views expressed in this work are solely those of the author and do not necessarily reflect the views of the publisher, and the publisher hereby disclaims any responsibility for them.

ISBN: 978-0-595-41631-8 (pbk)
ISBN: 978-0-595-85979-5 (ebk)

Printed in the United States of America

"Jean Cane weaves spiritual lessons throughout the compelling story of a woman's meeting with her tigress."

—Laurel King, author: "Women of Power."

In *The Hungry Heart,* Jean Cane embarks on a woman's journey of self-discovery and discovers a gift for healing along the way. Her unique experience provides a roadmap for readers to make their own journey, and the promise of angelic assistance waiting just beyond the shadow and substance of human existence.

—*R ev. Tana Chuhay, Minister, RSI (Religious Science International)*

Contents

Part II   White Feather's Clients

Foreword

Four years ago when I was going through a painful divorce, my mother said she had heard of a woman that did healing work and that I should go see her. So I went to see her, and that was the beginning of my friendship with Jean. She is a very loving and compassionate person with a delightful sense of humor and purpose. The last seven years besides her healing works her main motive in life has been to finish, *The Hungry Heart,* so she could help more people heal their hearts and have a richer life. I congratulate her on a job well done. But her work has truly just begun, because, next she intends to start a special horse ranch and other programs so that she can help children who need healing and spiritual guidance. I've been to a few healers in my life and definitely Jean has the touch. I always feel energized and fresh bordering on ecstatic when ever Jean has done a healing session on me. Jean calls what she does a channeled healing massage and she works with her guide or guardian angel she calls, "White Feather." She is a charismatic hands on healer who works on the body as well as the spirit or aura of her clients.

After her prayers, she goes into the spirit and she can see with spirit vision what the physical body needs. She sees colors and visions as she works speaking in tongues while furiously writing down notes from "White Feather," in between her guided healing effort. When she sees appalling colors and symbols, she replaces and realigns them with premium colors and healing energy. All the while singing and praying over her clients, she is guided where to look and what to do. In short, I believe Jean becomes a conduit that the higher healing energies can manifest through. Enabling her to merge with spirit and client to do what needs to be done on the physical level, as well as the spiritual plain.

In other words, Jean has spiritual insight. She has written true stories of her experiences, as well as other people's healing. Jean's book is filled with humor, sensitivity, and deep insight into the spiritual realm. Jean feels that the baby boomers are becoming more mindful and wanting to know more about spirit, not organized religion. *The Hungry Heart,* will give them a taste of more awareness in realizing their potential within.

When I have been on Jean's table, I have had many sacred visions and spiritual sensations. Are they out-of-body experiences or waking dreams? Perhaps I am merging with the spirit world also, seeing and feeling things from an extraordinary reality, normally inaccessible because of my hectic life style. Jean does a manual override on my inner dialogue freeing my spirit, my higher self. She turns the flow way down on the negative and increases the power on the positive in my life. In *The Hungry Heart,* Jean has shared and writes about seeing White Feather's healing light.

Jean abilities have helped me quit smoking as well as change my negative energy by helping me cope with the life changes from my divorce and other health issues.

I am praying that *The Hungry Heart,* will inspire and encourage people to grow spiritually and they will have a life-changing experience from reading Jean's book. I would like to see her lecture internationally to teach others to heal their mind, body and spirit. She gives an expansion of human perception beyond the normal five senses. *The Hungry Heart,* is an in depth book of how to survive the struggles of life as a result of healing one's soul.

Mr. Bob Figueiredo

Introduction

Through the determination of Jean and her spirit guide, *The Hungry Heart,* is finally complete after seven years. It was written for the benefit of every person who has an open mind and heart. Specifically it was written for people who desire to empower their lives and the lives of others through the practice of the spiritual techniques. By expanding our consciousness into the spiritual realm we get the privilege of obtaining our desires. It's the ground work, the building of the foundation within these spiritual realms that enables all of us to achieve our best potential. The spiritual benefits obtained from this book will benefit all who practice its principles. One of the spiritual lessons in life is to bless each other. As we accomplish this, in turn we bless each individual, and eventually the entire planet on this journey we call life.

The Hungry Heart, is about my encounters with my personal angel, "White Feather." This is her book, she inspired and encouraged me every step of the way as she resolved every potential difficulty in the development of this book. She also healed my personal life in a way that I could have never figured out myself.

The Hungry Heart, will help satisfy your heart's hunger by providing answers to your questions on your own spiritual quest. Practitioners have the opportunity to develop a higher thought pattern which will enable one to obtain blessings of love, hope, faith, and miracles. Subsequently, you will begin to grow in your understanding, as you discover the higher purpose of why we are here. These are times of uncertainly when people are searching for answers and,

The Hungry Heart, will provide the reader's help to nourish their spirit and lighten their hearts. It will heal their soul. Reading *The Hungry Heart,* will warm your spirit with White Feather's teachings.

The author has channeled much of the information in this book through White Feather her spiritual guide. Her purpose is to tell us how to fill our hearts hunger by growing spiritually so that you will have a powerful, dynamic life. As you learn to rely more upon what you learned in this book, your own self-esteem will gain momentum. Your life and the lives of people within your inner circle will be blessed beyond your wildest dreams. With God, White Feather's and the angel's guidance you will be following your true life path. I pray my book helps the reader overcome the tough times of their life. Many blessings.

I had a vision to have a CD with this book. I went to Mr. Joel Andrews (harpist) and White Feather channeled music of healing for her book. It is healing music for the heart. White Feather's music should be played as you first start the reading of Chapter Seventeen for meditation and healing.

Soon you will be able to order it through my website, Angel-Ranch.org My site is pending right now but should be assessable soon.

The best way to order the CD can be found is in the back of this book; please add shipping and handling. Thank you.

Acknowledgments

I give my thanks to the people, who provided instructions and other assistance for the preparation of this book. My greatest appreciation and love goes to Laurel King who believed in me and without her dedication this book would have been next to impossible to write. Her patience and encouragement has guided me every step of the way toward its development.

I am grateful to the many other people who have encouraged me by providing tips and assistance in The Hungry Heart's preparation: Joel Andrews International harpist for his insight and my CD music, Carter Sears, attorney, for his determination to win our case. Kenneth Baumgartner DDS, for proofreading my manuscript, Sheila Ryan photographer, who took such a great shot for my back cover, and Kwiah Light Safe for his ritual on healing. Mike Tosti, my car salesmen, for his assistance in getting my car. The owners of Creative Mind Computer repaired my computer so I could complete my book.

To my many friends and clients who have encouraged, motivated and helped I get through the seven years of the preparation of this book. I will be eternally grateful for the Figueiredo family, Jose Perla, Jayne Rodgers, Dina Ederer, Norma LaFavor, Ann Fisher and Mildred Boddy. Also, Cathy Underhill, Katie Matthews for their loving support. To Michael Riccetti who helped me in doing my author cards and press release, and with using computer programs. To my clients who are still with me and those whom have found a new spiritual path. I pray that you have a life filled with love, prosperity, joy and peace. I thank you from the depth of my heart.

Among the librarians and public relations people who went out of their way to help me learn the computer and to Rob Rahlf, who was lab instructor at the Senior Center. The staff at Beckman Printing, the staff at The Café who helped to inspire and keep me going through the years.

Special thanks to the ministers, of Mendocino Religious Science Center for Spiritual Awakening, to Reverend Tanya Wyldflower and Reverend Tana Chuhay for their inspiration. Both ministers supported my dreams; they are great women in their own right.

PART I

"We are not human beings
having a spiritual experience.
We are spiritual beings
having a human experience."

—*Drunvalo Melchizedek, 1992*

"Beware of false prophets who come to you in sheep's clothing but inwardly are ravenous wolves. You will
know them by their fruit."

—*Matthew 7:15-16*

Chapter One

The Hungry Wolf

"An old road ends, a new road begins."

—Anon

Never did I realize the power of faith until I met an outstanding American Indian Maiden. After that, I realized my life can never be the same, as faith is the force that shores up my life, my spirit. When this extraordinary Native American Indian Maiden unexpectedly came into my life it was at the time of my divorce from my husband. I remember it well. How can I forget it?

As I look back it seemed like any other evening. My husband was sitting in his chair reading the newspaper and I was clearing the dinner dishes off the kitchen table. Suddenly I heard a loud growl that chilled me to the bone. The growl turned to a scream. Stunned, my hand grabbed onto the table for support. Was it coming from outside or inside? Was there a strange animal in the house? Quickly glancing around, I looked at my dog Goldie. It wasn't her because she was quietly lying by the front door. Apparently she hadn't heard the threatening growl because she hadn't moved. I was the only one who seemed to have heard that shrieking snarl, and I was still shaking.

A cold shiver ran down my spine as the growl suddenly turned to a death scream, like an animal being slaughtered. My husband was still sitting with the newspaper covering his face just as though nothing had happened. I don't know how I knew the sound was coming from my husband.

Was he playing games with me? It wouldn't be the first time. I was living with a wild wolf, I thought, and he was hungry. He was hungry for anything he could get his teeth into—my money, my body and my spirit.

I was nearly eaten alive during our eleven years of marriage. I went from being a young woman filled with enthusiasm, to a beaten, discouraged woman who refused to see what her life had become. But I could no longer refuse to see. My husband had stolen my life and everything in it and he still wanted more. I knew in my heart my Little Red Riding Hood days were over. I had to get out of there, but my feet felt as if they were nailed to the floor.

Suddenly, the growling grew louder and turned into a shrill roar. I felt if my husband lowered the paper, a wolf would be staring back at me. In my mind's eye, I could see its snarling fang-like white teeth. Gripped with terror I tried to escape, but my feet felt like they were nailed to the floor. My body started to shake and suddenly I found tears running down my cheek.

Panicked, I knew I had to get away. Somehow, and I don't know where it came from, but I got the courage to take that first step. I reached down, picking up my dog and grabbing my car keys as I lunged for the door. I flung the door open and raced toward the car, running for my very life. I pulled the door handle, but it won't open. The car was locked. Putting Goldie onto the ground, I fumbled with the cars keys, while repeatedly glancing over my shoulder. He hadn't followed me—yet. Finally I shoved the key into the door, and twisted. I could hear the door unlock. Flinging open the door, with my hand and index finger, I motioned for Goldie to jump inside. She did. Immediately I followed, locking the door.

Once barricaded inside the car I felt a little secure. But I was still in a panic, because I could feel my heart pounding against my chest. Turning the ignition, the engine kicked over with a roar. Glancing again out the window, I looked toward the porch. He was just standing there, watching me, his face twisted with shock. I quickly shifted into drive. Suddenly there he was that fast, grabbing the door handle.

"Oh my God," I heard myself screaming. Instantly I felt my foot shoving down on the petal, and a second later I was gone.

In my heart I knew my Little Red Riding Hood days were over and I had to shed that red cape. I knew I had to escape.

That night I left my home, knowing in my heart I would never return.

Later I realized that it was White Feather, my spiritual guide, who had saved my life. I could not see how close to death I was, but White Feather knew. She lifted the physical veil which allowed me to hear my husband's growl so I could no longer deny his true nature. She knew once I saw and heard the truth I would leave behind my Red Riding Hood days.

I was shaking as I drove to a dear friend's house and knocked on her front door. If I had not had her friendship and knowing that God and White Feather were listening, I would have never had the courage to leave my husband.

"Sue, I left my husband," I confessed. She put her arms around me and I went inside. There was no suitcase. I had left with the clothes on my back, my dog, and nothing else. Three days later I filed for divorce.

I was in deep shock. I was devastated looking over my past. He was a wolf all right. Anything I did was never good enough for him. He never gave me a compliment, not once, about anything. I now feel he was jealous of me and afraid if I got some self-esteem I'd leave him which thank God I did. I had thought in my head, no guts no glory. I just know I had to get out no matter what it took. One word came to me, and it's called, "courage." I was tired of living with the wolf and walking on egg shells. Sometimes he is happy and exciting, charming and pleasant, but the next moment the wolf would be like a short fuse ready to blow. No one can live like that. He had to be in control and was always seeking power over me. He wanted to isolate me and I had to get his approval on everything.

I was determined to look ahead to my future and not look back but I know my healing would take time. The past was the past. I was moving forward. Right now even though I could not see the forest for the trees and I had been taken to the cleaners, still I had to believe in faith and know I was being led to higher ground.

The divorce took a little over a year but the financial settlement dragged on for years. I put my personal belongings in storage and started looking for a place to live. In the mean time I lived with various friends, sleeping on their couches. Besides finding a place to live I had the responsibility of housing my animals. Goldie, my golden retriever, Sammy my cat, Misty Moonlight, my Quarter horse, and a parrot named Geri.

As the months passed I wondered if I'd ever find a place to live. Then a dear friend named Meredith, a woman whom I had met at church a long time ago, offered me a private apartment in her barn on her ranch in Fort Bragg, California. Meredith that was a lovely older sophisticated woman that that was always dressed impeccable. We understood each other and had a deep spiritual connection. Meredith and I became close and we really cared for each other, so she could not stand that I had no place to call home.

I lived in that barn apartment for the following three years. During that time I mourned the loss of my marriage and what I had lost while with him. Once I got away from his influence, I was able to see what had happened to me. I was waking up. Did I deserve this kind of treatment? I didn't think so. No one does. Was I sorry I left? Yes, sometimes. I had mixed emotions, but I knew I was not going back. I was emotionally drained and discouraged.

Leaving my marriage was the price I paid for my freedom; nonetheless I could no longer live a nightmare. I realized then that the wolf had a chip on his shoulder and he took it out on me. The wolf had charm but he could turn it off and on like a light switch until he got what he wanted, then he'd turn on me, because he wanted control of everything. The wolf kept his own cash for himself. He would hoard his money and forced me to spend mine. The wolf was hungry and starving to come out because of the emotional stress of money. He showed me who he really was. He probably had the first nickel he ever earned and could make that buffalo squeal. He was afraid he couldn't make money himself. He was like a wolf who wanted me to crumble under the pressure of his roar. I realized that the wolf had not built anything for us but had been extremely hungry for what I had and gobbled it up for his dinner.

I had a lot to work out with the Hungry Wolf but the opportunity to do this never happened. The Hungry Wolf hated me so much for leaving him neither one of us could discuss the painful topic of divorce.

The wolf tracked me to the ranch and at times showed up without notice. Other times I believe he watched me from a distance like I was his prey. I'm not sure he really hated me. I believe he simply hated that he could not longer control me financially and emotionally.

One day he arrived at the ranch with a new cowboy shirt and boots on. He looked puffed up as usual as he approached me. I had to admit that he looked pretty good to me and for a moment I almost forgot how angry he could get.

"How about letting me take you to dinner?" he said. I looked at him like he was crazy.

"No thanks," I said while thinking I didn't want to be the wolf's dinner. Then, I asked,

"What's been on your mind? Have you found an attorney to handle the divorce?" My ability to hide underneath the naïveté of Little Red Riding Hood has caused me years of grief, but at the time it was the best I could do. This aggravated him because he thought he was charming and smarter than anyone else.

"I don't need an attorney," he replied in a nasty tone as he stomped away. That was the end of our discussion and we went our separate ways. Little did I know the deep secrets and the webs he was weaving behind my back to trap me into his lair.

I did not know at the time that the Hungry Wolf had already consulted an attorney and managed to transfer all his debts into my name. He was slick, devious and hungry.

I should have known what the wolf was up to, but I was in a lot of emotional pain and I did not want to look for more problems. I wanted to be finished with the whole mess but it just does not happen that way. I was still looking at the world through rose colored glasses and I did not want to believe the wolf was planning to trap me once again. This naïve behavior caused a lot of misery for me as I tried to sort out my life.

During this time at the ranch, I was completely alone except for my faith. This was a healing time for me, and I began to heal from the devastating effects of my marriage. I also had time to explore my spirituality, that perfect side of my nature my husband denied. My friend, a minister for the Church of Religious Science, taught me about prayer and positive thought. I studied the lessons in order to expand my spiritual growth. Praying and meditating daily, I was trying to get through the abuse from the Hungry Wolf who continued nipping at my heels, screaming his favorite line.

"I'm going to get you good!"

He was angry and hateful and nothing had changed about him, in fact he was worse.

As time passed I began to wonder what I was going to do with the rest of my life. I knew God had a plan for me, I just didn't know what it was. I often prayed for guidance and wisdom often, but like anything else it comes in its own time. Yet I became even more nervous, impatient and even discouraged. I had been searching for the next step in my life, but I began to doubt that I would ever receive an answer. Then the answer came in a very mysterious way.

Flopping down on the bed, I started crying. Suddenly I heard a soft rustle in the far corner of my room. I stopped, holding my breath, looking around. That's when I saw three very tall, lean men standing there wearing loose flowing light brown robes with hoods draping over the front of their faces. I was surprised, not scared, as they brought calmness with them. I knew they were here to help me.

Who are these men? I thought to myself, and how did they get into my room? Curiously, I got up from my bed and walked over to take a closer look. 'Who are you?' I thought as I reached out to touch one of them. I wanted to see if they were real, solid. One of then stepped back and would not let me see beneath his hood.

Then he spoke unexpectedly. I cowered back. His spirit had read my mind.

"We are your wise men and we have been with you all your life," one man said. I was astonished, overwhelmed with amazement! I could hardly speak.

"You're my wise men?" I squawked, looking in awe, "What do you want?" I said nervously.

"Nothing," he said. Light was pouring from them.

"We are here to give you encouragement and to tell you, not to give up on life. You are needed in this world. We will be by your side. Hold onto your faith." he said.

"We are here to guide and protect you," the second wise man spoke.

I tried to look into their faces, but they would not let me see them. The third wise man spoke and added,

"Things will change for you in a good way. We are your wise angels."

I was speechless. Still I was listening very closely and my heart was beating fast. At last my angels were with me and I could see them yet still not see their faces. I stepped back and looked at them. I was rubbing my eyes to make sure they were really there. They were. I was in amazement but yet I knew the truth of the angels. My heart was being filled with love. I knew in my soul they were there for only my good and protection.

I went back to my bed. I couldn't believe what I had seen. I felt what they had said was true. I had been given a great gift of their love. I believed that their coming was a sign that I was on the right path and that something good was coming my way. I was inspired to keep going. My part was to keep moving and believe in God, the angels, and most of all myself.

I was moving forward into the light. This was good. I was happy.

Yet I was not prepared for my next visitor.

"What we are is God's gift to us. What we become is
our gift to God."

—*Author unknown*

Chapter Two

The Gift

"Dream the possible dream and then make it happen"

—White Feather

I met White Feather in a dream on December 10, 1992. It was very late in the evening. I was asleep when I heard the wind whirling around my small house, back in the alley. For long moments I lay in my bed recalling a magical dream. I had just met the most stunning Native American Indian maiden. The dream was so real and the colors so dazzling I thought I had left my body and was actually in her presence.

The Indian reservation in the dream seemed familiar to me, and as I looked at the shimmering scenery, with its green rolling knoll, it felt like I had been there before. The mountains that were immediately in front of me, reminded me of Mount Shasta in Northern, California. Only in my dream they were more exquisite and breathtaking. A deep blue lake, with the crystal clear water reflected the mountains in all their elegant grace and grandeur. Directly in front of me, I saw a Native American white Indian tepee. Beside it stood, in all her grace, a young Native American Indian maiden, wearing a white buckskin dress with beads of gold and turquoise on the front.

I intuitively knew who she was. I knew I was looking at White Feather even though I had never met her.

I realized now that White Feather was the spirit who had showed me the face of the Hungry Wolf—my ex-husband's true nature.

White Feather's hair was coal black, long, and braided down her back. Pointing to the sky at the back of her head was a white feather, trimmed in a lovely shade of turquoise, held to her forehead by a white leather band. Her eyes were brown, reminding me of a young fawn. Her skin was a golden brown. She was about five-feet-five and her slim body was elegant. Her arms were crossed on her chest and she held one golden medicine stick in each hand. They had turquoise beads, held by strips of leather dangling from them. White Feather was the most graceful, stunning creature I had ever seen and I was in awe of her. I felt no fear, rather I felt honored to be standing in her presence.

Next to the tepee, a ceremonial fire was lit within a small circle of rocks. White Feather turned suddenly, looking into my eyes for a long moment. I couldn't look away.

"Please come and stand next to me," she said with a gentle but authoritative voice.

"I am White Feather, a 'healer of the universe.' she said, and I am giving you a gift of healing through your hands." she said.

As I started to move closer, I could sense a power radiating from her, almost like a warm energy.

"I will place my white gloves that are not of earth, but of my light, upon your hands. You will have great healing power through me," she said, her gaze still locked on mine.

As she continued talking to me in her soft spoken manner she gave me her medicine sticks and placed them into each of my hands. Immediately I felt their power. It was like—they were alive! I felt privileged to be with White Feather and be receiving these precious ceremonial gifts of love and healing.

"Here is the healing power I am giving you through my medicine sticks. Do not be afraid, accept and believe," White Feather again took her golden medicine sticks and kneeling slightly, carefully placed them on an ashen rock next to her. Then she turned and without another word, briskly walked away.

I felt honored. White Feather had given me her gift of healing. The next thing I knew I was back in my room. As I awoke from the dream, I heard her speak again.

"Write down your dream," she said in a gentle voice.

Immediately I reached into the drawer of my night stand and wrote as fast as I could for fear of forgetting the dream.

I was not surprised by the dream. In fact, it seemed very natural to me. If felt like the gift I was given and my meeting with White Feather was the next step in my spiritual journey. I was discovering who I really am and as White Feather would heal me on many levels, and in return, I would learn to heal others. I was beginning a journey of self-discovery.

White Feather came to me in various ways. The first time was while I was massaging my friend on the ranch. The gift I received in my dream started to appear in my life. At the time, I was giving horseback riding lessons to adults and children in order to add to my small income. My clients paid me what they could.

One day Danielle, a small framed mature woman with blonde streaked hair came out for a riding lesson and after the lesson, she said in her small voice,

"Jean, my back hurts," she said.

Instantly I felt like I was on a higher plane and it was time for me to help her, but I did not know yet how. I placed a blanket on the grass under an old oak tree.

"Please lie down on this blanket," I said gesturing, "on your stomach,"

She knelt down slowly, probably because of the pain. I immediately bent down beside her and put the palms of both my hands on her back. From the small of her back, I could feel heat radiating right through her red sweater. As I rubbed my hands over her back, I was amazed at how the feeling felt so natural. For some reason, I also felt warm in my heart. It was a lovely feeling. Again I put my hands on her and gently started massaging her, helping her to heal. This intense feeling of love and knowing

I was helping her heal, I knew then that I wanted to continue doing massage therapy for the rest of my life.

When I finished Danielle looked at me and said,

"I had the best massage therapy in Los Angeles and you're are far superior to all of them," she said

I just looked at her in amazement!

"Why aren't you doing this for a career?" she asked, in a soft voice and I told her,

"I never seriously thought of it," I said.

Then, Danielle looked at me with her intense blue eyes and asked,

"Jean, what spirit is with us?"

It was amazing and remarkable. Apparently Danielle had also felt a spirit moving through me and was curious to learn more. I grew quiet and I asked the spirit her name, and in my heart I heard, 'White Feather, a healer.' Danielle was staring at me waiting for my answer.

"My spiritual guide,

White Feather is here," I said. In that moment, I knew my spirit guide had been born. Then, I remembered the dream I had a few months earlier when I received White Feather's gift of healing. I had begun my own healing journey with White Feather. I was in awe, but loved the idea of this new spiritual and healing adventure.

My healing hands are the most incredible gift. White Feather granted me the privileges of working with her and it's always a blessing.

"The Secret Place of the Most High is within me."

—Doctor Earnest Holmes

Chapter Three

Healing Light

*"We look for many to give us
what we can only find inside."*

—Jacob Needleman

People heard about White Feather's healing light. From all over, they began to come to the ranch for massages. The barn, where I stabled my horse, Misty Moonlight became a popular place for a healing experience. The smell of fresh hay and alfalfa and the sounds of the birds and Misty Moonlight eating her hay were extremely comforting to my clients. I could hear White Feather's voice so clearly and I knew miracles were happening of a super-human nature.

At first I questioned the gift but eventually I felt it was better to accept it than to deny it. I had nothing to lose by believing in the healing gift she gave me. As it turned out, I had no concept of the precious gift until much later. What I've seen is that everyone that has White Feather's hands on them had received some kind of gift or healing. White Feather is very powerful and loves the human soul. I've have never seen White Feather make a mistake about anything and this is truly astonishing.

Prior to meeting White Feather, it had not occurred to me to be a masseuse or a healer, but when I felt her energy move through me I knew that I couldn't do anything else.

I do not have a formal training in massage therapy, nor do I need this back-ground because of the healing gift I've received from White Feather. White Feather knows all forms of body work and she shows me what to do and what to say. She uses me to channel the gift to others.

In the late eighties I also received acupuncture treatments from a Chinese medical doctor in a town near by. Over a five year period I went every other week for treatment. I loved every treatment and I believed in the healing power of acupuncture.

White Feather and I utilized this information to balance people's energy. She incorporates this knowledge into her healing massage. Some people stay away from the needles of acupuncture, so an alternative to this acupressure, which works on strategic body points. These points are located along the meridians, which relate to the organs and body functions. Each acupuncture point is said to have a specific therapeutic effect. The goal of acupuncture and acupressure is to restore the smooth flow of energy through the body. This, too, is White Feather's goal.

To know White Feather is like riding a roller coaster full of the twists and turns in life, the ins and outs, and the ups and downs. But, White Feather holds me secure with a safety belt of love. She helps me see the humor in just about everything life throws at me. She shows me the joy, instead of the sorrow. Believe me if we don't keep our faith intact, I would have never been able to complete this book. She taught me that if I kept a smile on my face, the joy would come.

White Feather did not pass on her healing power all at once. I had to take baby steps toward developing this powerful gift. I learned to listen so I could hear her soft nurturing voice encouraging my potential within. Even though I trusted White Feather, I was often surprised by what was happening to me. Eventually I learned of the blessings for everyone who has been fortunate enough to be under her hands. She has the hands of a Native American angel, which she is.

As time passed I heard White Feather's voice with increasing clarity and the power of her gift grew stronger within me. Over the years, I witnessed many kinds of healing, several of which stand out in my memory. A woman client with a vulnerable health condition asked me to help her change her life.

She also was very lonely and wanted to meet the right mate. I told her after many healing massages that White Feather would help her only she were willing to help take action for her life.

When she came to me, she was nearly ready to give up on her destructive habits. Her problems were low self-esteem, smoking cigarettes and pot. Her addictions kept her on the lower spiritual levels.

One foggy afternoon during one of our massages White Feather told me to pass on the following information to her.

"I can see and sense some kind of dark spot under your lungs. If you don't give up all this junk you will be dead within two years," I said. She sat up, leaned back and looked at me with her piercing brown eyes. I could feel fear penetrate her soul.

"I can't keep coming to you for a fix and then go home and keep my same old patterns," she said.

"That's right. You will not get completely healed if you continue in your same old ways," I said

"That would be a shame because you are very talented," I told her.

She decided to continue coming to me until she was strong enough to quit her destructive habits. Gradually she stopped with the help of her treatments and told me her of her progress.

"It's amazing," she confessed,

"I have never felt better and I have additional energy but will I ever meet anyone?" she asked.

"You will," I said,

"If you give up these risky habits." I said.

She did. A couple of months later, in another treatment, I began to gently touch her lungs and I felt her healing had taken place.

"Your tumors are gone," White Feather just told me,

"Would you please put this into your Bible and pray for me?"

I did. A month later we ran into each other at the Fort Bragg library. She was happy to see me and she took my arm and guided me to a private corner of the room.

"I met him, I met my new boyfriend," she said, bouncing up and down with joy.

"How did you know it was him?" I asked.

A bright smile came upon her face and she looked at me with such love in her eyes.

"Jean, when he took me in his arms and kissed me for the first time I knew our love would last a lifetime," she said. She was radiant, and I was overjoyed for her.

I remembered the letter and realized that it probably had to do with her wanting a mate. Knowing White Feather had a hand in meeting her mate, a smile lit up my face as well. If this client had not done her internal spiritual work, I realized she would have never met her mate or changed her life. She was indeed very blessed.

I was more than a little surprised the first time I saw my hands dressed in White Feather's healing gloves of light. One night I went too a client's home to give her a massage and when I entered her front room her cat Snowflake got up and came toward me. She called her Snowflake because she was all black except all four paws were white like snow. When she rubbed against my leg, I knew Snowflake wanted me to touch her, so I did. Suddenly I looked over her head to see a space opening in the dark corner of the room. I was startled. The space forming was about the size of an 8" by 10" picture. Curious, I squinted and looked closer. I could see my hands were crossed, and I was wearing white gloves. I knew that the gloves were not from this earth and that they were special gloves, gloves of light, from White Feather. Again looking closer, I could see my hands were still criss-crossed, but this time I could see a line of bright white light tracing their form.

Then I heard White Feather speak to me, her voice was gentle,

"Jean, when I do healing on the table, I place my gloves of light on you. This is why you can see the healing colors and why you are able to heal through me. The healing energy illuminates the gloves," she said.

Slowly the space dissolved and darkness returned. Snowflake was still looking at me, and I knew she had received her own healing. She wanted to stay in the living room and bask in White Feather's healing energy. Her healing aura was all around the room, so feeling comfort, Snowflake decided to lie down. I could feel her peace.

Now, when ever I do a healing massage I wear White Feather's gloves of light on my hands. I trust White Feather and never have to worry about her healing ability. When I do White Feather's healing work I feel happy and safe because I always know within my heart, that the healing is perfect no matter whom I am working on.

At the same time Jenna came to the ranch for a massage and she told me,

"Jean, everything is going to hell in a hand basket, and I am sick of being sick and tired. Please help me. I need White Feather's assistance," she said.

As she lay down I saw she was very upset. She told me about a business she had invested in. She explained that she and her business partner had decided to end their business relationship but they could not come to a financial agreement that suited them both. She was in a position to lose a lot of money. As I massaged her, I heard White Feather's voice,

"Tell her the partner is going to buy her out! Not to worry. She will get her money back." she said.

When I told Jenna what White Feather had said, she cried with relief. As we walked out of the barn she gave me a hug.

A couple of weeks later she called me very excited,

"Everything you said came true. My partner is buying me out. Thank you for seeing this for me and knowing things would work out. I have never been so relieved in my life." she said with a big smile on her face.

One of the most dramatic healings done by White Feather was on a client named Carol. This healing was truly dramatic, but there is one I'll tell you about later, that was an absolute miracle. Carol was a mature woman, while I was massaging Carol, White Feather showed me a dark sticky tar between her breasts. In fact, my hands actually stuck on her chest.

"Carol, I see something dark between your breasts," I told her. "Do not worry. White Feather can heal this if you have the faith to believe that you can be healed?" I said.

A week later her doctor called and asked to see her. He was going to take X-rays and start treatment. He did not know exactly what the health problem was, so he wanted to run more tests.

Carol called me to make another appointment with me. When she came in her face looked very pale and I could tell she was upset. She told me the doctor had told her she had Valley Fever and there was not much he could do about this. I consulted with White Feather regarding Carol's situation. White Feather had asked that she come in for treatments every week for five weeks.

"Are you up to it? Do you have the faith to believe that you can be healed?" I asked her,

"Yes, Jean. I do believe through our own faith and White Feather's healing light I can be healed," she said.

I suggested she come back for more treatments and pray about this.

Carol called to make another appointment with me.

"Carol, through your great faith and White Feather's healing hands of light, you are well,"

She gave me such a loving smile. When she saw her doctor he could tell she felt better although he could not understand what happened. A few weeks later Carol came back in for another healing massage.

"Jean, the doctor found my Valley Fever has returned," she told me.

I took hold of her shoulders with great intensity, and said.

"Carol, when God or White Feather heals a disease, it should not come back. You just got off the table and I did not see anything. Do not tell me you're not well," I continued,

"I have the faith to believe there is nothing wrong with you at this time. You are well. Do not put any negative vibrations on our work together with White Feather." I gave her a hug and she left. A week later Carol decided to came in for another healing massage.

"Jean, the doctor read the wrong X-ray on my lungs," she said.

I looked at her in disbelief.

"White Feather is a great healer and when she said you are well, and believe it because it's true. It was a miracle from God and White Feather has the power of healing," and I continued,

"But you have to maintain the healing light in your body," I said.

To this day Carol has been in remission while she was coming to me. I just heard from one of my former clients that Carol health has changed. She has not been in to see me for years. Things can change in our lives to alter our health. It is up to you.

When my boyfriend left me in 2000 for the millionth time I was heart-broken and miserable. I, crawled into bed to nurse my wounds, when I heard White Feather's voice,

"Why are you on the bed and not on my healing table?" she said.

I cleared off my massage table, climbed on, and lay down on my back. When I looked up I saw a bucket suspended in mid-air with gold and green light pouring down onto my head. I knew I was receiving a tremendous healing. Gold and green are colors for emotional healing of the heart. I lay on the table soaking up the light like a sponge. Then I closed my eyes and went to sleep. The angels came to me while I slept and told me,

"Your heart will mend in time. Please don't rush your healing!" she said. I awakened feeling calm for the first time in months. I had slept almost two hours, which surprised me because prior to this my heart had been racing and I had been unable to sleep. I felt that my soul was once again graced with protection, the same protection that had been with me all my life. I felt like I would survive this ordeal and I did.

"He who knows much about others may be learned
but he who understands himself is more intelligent
He who controls others may be powerful, but he
who masters himself, is mightier still."

—Lao-Tzu

Chapter Four

Little Red Riding Hood and the Wolf

"When the heart weeps for what it has lost the spirit laughs for what is has found."

—Sufi Aphorism

I became more aware of my gift from White Feather after leaving my husband. The healing gift and leaving him seemed to come all at once. I believe this is because White Feather was waiting for me to rid myself of the wolf's negative energy.

Even though I left the wolf, he continued to come after me with fierce unyielding energy. At first he was determined to get me back, but instead of courting me with some kindness he used an arrogant, "I'm entitled to you," attitude. His attitude and the memory of the Hungry Wolf's growl did nothing to warm me up to him.

I did everything I could to stay away from him. When I was forced to be in the same place with him I made it clear to him that I was not interested in returning to wherever he thought he could house us. When he finally understood that I was not coming back to him, he then came after me financially.

The first thing he did was signing a quick claim deed and put our house in my name only. I wondered why he signed it so easy but later I found out the wolf could never do anything unless it was for him. He then refused to pay his share of the payments, which sent the house into foreclosure. I thought he was going to do something good for a change, but I quickly saw the deviousness behind his deed. He then hired a sharp attorney who made a case for half of my property and said that I owed him spousal support, not the other way around.

The divorce was a disaster and it dragged on for over a year. Neither the attorney nor Little Red Riding Hood was a match for the wolf. Help was needed or I knew I'd be in trouble. To defend my rights and my property I hired a toothless old wolf as my attorney. I did not realize that he was toothless until I came in one day to see him, but I knew when he smiled. To make matters worse, he was apparently senile because he did not remember who I was, even after I told him. He looked at me like,

"Who are you?"

This guy must have been over eighty, and he had long forgotten how to defend his client.

I was too naive to realize what was going on, but quickly discovered he was unable to battle with the Wolf. At the time, I was also very scared and did not know what to do. The old wolf let the predator wolf take everything I had. I had already paid the attorney all my savings so I had nothing left to hire another one. I lost my house and property plus our debts and his business arrears were put in my name. I was in such a state of shock I did not realize what was happening to me, so I was easy prey to the wolf.

The wolf had dragged me into his den and ate his fill.

I was really angry. In my frustration I asked White Feather why she did not warn me that my attorney was a useless old attorney who would take my money and leave me open to more abuse from the wolf.

"I saved your life," White Feather answered. "I don't watch everything you do. Some of this is your life's lesson," she continued,

"If after being eaten alive by the Hungry Wolf, you could not see with your own eyes that this man was a toothless old wolf what do you expect me to do?" If I had shown you this, you wouldn't have gotten the lesson you needed, which is boldly go out and trust again. You had something to learn in this, you needed to become stronger in your character not whimper around like a little girl. It's time to let Little Red Riding Hood grow up and become a strong woman. It's time to wake up and see the wolf behind grandma's hood.

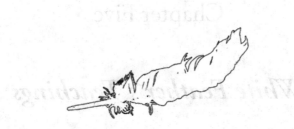

"To live is to sleep to die is to awaken."

—Author Unknown

Chapter Five

White Feather's Teachings

Metaphysical teachers tell you,
"Grace is one wing of the bird; your effort is the other wing."

One summer afternoon, I was sitting at my desk pondering what to write next when White Feather arrived and began singing a show tune from *The King and I*. "Getting to know you, getting to know all about you," she crooned.

I was about to ask her what she was up to when she stopped singing.

"Tell your readers about us, our relationship, and our deep friendship," she said.

I responded with an, "Okay," while thinking this is easier said than done.

Trying to describe a spiritual experience or a relationship with a spiritual being is a challenge. Lynn Andrews, author of *Medicine Woman*, said in an interview that our culture does not have the words to describe a spiritual experience, so we sometimes have to write a story around it.

A few years ago White Feather very softly mentioned to me,

"Jean, you're going to write a book about our work,"

"Oh, sure, White Feather I'll just go out and write a best seller. There's nothing to it," I responded sarcastically. Are you serious? I thought. I knew that she couldn't be serious. After all, she knew I did not have any writing experience and I thought she had forgotten about it.

I tried to push the thought of writing way out of my mind because it was too impossible for me to think about it. Then, one of my clients took a creative writing class, at a college and when White Feather heard this she said,

"Jean, when are you going to start my book? I want you to attend this class,"

"You want me to what?" I squawked.

She kept at me about this, not like my mother, but as a good friend, nudging me gently. White Feather would absolutely not give up until I signed at the College of the Redwoods. This was the start of my first writing adventure. I prayed that maybe there was some talent buried in my heart in this area but I doubted my ability to channel anything. Gradually I discovered that I had the ability to tell a good story, so I began to write the way I talk. I also learned that I didn't have to write alone. White Feather had become my co-author.

White Feather is a mystery to me; I never know when she will come for a visit. I can be in my car or in my bathtub, dreaming or even riding my bike when she just pops up with "Here I am. Aren't you a lucky woman?"

One night, I was watching television when I heard White Feather say,

"Turn that noise off. I can't hear myself think."

I jumped out of bed in shock and turned off the television set. When I realized it was White Feather, I went back to my bed and sat down eagerly waiting her instructions.

"Jean, you are writing your angel chapter tonight," she said.

"What?" I said. White Feather had never done this before. I felt in my soul I was going to receive valuable information from White Feather. I wanted to be open to the flow of energy from Heaven.

I wrote for four solid hours. Paper was strewn all over my bedroom. It looked like a paper mill and I was the only human working. I kept writing and writing. Words were flowing out of me like water off a duck's back. I wanted to record every drop of water that contained her words.

"You did a great job and followed my instructions correctly," White Feather said unexpectedly. In the next instant, she was gone. I was wondering what White Feather was going to show me next.

"Outside the open window the morning
air is all awash with angels."

—Richard Wilburn

Chapter Six

Angel Watching Over Me

"For he will give his angels charge
of you to guard you in all your ways.
On their hands they will bear you up,
lest you dash your foot against a stone."

—Psalms 91

White Feather always watched over my shoulder. She was with me when I grieved the loss of my parents. I remember the first time I heard the word divorce. My parent's terrible fights, their voices grew louder and they used that "D," word. Then, when they separated I knew what divorce meant. That was a very painful period for a young ten year old spirit to deal with. I was the one who would suffer most as I grew older because I had lost everything and nothing would ever be the same. It was an almost unbearable loss and heartache I felt as a young child. It was especially difficult since my grandmother lived in another town and we loved each other dearly. I was her only granddaughter. I would need courage beyond my years to get over the loss of leaving my grandmother whom I loved so deeply.

Even though I suffered and was in grief of my family's separation, I became a happy-go-lucky spirit. I always loved animals and wanted to be around them, all the time. I had a special love for horses and dogs, and later cats. I feel today that this was the healing spirit of White Feather coming out in my nature. I also think that White Feather had something to do with the development of my sense of humor and my gusty attitude toward life.

When I was a child my grandmother, told me,

"A sense of humor comes from the angels," and I never forgot that because it comforted me.

I believe this to be true, because humor is a healing tool of the spirit. I use her wisdom and it always lifted my spirit.

As I adjusted to my new life it was not as terrible as I first thought. I met new friends and even had a horse to ride. Sometimes I would feel I had an angel walking beside me along my path and she was protecting, guiding me, along the way.

For some unknown reason these true protection stories started to flood through my mind and I wanted to share them so people would realize we do have powerful angels around us who protect us from all kinds of situations. I feel these true stories were healing my heart. Here they are from a scary trail ride to a tender teenager's tale.

As I look back through the years there are many, many times that White Feather had protected me and looked over my shoulder. One of the most important times was when I took a trail ride and almost got lost. I have ridden many years and was never hurt. I know it was because of White Feather. These stories are important because it shows that angels love us and watch us everywhere we go.

I loved my horse Misty Moonlight because she was always there for me and we had a deep connection. I remember the first time I saw Misty Moonlight in Novato, California when I was visiting my dad. I saw an ad in the local newspaper for horses for sale. I decided to go out to the ranch and see them. The man who owned the ranch brought out Misty Moonlight. She strutted out and looked me right in the eyes, and it was as if I was looking into her heart. She was a bloody bay with four black legs and a flash of white down her face. She was Half Quarter and Thoroughbred, and very lovely and intelligent. I bought her on the spot and I was never sorry. We were the perfect match. She was so wonderful and always willing to do whatever I asked. She was with me seventeen years. Misty Moonlight has been gone a long time now but in my heart it feels just like yesterday. This is the way I commit to memory this dangerous ride I had.

One sunny warm afternoon my mare, Misty Moonlight, and I were going to take a trail ride. It's always invigorating to hear the sound of Misty Moonlight's hooves hitting the ground, the smell of the outdoors and the feel of the saddle under my butt. To me, it's how nature heals my soul.

As I was I was saddling her, I wondered what adventure we could have today. I gently climbed on her back and started out of the ranch that was her home. As I was riding down the road I saw a trail where I had never been on before. I headed in that direction, but I suddenly realized that one trail led into another. This was a forest-like setting and I was a little concerned because there were no landmarks in case we got lost. The trail zigged and jagged and we wandered further than we had ever gone.

On this particular trail ride there were a lot of trees on both sides of the trail. I was taking in the grandeur of the ride when suddenly with a jerk I was brought me back to my senses. Misty Moonlight was walking slowly, cautiously. This usually meant trouble ahead of some kind. I was riding toward a clearing and I looked around carefully. I noticed the fence on the left side of the trail came to an abrupt end. As I rode around the corner, Misty Moonlight's ears shifted forward, which told me that she was looking at something strange and that usually meant trouble. Her hooves were fastened to the ground and her ears were saying, 'Take a look on top of the hill. I'll protect you.'

I rose up in the saddle and before my eye was the biggest humpback camel I had ever seen!

Slowly I lowered back down in the saddle. Now I knew what was brothering Misty Moonlight. I feared that she or the camel would charge. My heart felt as if it was going to jump out of my body. I was scared. Misty Moonlight did not like this huge smelly animal that she had smelled two miles away. I prayed to White Feather for courage and guidance. I gently pulled back on the reins and had Misty Moonlight turn her head away from the camel and head toward home.

Being scared, I wasn't thinking clearly and I didn't know where we were. All I knew was that home was about two miles away. Misty Moonlight had now broken into a gallop when the fork in the road loomed up ahead of us. I couldn't think clearly, which way, but then I thought I heard White Feather whisper to loosen up on the rein and let Misty Moonlight find her own way home. I slackened the reins and she galloped as if she knew exactly where she was heading.

After that, we made it home in a flash. I was praying the camel did not chase after us and it didn't. It just stood on the hill watching us leave. I got off my horse and tied her to the hitching post and ran toward my trainer screaming,

"Judy, Judy, Misty Moonlight and I saw a camel on the trail," I said.

She looked concerned,

"Jean, the camel has been there for years. Thank God you are safe. Others have been hurt when their horses have been startled by him," she said.

I think the reason Judy did not warn me about the camel was because she never thought I'd take a trail ride that far out in the forest. I had always ridden just around her ranch.

As I led my horse into her stall for the night I thanked White Feather for always being there when I needed her most. She definitely was looking over my shoulder that day.

Sometimes knowing White Feather can be like having a direct line to the spirit world. I'll think of something I want or need and she'll be right there. Sometime she shows up when I don't even know I need her. Then, other times, I'll want to talk to her and she's no where to be found. I don't worry about this because she knows when I really need her and she lands right on my shoulder with her love and protection. White Feather always cared for me.

One of my fondest memories was when I was a sophomore in high school. I was struggling to fit in that year, but failing miserably. One day in gym class I went to take a shower and the 'popular girls' decided to play a trick on me. Three girls came up behind me and pushed me into the shower with my clothes on, while they stood there laughing at me.

My temper flared and I lost control. I grabbed one of them and pushed her into the shower and held her up to the shower head. I screamed,

"Is this funny to you? It's not funny to me, how do you like it? Does this feel good to you?" In shock she just hung there like a wet noodle, as the other girls ran off. I finally released her and went looking for a towel to dry myself.

Class was due to start in two minutes. My clothes were stuck to my youthful frame like glue. I looked like a plucked chicken. My makeup was off, and my hair was flat against my head. I felt like running away, but an idea came to me. I thought I am going to walk into English class like I own the place.

It was late when I stepped through the door of the classroom. The kids looked at me and laughed. The teacher gave me a stern look and a slight smile crossed his face.

"Come in, you're late," he said in an irate voice.

"I was so late I didn't take my clothes off to shower!" I said trying to smile.

The whole class kept laughing out of control. I was so embarrassed; I could feel my face turning beet red. When I sat down I noticed one of the most handsome boys in school sitting in the next chair. He had a quizzical smile on his face. As he looked at me a small puddle formed under my chair.

"Did you bring a mop?" he said. He came up to me after class with a mischievous smile on his face,

"May I carry your books to your next class?" he asked.

We became a couple and after that day, my struggle with fitting in is over. I can see now, that White Feather's humor and protection was with me that day, and that she turned the whole situation around for me.

Recently, I asked White Feather why she waited so long to reveal herself to me,

"Because you wouldn't have understood, back then," she said.

"I knew you were with me as a child, so why didn't you let me see you?" I asked.

"You weren't mature enough. I would have scared you," she said.

I think she was right. I would not even know what a spirit guide was. It would have been strange, early on, for me to accept a Native American spirit as a spiritual guide. I hadn't been exposed to much spiritual information. Today, spirituality is more in the open. People who have any knowledge of spirituality understand the definition of a spirit guide. This atmosphere made it easier for me to accept that I, too, had a spirit guide working with me.

There is no doubt in my heart that angels protect us from harm and evil and we are never alone. Nothing will make you feel more secure in your heart and drive away negative feelings then knowing our angels look over our shoulders.

Our guardian angel puts a protection shield around us. The angels protect and talk to us through our gut instinct everyday of our life. It's up to us to listen and react in the right way and then take the action that we received from our guardian angel. When we take the right action we will be happier. When the angel talk to us through our gut level, do not try to change what you hear because the angels are not contacting us for nothing. It is always important, so pay attention and follow through with their guidance.

One summer day while I was driving in my car I saw this on the back of a bumper a sticker; *'the bigger the risk, the deeper the trust, the louder the prayer, the more angels show off.'* I mentally wrote it down. That is a reminder our angels are truly flying around us and do land on our shoulders.

That put a big smile on my face for the rest of the day.

"The journey of a thousands miles begins with a first step."

—Ta-Tzu-Te-Ching

Chapter Seven

White Feathers Waltz

"If Thou standeth beside me nothing can prevail against me."

—Howard Thurman

I appreciate White Feather's patience as she waited for me to accept her new ideas. She gradually brought me into our spiritual relationship by giving me baby-steps to follow.

The first step White Feather asked of me was to simply get used to her being with me, and to simply acknowledge her presence. Even today, I can be in my car or bathtub, riding my bike, or even sleeping when she just pops up with a,

"Here I am. Aren't you a blessed woman?" Overtime, I was able to do this. Having her with me became second nature. When White Feather visits me, I feel her presence, just as if she was a person walking into the room, but it's not an everyday thing to have a spirit become a part of one's life. It took awhile for me to get attuned to her arrival and departure. I knew that when I gave a healing massage she was always present, but other times, when I'd be alone, I never knew when White Feather will come for a visit. That always brightens up my day.

Fortunately one night, while I was relaxing in a warm bubble bath she dropped in on me and began chanting. I felt the warm water envelope me and I closed my eyes to listen to her comforting voice. She continued chanting for a while and then she said,

"Jean, be at peace within. You're moving down your spiritual path faster than you think. It's important to remember to listen to your heart at all times, but especially when you meet the big lumps and bumps of life." she said. Pondering what she said to me, and just about the time I was understanding what she was telling me, I heard a deep chuckle, followed by,

"Jean, it's time to lighten up and enjoy these bubbles.

"Splash, splash, I was taking a bath and a Native American spirit sang an old country song to your heart," she said.

Then, as quietly as she came, she was gone. I stayed in my tub a little longer and closed my eyes again and I said to myself,

"You have the most blessed experiences."

Then, one morning White Feather showed up in my dream, I was praying for my life to straighten out. I was dancing around the pearly gates asking God and my angels to help me get my rent paid.

"Jean, do you know who you are praying to?" she asked.

I was very surprised to see her in my dream.

"Yes, White Feather. I am praying to God and his angels," I said.

She questioned,

"Why are you not making your prayer a little larger?"

"What do you mean?" I asked.

"Then, why don't you make your prayer bigger?" she said.

I didn't know what she meant.

"I mean you are asking for puny things. Why not enlarge your thoughts to ask for more?

She continued,

God made Heaven and the universe, so he can certainly give you more. What's this rent thing? God can give you a house by the ocean. It's his pleasure to do so," she explained.

I was taken back. 'Ask for more?' I thought. I believed I should ask for just enough to cover my bills and I thought it selfish to ask for extra. White Feather did not agree with this perspective.

"Jean, selfish, smell fish, where do you get your ideas? That will get you no where. When you ask for so little you stay in your own little puny world consumed with your little bitty thoughts. Expand your thoughts, expand your prayers, expand your world," she said as she continued,

"God made Heaven and earth; she repeated. In other words, you're talking to the big boys and girls, now, the spirits in Heaven. Make your prayers bold. You have their attention now, so don't waste it with little trivial things." she said.

Then, this remarkable thing happened. White Feather showed me what I believe were the *Keys to Heaven.* They were unbelievably breathtaking. Angels were holding three keys above me as they gleamed brightly in the sky. The keys were made out of stars and the stars had names and colors. Shiny pink was for love, pure white, for hope and shimmering silver, for faith. The angels held the bright and gleaming stars about me. I just stared at the keys.

"White Feather, this is an incredible vision I am having," I said.

"Yes," she responded.

"I'm showing you the keys so you'll remember that all you have to do is ask for more and believe and then, just wait for the miracle," she said.

I didn't know what to say. I knew what I had seen and what I had heard, but to really believe I could ask for more than I needed, this overwhelmed my emotions and spirit.

White Feather continued,

"Jean, ask and you shall receive. Knock and the doors to Heaven will open and God will pour in more blessings than you ever imagined but you have to have faith to believe it first," she repeated.

I remembered my favorite Bible verse. *"Faith is the assurance of things hoped for and the conviction of things unseen."* From Hebrew 11:01.

I felt the truth and power of the information White Feather gave me and this frightened me. I did not know if I was ready for her complete work. I felt that if I really believed what she said, my whole life would change and I would have to put angel power beneath my wings. Despite my fears, I prayed as White Feather suggested. I asked for love. I prayed for happiness, prosperity, joy and the right guidance for my life. I thought of Psalms Twenty-Three from the Bible; *The Lord is My Shepherd, I shall not want.* I felt the answers were coming and they were coming fast. I knew I needed to be ready, to receive them.

White Feather came to me once again,

"Jean, this is a powerful prayer. Now look for the silver lining and for your prayer to materialize in your life. Do not doubt your prayers.

She continued,

Your prayers will help many people on the planet, including yourself. I love you and I know you will fulfill your dreams with my help of course," she added.

Once again she was singing,

"You have to give a little, and love a bunch and your hungry heart will be filled with love, passion and purpose," she said. Then, she was gone.

Wow! I thought here is the title for her book. What a great title, only White Feather could have thought of this catchy name.

When White Feather sings I knew she always has a gentle smile on her face. When she was finished she leaves. Again, I prayed, this time I prayed boldly with the conviction that I prayed for would come true. As a result, I felt more at peace about my life than I had in a long time. I stopped worrying about the money and a few days later I received a bonus from a client of mine which more than paid for my rent. I was so appreciative. Then, I nearly fell off my bed when I opened my ex-husband's Christmas card and two alimony checks were inside! When this happened, I knew for sure my prayer was heard and answered. I always gave my thanks.

Overtime, my trust in White Feather strengthened and as she requested, I adopted to her coming and going in my life. I grew to know that White Feather is here for me in every way. She gives and never takes, which I had to get adjusted too, because most people want something from you.

Initially, I had my doubts about her, but she always comes through with amazing special gifts. No matter what the situation, White Feather gives her finest and has never let me down. She's never failed to show up; in fact it's the other way around. I think sometimes I let her down by not completing her spiritual work.

When White Feather knew I was comfortable with her she moved our relationship to the next step. In the second step, she asked of me to trust her even more deeply. She asked me to let her join with my spirit, not take me over, but join with me. She knew I'd had to think about this. White Feather didn't ask this of me again until I was ready and until I knew in my heart that I was ready. She was already channeling her healing energy through me during a healing massage, and I was feeling more comfortable with her being in my life.

When I was ready, it happened naturally. When I was searching for the words to describe this experience, I didn't know where to start, went over to my couch, lay down and closed my eyes I took a deep breath and consciously thought about how I feel when listening to White Feather's voice. When doing this I can feel her healing energy around me. Oh, I thought of all the times I have seen her help others. In focusing my thought on this spiritual level soon I felt the love, joy and power moving in my spirit. A deep calmness and awareness come over me. I felt enlightened. White Feather had given me this gift to share with humans that needed healing.

My senses heightened and I felt White Feather's gentle warm loving spirit enter my soul. I received a warm toasty glow that was filled with electric healing energy. Her healing energy is pure white and compelling, yet at the same time gentle and loving. 'That's what it's like,' I thought as I experienced this event. This was the blending of two spirits, yet it still left me with my own consciousness and a sense of self.

However, I'm aware of her energy moving through me as she channels her energy into me. In a way, I am a conduit for her energy. We are one in spirit. I had to clear my mind and trust her completely. My whole body had been touched and I am enraptured by White Feather's love of the human spirit. I feel this why she gave me her gift of healing, so that I can put myself on her spiritual level. White Feather has also asked me to have more faith in her.

This was a large step because when this occurs, White Feather takes over my mind, body and spirit and this takes complete trust in each other. White Feather didn't ask this of me again until I was ready and until I knew in my heart that I would trust her with my life. I know I already trusted her, but this was complete trust.

After I mastered the first two steps, she gave me a third step which was a spiritual step perhaps more of a challenge than the other two. White Feather asked me to grow beyond seeing her as a spiritual guide and teacher, to seeing her as a spiritual friend and co-creator of our experiences. White Feather is not only the best spirit that I know; she is the greatest friend I've ever had. She always knows the exact time to tell me to 'Hold them, fold them, and let them go.' White Feather gives me her entire love and essence of her heart. I just had to learn to accept, trust and believe in our work together. I never felt that, I was completely worthy. Now, I totally believe she is with me and is guiding my every step of the way.

White Feather taught me that when you change the way you look at things, the things you look at change.

"Beware of false prophets who come to you in sheep's clothing but inwardly are ravenous wolves. You will know them by their fruits."

—*Matthew 7:15-16*

Chapter Eight

Dr. Jekyll and Mr. Hyde

*"We either make ourselves miserable, or
we make ourselves strong. The amount
of work is the same."*

—Carlos Castaneda

My Mother never really liked the wolf.

One week-end my Mother and I were visiting the wolf at his place in Sonora, California. My mother saw though the wolf's charm and saw how self-serving the wolf was. Everything was about him and for him. The wolf and I planned to marry, so I planned to give up my position at Doctor's Hospital, gave up my friends and everything to be with him. My mother did not approve of this. She could see the writing on the wall.

"I'd give this some serious thought if I were you," she said.

"He's not exactly who he says he is. He makes himself out to be more than he is." she said in and anxious voice.

My mother knew he could be charming and she knew that is what I fell for. This made me mad because I did not believe what she said. My Mother and I were never close, so I did not take her too seriously. I think my Mother's caution about this situation was right but I did not know this at the time. My eyes were covered and I saw only what I wanted to see, a man who I was in love with. I thought he was my Prince Charming and I was tired of kissing frogs.

The Hungry Wolf won my heart when he planned a special trip to Monterey, California where he arranged for us to be married at the Highlands Inn. I was swept away and pulled into his lair. I left the wolf because he was verbally abusive and had started pushing me around. A couple of times he had thrown me down on the ground and when I looked up at him from the ground he looked angrily at me with no remorse. When I heard the wolf that horrible night I knew I had to leave. Our marriage had lasted eleven years and later he spit me out with passions and finances depleted. Everything I had disappeared as if by magic but I knew it was not magic, it was the cunning wolf.

White Feather didn't think much of the Hungry Wolf either. One time I asked her what she thought.

"Jean, the wolf is capable of anything. He has negative vibrations around him. You were bumping along a very destructive path. My communication with you would not have developed fully. The negative vibrations around you would have destroyed your ability to listen and to write and this would have kept me from giving you the total gift of healing. This is your true spiritual path," she said.

I was disturbed for a moment but then it hit me like a led balloon. White Feather tells me just what she wants me to know when she wants me to know it. I laughed when I thought about this. This sounded more like a human relationship than a spiritual one. White Feather has her own ways and she has reasons for everything she does. If she felt the wolf was a negative influence, then most likely he was. She was never wrong and I trusted her because I could feel his anger and hatred. This really scared me.

White Feather and I dealt with the Hungry Wolf for a long time. She knew when I married him and when I left him. She also knew I was in a fight to the death with the wolf and that it was my desire to hide in my own delusions, even though it was going to kill me. At first he was determined to get me back, but instead of courting me with kind words, he was once more hungry and after me with his fierce unyielding energy. White Feather never trusted the wolf but, unlike my mother, White Feather kept her opinions to herself. She did however save me that night from the wolf.

Little Red Riding Hood did not want to see the face of the wolf, but White Feather knew it was time for me to face the cold hard truth. So she lifted the veil of my denial just long enough and allowed me to hear that hungry scream the night I left him. But, White Feather knew the battle with the wolf was far from over. Even though I had run for my life away from the jaws of the Hungry Wolf, I continued to encounter him.

The wolf hated to part with money. Once the Hungry Wolf knew I was not coming back, his thoughts turned to money and revenge. The wolf was always in him, but the wolf was hungry and starving to come out because of the emotional stress of money. He showed me who he really was. He began to focus on how much money he spent on me and how much money he was going to get from me.

Once I thwarted his advances, the conversation again turned to money. He insisted on meeting me at local restaurant for coffee before he would give me my alimony check. During one of our meetings at the restaurant he sat staring at me with an angry hateful look on his face. He sat there staring me straight in the face and told me,

"I have spent a fortune on you and I am tired of it," he shouted.

"I want you to go to work. You have been on the gravy train far too long," he yelled.

"That's it," I said.

I could feel people's eyes staring at me as a hush fell over the restaurant.

"The Realtor, Karen, told me that you were going to marry John," he continued,

I was stunned.

"No! He was helping me with a project, but we were never an item," I said.

"Don't lie to me," he shouted.

I looked around in embarrassment.

"This is no place to be discussing these matters. I'm leaving," I said.

In the next instant as we were getting up to leave, he moved closer to me and whispered in my ear so no one else could hear.

"You could be found in an alley with your throat slit," The wolf hissed at me.

I could not move or say a word for a second. I wondered if I had heard him right but I know I had. It's just that I could not believe he had just threatened my life. I knew then that I had been told in divine timing to get out of this marriage and if I had not maybe I would not be here. You never know when the wolf could flip and go too far and I could have been found in an alley dead. Shivers flew up my spine and at that very moment I knew in my heart this wolf was evil and had more devious thoughts in his mind then I had realized. Now he was acting out his feelings on me and trying to punish me like I deserved this kind of treatment.

My face felt white as snow as I pushed back my chair and nearly ran from the restaurant with him hot on my heels. He was becoming nastier and nastier. Thanks to White Feather I had heard her voice and was saved.

Once outside, he started yelling at me,

"I've spent one hundred thousand dollars on you," he screamed.

I turned and could see people from the restaurant staring at us. They probably thought he was going to hit me. I'd had it. I jumped in my car, rolled up the windows and drove away. I was never going to agree to meet him again so I could get my alimony check. In reality it was my money anyway. I was just trying to recoup what he took from me. When we married I owned a house which was nearly paid off. I had a nice car and money in the bank. I was enrolled in the nursing program at college. My future looked promising.

During the marriage we decided to sell my house in Modesto, California that I had before this marriage and purchase a house in Mendocino, California. A lot of my money went into purchasing that house so now I was without any funds. The wolf had eaten my money and my spirit leaving me high and dry. Devastated by it all, I'd find myself walking around in a state of shock.

After the divorce I was in no condition to get a job right a way. I needed time to recoup. Even so, I tried to get work, but it had been too many years and my work history was all in Modesto, California. I also realized that if I had gotten a job it wouldn't have been enough for the ravenous wolf. No matter what I did, it was never good enough for him. I was not trying to please him anymore, I was becoming much stronger by shedding that weak skin, and I was determined to not be a victim any more.

"It is by spending oneself that one becomes rich."

—Sarah Bernhardt

Chapter Nine

Charles

"The really valuable thing is your imagination."

—Albert Einstein

I was having coffee at a local coffee house when I noticed a tall, lean man with blond salt and pepper ponytail sitting next to me. He turned around and our eyes connected. We gave each other the once over.

"Will you join me for a cup of coffee?" he asked.

"Yes," I responded as I brought my coffee over to his table, as his dark brown eyes remaining locked on mine. He raised his hand palm up, gesturing for me to sit opposite him. Still smiling, I slide onto the red leather booth and we immediately introduced ourselves.

We started talking about different subjects. I told him,

"I was a License Vocational nurse and an assistant, at Doctors Hospital in Modesto, California and I enjoyed the work because you never knew what was going to happen. The work is exciting but yet serious and it could be a matter of life or death. I worked in the orthopedic ward and we took care of a lot of accident cases.

"I'm half Pomo Indian and half white. I did a lot of work for the Native American community here in Fort Bragg, California but I work in different communities, some of which are not for the public.

I liked him; he had such intense and wonderful eyes. I'm glad he felt comfortable with me right from the start, but he was a little coy, but also a little sly, so I decided to nickname him Coyote. We decided to meet for coffee again. We did this for several months. One day at coffee I said,

"Charles, I'd like to know more about the Indian magic." His lips upturned, he was displaying a coy smile.

"I'll give you lessons on the animal totems," he said finally.

I liked this idea. I knew that he was offering to teach me about the spirit or essence of the animals. Instead of the coffee shop, we agreed to meet at the ranch the next time. Sometimes we met there and other times I met him at his apartment, which was strictly for teaching.

Charles went into great detail about each animal. For example, he told me that I was about to experience a change of consciousness and it could involve walking inside the Great Mystery on another brighter path.

"What does that mean?" I asked.

"It could be a sign of the Raven that says you have earned the right to see and experience more of life's magic. The Raven's color is the dark color of the void—or the road of the spiritual or nonphysical. Its dark blue-black defines the magic of darkness, and that helps bring an awakening," he said.

This was starting to sound fascinating. "Is there anything it does on more of a, ah, practical level?" I asked.

He continued,

"Yes he said with a serious intense look. The Raven is a sacred bird and guides the magic of healing. It guides a change in consciousness that will bring a new reality and dispel disease. Also when you see a raven you can expect to receive an important message of some kind or have an important experience." he said.

I could never forget what he said about that scared bird. One day I was at home waiting for a special phone call. It hadn't come so I went to a movie. After the movie I was sitting in my car when I saw a raven sitting on top of the movie billboard. We stared right at each other eyes for one second. Then, this large raven flew right at my car window. I knew that he was bringing me a message of the highest level. In that darkness of the void the raven was bringing me a message. Something magical was going to happen.

When I got home the telephone rang and it was the person I'd been waiting for to call me. It was more than just a phone call. I received information of great value to me on a personal level. I thanked the raven I saw that day. The raven brings messages of good news. In a sense, it is a healer in its own right.

At one point I had four ravens hanging out around my house. They were croaking in their blue-black suits and they woke me up regularly at 6:00 A.M. The neighbors asked me what I thought was going on; nobody could understand why the ravens had suddenly appeared and why, why on earth, they were hanging around my house. This went on for three months. Then, they started defecating on my car. Now, this angered me. In a flash I was on the phone with Charles.

"It was bad enough that they woke me up," I said, "but now they are relieving themselves on my car," I complained.

"I thought they'd leave on their own, but they've been here for months," I said.

"Go out and put food on your car," he responded calmly.

"Why should I do that? It'll only encourage them to stay," I said.

"They're hungry. If you feed them they'll leave," he said coyly.

I was becoming more aware that Charles had a trickster personality in him. I felt that would only make them stay because food does not get rid of birds or any other animal for that matter. I was thinking Coyote gave me a break and I laughed to myself. Charles might be his name but Coyote was his game.

"I'm not going to do that. I called you to use your magic and ask them to leave," I said, hoping he would help me.

"I'll think about it," he said

I don't know if he did this or not, but a few weeks later they were gone.

By then, however, I had continued to call him Coyote because of his trickster nature. For example, I made the mistake of asking him what my totem is, expecting it to be a tigress, or a beautiful deer, or a horse.

"A bumble bee," he said.

"You're crazy," I said. I did not like the idea of being a bumble bee.

"Why am I a bumble bee?" I squawked.

"Well, well," he said with a sheepish smile on his face,

"You've got honey in you and you go from flower to flower," he said.

I was very upset by this.

"I'm not a bee. I don't know what I am, but I'm not a bee," I answered.

Charles just kept on smiling. From then on, I for sure called him Coyote.

Coyote never tells you how much he knows. He just lets me fall into a pothole and then, if I'm lucky, he'll help me out. With Coyote I never know which way it will go. He is a Coyote trickster but, he does have a great heart. He does play tricks on me, but he would never let me be hurt. Another thing about Coyote is if he doesn't want to be found, he won't be.

One day I was looking all over town for Coyote. I went to all his haunts, but no Coyote. Then, I drove by our small grocery store in the middle of town and saw his car parked in front of it. I went inside to find him but he was nowhere to be seen. I walked up and down every aisle. I looked all around that store, but I could not see him, yet I knew he was there. I stopped and looked at some magazines. I pulled out The Globe and started to read the star gossip. I could swear he was right behind me, but he was nowhere to be found.

"Coyote, where are you?" I said out loud. No response. Nothing happened. He would not show himself that little Coyote trickster. It made the hair stand up on the back of my neck because I knew his energy was around me and he would not respond. He was getting to me and he knows it. I stood there for a few minutes contemplating and I flashed on what I was going to do.

I was thinking as I left the store that I was going to make a telephone call to Coyote and he better have a great answer as to why he did not respond to me when I called his name. I knew he would have *some* answer to my question because he always does.

When I reached Coyote he invited me over. I was at his home in minutes and immediately confronted him. This was better face to face.

"Why didn't you respond when I called your name at the store?" I asked.

"You were there weren't you?" I said.

He had a coy look on his face.

"I wanted you to find me," he said.

"Coyote, you are so full of it. I really needed to talk to you and you kept evading me. Please don't do that to me again," I said.

"Oh, I'll try not to," he said.

"But you could have found me if you had used more of your instincts. You don't use them enough and they are lying dormant," he said. Then, he pulled out his Coyote bag of tricks.

"How did you like the article in The Globe?" he asked.

All I could think was how he had done it to me again. Oh, well he was just a man.

One day we were sitting in the restaurant when Charles (Coyote) told me I was going to write a book about wolves.

"Oh, no," I said. I looked at him like he was crazy. What could he be thinking?

"I am not going to write a story about wolves. Why should I do that? I don't know anything about wolves and plus I do not write." He gave me sly grin like he always does, maybe he could see the future, but I never knew with Charles because he was a trickster, but with a kind heart.

"Upon awakening every morning, I ask my Higher Power to use me for something greater than myself."

—Oprah Winfrey

Chapter Ten

Potholes

"At last it dawned on me that these obstacles were my life."

—Alfred D'Souza

I know that there are potholes in life because I have hit most of them. I can be in a car or my bedroom or a café or a movie theatre—I can be anywhere and a pothole can appear. I've learned about traps and potholes that might be hiding anywhere. These potholes sure can have a rippling effect in you're life. It's easy to get into a pothole but it's a million times harder to get out.

They are the hole one falls into when you're are not looking or the hole you purposely dive in just because it seems too good to pass up. Potholes are the curves and detours along the way.

Potholes are the bumps in ones road of life. They are the financial problems, health challenges, relationship issues, work concerns, or any other challenge one is asked to face. They are the problems, troubles, suffering, and ultimately ones' spiritual lessons. Potholes have power and I have learned that some of the most difficult ones may offer you understanding because you are learning to fine-tune your perceptions and judgments in life.

My biggest potholes have been men.

No matter how smooth a road appears we all have potholes and man-holes. Then we do it again, again, and again. What did I learn from it and how can I improve myself so I won't do it again. All though my Hungry Wolf episodes, I discovered my ex to be the biggest pothole of them all—yet I still had time to meet a few others.

I was determined emotionally to move forward on my spiritual path, to grow spiritually, but instead I took a path full of potholes and challenges. I still had not learned how a wolf will conceal their true nature. This blindness is what gets me into trouble.

Unwavering to move to a higher expression of my life, I took a creative writing class at the College of the Redwoods, in Northern, California and explored career options for my life. Nursing or teaching children, as a career, was over, I couldn't go back but I didn't know what my next career move would be.

During this time in my personal life I was looking for a new adventure in my life, so I began to answer personal ads in a Northern California publication. In 1994, I met a man who I will call, Gary. We had a lot in common. He was a physician and I'd been a nurse. We communicated by letter for over eight months and finally we planned to meet.

Gary called me for the first time right before we met. He spoke into the phone with such enthusiasm,

"I'll be carrying a gift, so you can recognize me," he crooned in his smooth masculine voice.

I was so excited I could hardly sleep that night anticipating the next day. I could not turn my mind off. Would he like my looks? How would the date go? I wondered.

Jean, just be yourself, I kept telling myself. I finally went to sleep my thoughts were on cloud nine.

We were scheduled to meet at 3:00 P.M. at a historic hotel in Mendocino, California. I was dressed to the hilt. A red and black knit suit swallowed up my luscious body. My red hair was immaculate and my make-up was put on with impeccable care. I was ready to meet this Gary. Bring him on, I thought. I was dressed to go out with a movie "star" or at least a God in physician's clothing.

It sprinkled rain as I got in my car and drove ten miles to the hotel. I was trembling with excitement, tears of anticipation splashed down my face. Questions poured through my mind. Is Gary the soul-mate I have been searching for all my life? Is this real or just a romantic fantasy? I pondered.

I arrived at the hotel and pulled into a parking place. A good looking man six feet tall with salt and pepper hair, holding a black umbrella that was open walked over to me. He leaned over and opened my Cadillac door. We made eye contact for the first time. What I felt is a definite physical and spiritual connection. His tender smile and light blue-green eyes were staring at me. I was spellbound.

"I am Gary, you must be Jean? I would know you anywhere. He stepped back like he was looking me over,

"You're an attractive woman," he admitted, looking into my eyes. I could not move or say a word for a second. I wondered if I had heard him right but I knew I had.

"Yes, thank you," I responded softly, as a delightful smile lit up my face.

"I have a gift for you," I said as I reached into the back seat of the Cadillac for a red gift bag, which held my present for him.

We agreed to go back to his suite for a drink before dining. But in my mind I was thinking, should I go? Should I take the chance? Then I thought, why not, it'll be fine. I felt I knew him because for the past eight months, everyday he sent me a letter. That says something about him. In my heart I felt I could trust him so I decided to follow him to his room.

Gary led me up a flight of stairs to his room. Everything seemed fine as he was very gracious. With the sweep of his arm, he motioned me to have a seat, obviously attempting to make me feel comfortable. He was not pushing me, and that was good, because I felt excited being with him. His suite was painted a light green with multicolored flowered drapes on the window. A stone fireplace was set at the far end of the room, was lit. Elegant antique furniture completely filled the room, making the room look like a show case.

My eyes focused on the coffee table where it supported a red gift bag filled with red roses and celery sat. Were they for me? I took my gift and placed it on the coffee table and then, as if by magic, there were two red bags containing the exact same gift. I was speechless. Strange, as this was a very unusual combination. I had purchased my gift locally and Gary had brought his out of town. It was such a coincidence, I was speechless. We stared at each other. His smile was warm and gentle, and his intense bluish-green eyes warmed my heart. He glanced back at my gift to him.

"I see you've been busy thinking of our first date," he said.

"This is a sign that we were destined to meet. I think we are soul-mates. Our gifts are from our hearts," I said.

He walked across the room and put his arm around my waist. He led me to a small love-seat where we sat. He slowly put both his arms around me. With one arm he turned my head toward him. His kiss was soft and tender, I slowly pulled away.

"I am not ready for anything more," I told him. He looked at me intently and said,

"When you're ready, Jean. I'll wait you are worth it," he said.

We got up from the love-seat and Gary took my hand and led me down to the restaurant. Within a week, we were a pair in every sense of the word.

When Gary asked me to marry him I was surprised, and happy.

"Yes, I would be honored to be your wife," I told him. I thought everything was just flawless or so it looked on the surface. I did not realize how slippery and full of potholes a situation could be.

It was Christmas, which is my favorite time of the year and with Gary's marriage proposal, I was ecstatic. He took me shopping everywhere and bought me some very expensive perfume and a nice silk coat. For a surprise, he had the expression, 'You are mine and I am yours. Love, Gary,' engraved on a lovely gold heart pendant for me. This thrilled me! Yes, Gary knew how to please a woman and I fell for him completely. I was in another deep and treacherous pothole and never even know it.

I introduced him to my friends over the holiday and some of my friends did not care for him. They said he was arrogant and that he thought he was better than them. I only saw what I wanted to see—a kind, very intelligent professional man who was in love with me. I loved him with all my heart. I did not know the heart wrenching pothole I was falling into.

When I accepted Gary's marriage proposal I agreed to move to Washington to help him sell his million dollar house, then we planned to return to Mendocino to live. I did not know it then, but, another ravenous wolf held me in his clutches, and as I was smiling his teeth gripped my heart.

Gary's 7,000 square foot home had been on the market four years without a buyer. When I arrived we redecorated the entire place and did quite a bit of remodeling. When we finished it was a spectacular show place for the rich and famous. I always had great decorating ability that I had inherited from my father who was an architect. The 7,000 square foot house had three floors and a three car garage, an entrance way laid with black marble, and the main floor decorated with two black marble fireplaces. I knew it would sell in the near future. I consistently prayed that the house would sell to the right buyers. Four months later his house sold. That is what prayer will do, not to mention all the hard work and energy we put into the house. But you also need faith.

Fortunately, we did not marry right away. This gave me time to see Gary for who he positively was—a wolf in sheep's clothing! Again! Not long after I moved in with Gary, I was rudely awakened by some big potholes they suddenly flared up. Would I ever learn not to be so delusional? I asked myself.

Gary was deeply in debt. He owed his brother a large sum of money. He planned to pay off the loan from the sale of the house. Mean while his brother grew impatient and was applying pressure, and as a result Gary grew increasingly difficult to live with. He revealed mood swings and personality changes that astonished me. He'd be wonderful one minute and then, angry or sulking the next. I discovered he was a closet pill-popper and an alcoholic.

I wanted out of the relationship, but I was not sure how to get out of it. The wolf had me by the throat. I wanted to stay because I loved this man but at the same time I knew I should go. My heart was being torn in two. Gary's fangs were starting to show, and it quickly turned into a dangerous push-pull game of the heart. This brought back vivid memories of another wolf I had dealt with.

One sunny afternoon Gary and I were looking out the dining room window when suddenly we saw a white dove. I knew in my heart that White Feather knew we needed more understanding, love, and harmony in our relationship. She was preparing us for grand finale which was rapidly approaching. The dove was pure white, and lovely. The dove stayed all evening which surprised me, because doves usually stay for a while and then, leave. The succeeding day I went down to see the dove which was perched in a small pine tree in the yard. In my heart I knew she was waiting for me.

"Why are you here?" I asked.

She responded in a soft voice that only I could hear,

"I came to bring harmony to you and Gary and to tell you that your time here is nearly completed," she said.

Then she spread her wings and gently flew into the electric blue sky until she disappeared. My heart ached knowing I would be leaving soon and warm tears of sadness ran down my face. I knew my future was not with this man, one whom I believed I would marry. I was so hurt and sad I could hardly believe what she told me, but I knew spiritually that the message she gave me, would happen.

Back in the house, Gary was coming downstairs when I confronted him.

"The white dove has left," I said. He didn't respond immediately, almost as if he could sense my sadness, but he didn't mention it.

"Jean," he answered,

"I've never seen a white dove at my house or in this area.

"It's very unusual," he said.

"Well it was White Feather's doing, but I didn't mention the message that the dove delivered. He had nothing to say about White Feather.

As I said this, I knew in my heart that this was White Feather's way of telling me it was time to say good-bye. I felt deep hurt and betrayal because he hid his addictions from me. I was in pain from the separation of love, I knew in my heart that it would take years to get over. There was no other choice but to let go of the future that I had hoped for with him. It was a nasty trick of fate.

In my heart I knew I would never see Gary again. I also knew something or someone had changed his mind, I could sense it. Possibly it was his past, perhaps his grown children, or possibly his brother.

I found it odd that he told me not to pick up the telephone while he was out. One time I did pick up the telephone and I didn't say anything. Later I told Gary what I had done and he got very upset with me. Then I learned it was his brother who had been on the telephone. I felt he was hiding me from his family and that made me very uncomfortable.

After, all I was in love with him, I thought Gary was in love with me. You do not hide someone you are going to marry and are proud to be with. His action was suspicious and that made me feel very gloomy inside. I realized that I just trusted him too much and I had left my home to be with him. I had to hold onto my faith in White Feather I know she was their too protect me and lift me with her wings. I needed all the soul coverage that I could get for my protection.

Gary was just what the doctor ordered, a pothole for me. I clung to my illusion of the perfect guy and our exquisite future together. Although I wanted to leave, I could not let go of the dream. Finally I thought I had found the right man. He was the perfect package a position in society, intelligence, personality, handsome, and fun to be with. What else could one ask for I thought? I refused to face the reality of his drug addiction but the more I ignored the pothole the bigger it got. Finally, I had four wheels in the hole and I was stuck, stuck, stuck. I could not believe this had happened to me, yet again.

My refusal to let go of the illusion was the pothole. Even though I wanted to leave I just could not let go of the dream. It took years to find each other and I did not want to admit the truth of our relationship. Another starving wolf had taken hold of me, I felt trapped inside of Gary's lair. Finally, in desperation I cried for help.

'God, White Feather, what should I do?' I cried.

I was in such shock and had just finished an Easter prayer outside his house.

A few days later, on Easter morning, Gary came home and I could tell he was deeply troubled.

"Pack your bags. I am taking you home," he said in a very stern, hateful voice.

"I knew the time has come," I answered, resigned to the inevitable.

"There is no use talking about it," he said.

His whole face was twisted in such a distorted manner I knew it was the drugs talking. He scared me to death and I knew I had to get the hell out of his way or I could get hurt. He was going to take me home. For me once more, tears were streaming down my face. I wondered how I was going to survive it. I knew Gary was now on the dark path and had no compassion for me at all. My tears almost turned angry but I knew that would not do any good, I had to use a cool head. I wondered if I was going to survive.

My illusion of my perfect relationship with the perfect man kept me from facing how alone I felt when this relationship ended. I had to rely on my faith and I knew that White Feather was here and she was protecting me. No matter what it looked like on the surface, I knew it would be all right. My angel was there and this comforted me.

I was being hard on myself. I wondered how I could have been so blind but love can indeed be blind. Therefore, I was filled with self-recrimination and self-pity. White Feather heard my cries and did not let me stay there long. White Feather, in her compassion, finally pulled me out of that relationship pothole. I was struggling to stay but wanted to leave my emotions were going wild.

"Jean, true love makes you know your strength and weakness because during times of intense stress you are experiencing your most personal growth. Your character will become stronger and you will feel your personal growth in every way. If you get through all of the difficulties a relationship throws at you then its real love," she said.

"But there were moments the relationship felt so real," I said.

"Gary did not want to put the time and effort into your relationship, so he bailed out. And I'll tell you his family was against any relationship Gary might have had. He was not in the best financial situation. It was not your fault and I know this does not make the hurt any less," she said.

"No it doesn't," I responded.

"I am setting you free now and someday you will love again and this time it will be real great love. It will have chemistry, joy and bring the both of you happiness. I promised you, years ago I will save the best for last and I have." she said. Once more White Feather was giving me inner strength to move on in my life. What would I do with out her? I was thankful for her being her to help me get over this huge hurtles of my life.

It is hard to believe that after the Hungry Wolf and Gary I would fall into yet another pothole, but it did happen. I still hadn't learned my lesson or it would not have happened unless I was just too hard headed. If we do not fill the potholes with the spiritual, the pothole will remain before us for us to fall into over and over again until I learned the hard lessons White Feather was showing me.

I had been out of a relationship for five years and then I met Mark in April of 1999. Mark had more romance and fun in his soul than anyone I had met in years. I fell head over heals in love with him. I did not know at the time, but this was going to be one of the biggest potholes in my life.

I met Mark at a Single's Club meeting in my area. In fact, I sat right next to him. I had no idea how many women he had finessed before me and that he had a dreadful reputation. I just knew that I was sitting next to a very attractive man. Everyone sat and listened to the music and no one danced because the music was so bad. I did get one dance but not from Mark. He didn't dance at the club. When the music ended Mark got up to leave. I followed him. As I walked out the front door I saw him walking past my car a little way down the street. I wondered where he was going. He's been sitting with me for two hours, so I shouted in a loud voice,

"Where are you going?"

He turned around.

"I'm going to a Cantina where they have a band that plays decent music," he answered.

"May I join you?" I asked.

"You might as well," he said.

I followed him to the Cantina and we sat down at a table. He asked me to dance. He put his arms around me and began to lead me around the floor. It felt so romantic and comfortable. I felt like I had danced with Mark all my life. Our bodies blended together with such fire and passion we danced many dances that night. Then, he walked me to my car.

"I'd like to call you Monday for a date. Would that be all right with you?" he asked.

Boy was it ever, I thought.

"Yes, that would be fine," I said.

I was very attracted to Mark; he was a handsome man with a sexy smile and nice personality. I loved to dance and so did he. As our dates progressed I also realized we had a lot in common, plus Mark was amusing and fun. We both liked to dance, camp, and travel but it was not intellectual. We spent a lot of quality time together. He took me everywhere with him. My life became richer and fuller because we enjoyed all our hobbies together. We were gone most week-ends boating, camping and dancing. Love and romance were in full bloom, filling my hungry heart.

He was very smooth in the way he pursued me. I had no way of knowing how many women he finessed before me. Nor did I know of his terrible reputation until once again, I was hitting those potholes after potholes. The passion we had for each other was out of this world and he was a skilled lover. I walked on the earth, but my heart floated in mid-air on clouds. I didn't know it at the time, but this was going to be one of the biggest potholes in my entire life. With my head in the clouds it was impossible to spot the bumps.

One time Mark expressed to me,

"Jean, you have gone with doctors, lawyers, merchants and chiefs and now you are going with a beach bum," he said.

"That is not true," I said.

"Just because you do not have a big college education does not mean you're a beach bum," I said.

His profession or lack of professionalism did not brother me. I was willing to live with our lifestyle differences, but what became increasingly apparent were his problems with drugs and alcohol. As we kept dating and became more involved with each other, he showed me his true colors. I did not realize he had so many serious addictions. I thought love would concur all, so I let the sweet romance rage on.

One night we scheduled a date and I got all dressed up. He didn't show up. I waited until finally Mark called.

"Jean, I can't come over tonight," he said.

"Why?" I asked.

He would not tell me and hung up. That made me so mad I jumped in my car and drove over to his place. I knocked on the door and he opened it.

"May I come in?" I said.

"Oh, I guess," he said as he squared his shoulders.

"I'd give you a kiss, but I smell bad," he said.

"Yes you do, it is too bad you can't control yourself. You missed a good date," I said.

As I walked by him I smelled alcohol all over him. The smell was strong and I was very upset. That is when I knew at that moment he had a terrible problem with alcohol.

Running out I slammed the door behind me. I jumped in my car and cried all the way home. He had so many serious addictions and I never realized it. I was getting mad at myself for getting into this painful situation. At first, I thought we could fix his problem. I finally realized Mark was not interested in doing anything about it.

"I like myself the way I am. I am too old to change," he said.

I was thinking to myself, what a cop-out. What a weak man, and he was going to stay that way. He really was not that smart and he was not going to change for himself or me. Love was not enough in this scenario. White Feather was giving him a chance to change his life for a higher purpose but he was fighting it. He tried for a while but he gave in to what he thought was his true nature because he had been that way for so many years.

Love is blind, but it could not harmonize the mood swings of Mark. When he was clean of alcohol and drugs he was a wonderful, fun-loving, responsible guy, but when he started drinking, he became completely different. It was like dating Dr. Jekyll and Mr. Hyde. When he drank I could not rely on him at all. He would stand me up for a date and not remember to call until the next morning. Once in a great while he would remember, but not often.

When we had a misunderstanding, instead of staying to talk things out, he would stomp out. Sometimes he would disappear for days and months at a time and I never knew why. I agonized over his disappearance thinking it was maybe something I said or did. Finally I knew it was neither of these things. It was like living in a total nightmare. Mark did not want to face the music or be responsible for problems in our relationship. He was a so-called free spirit and that is where the problem came in. He had not learned yet, you cannot have your cake and eat it too. Mark did not want to grow up and have a mature relationship. I was laughing on the outside and crying on the inside. I had begun to question our relationship.

One New Year's Eve, Mark made all kinds of plans for us. He made dinner reservations and he purchased tickets for a New Year's Ball. He made these plans when he was sober, but then a few weeks before the event he started drinking again and he disappeared. I didn't know that to think or where he'd gone, but I looked for him everywhere. It was the night before the ball that I finally caught up with him in front of a restaurant. We agreed to go together and he stayed sober. I had one of the best times of my entire life at that New Year's Eve Ball.

But, I saw the writing on the wall. His problem with alcohol and drugs was not going away. Did I want to spend the rest of my life being in a sick relationship never knowing where he was? Did I want to spend my nights running down alleys to find him? I knew this would definitely break my heart. Then the awareness came to me. I was in a horrible pothole. I saw the truth—but, I did not want to leave—not yet. I was not ready to let go.

The good times became fewer and farther apart. White Feather tried to warn me.

"Mark is not all that he's led you to believe. If a man is on the shadowy side, you will not have a lasting relationship because he is only thinking about himself. He does not want to see the truth or change his old ways, because he's selfish and weak in spirit," she said.

For a long time, I did not listen to White Feather. I did not want to go through the pain and heartache of letting go. In my heart I knew that drugs and alcohol was Gary's God. He tried to quit but his demons made him weak and he didn't want to fight them. It was easier for him to give in, than to believe, to have faith that he could fight his addictions. He was just a weak man and did not feel he could or that he even wanted to change. There was nothing I could do except pray for him, which I did. He had to make a choice. While he had tried for a while, nonetheless it obviously was too much work. Unfortunately he had friends who had the same bad habits, so he just gave in. He had no back bone.

Mark was like having a taste of honey for the first time in my life. Once I experienced that sweet taste I wanted more. But, I also wanted more of the romance, not the mood swings that accommodated his drug use. Finally, I had to admit to myself that Mark and his addictions had beaten me. He did not love me enough, he loved himself and the drug's more. Living with that lifestyle was impossible. No matter how hard it was, I wanted to be with someone who loved me and was committed to working things out. I wanted someone who would compromise in a relationship and never leave me. Someone who would talk things over not just walks out and get drunk.

Mark did not realize how much he hurt me; either that or he did not care. He was destroying my love for him and I was loosing respect for him and myself. I was in a lot of emotional pain and I could not sleep at night. I was fighting my emotions and myself.

True love is a gift, not an obligation. True love makes your life sweeter because you are able to work things out and respect each other. It's my belief that sex is sacred and although I wanted to believe that I had this with Mark I knew that this was not so. I was brokenhearted. I was suffering. I was in agony. This relationship was coming to and end and I knew it. I had to accept that fact and I finally did, but it was not easy. It took me three years to get over it, but as a result I became a wiser and stronger person. The pain lessened when I was able to look at what Mark had taught me. I had learned a hard lesson and I was not going to dig my way into another deep pothole as the one I climbed out of with Mark. I learned you can't make someone love you, and that's a fact!

Real love stands the test of time and becomes stronger and more fulfilling with time. True love makes your life sweeter because you are able to work things out and respect one another. The sexual energy becomes more natural and enhanced because you know each other's likes and dislikes. This does not mean the passion goes away. It is just deeper emotionally.

To have love and a sexual connection is sacred and although I wanted to believe that I had this with Mark, I knew this was not so. He was only a skilled lover and I knew he was pretending to love me for whatever his reason. I felt grief-stricken. I had found faithful love or so I thought, but now the relationship was vanishing like the wind. Still bouncing along life's highway, I was still hitting those potholes. This relationship was over a long time ago, but I did not want to accept it. How could I accept it if I was still in love with him? That meant fighting rejection and I was not ready to suffer heartbreak and loneliness. Knowing it was coming, I just could not let go as yet. Who wants to be dumped, but I knew there was no way to avoid it.

Why did I have to travel the bumpy pothole once more? I knew why. Mark had already made his choice. He was unwilling to change even for himself. It was time for me to get on with my life.

. My heart was breaking. I thought Mark was my soul mate, but it turned out he was just another big pothole. I was miserable, and my heart felt anguish from the loss. It is good fortune to find love and trust in a relationship and I was not ready to find another man. In my heart I knew this was my last relationship unless God or White Feather chose a mate for me. I had no way of telling how long that may take! I hoped Mark is not the last man I would ever love, but, I am unwilling to stumble into another pothole. I now realized that I needed to heal that part of me that was laid out for a wolf's feast.

I turned to White Feather for comfort and she was right there for me. After all, she had watched me run into the pothole. She lets me have these experiences so that I'll build wisdom, grow stronger in spirit and help others with their heartaches.

After my relationship with Mark was over White Feather said to me,

"I am nobody's dinner to be eaten and then tossed aside," she said.

She reminded me that I am a strong woman, who simply chose to ignore the warning signs. I had not loved in vain. Past relationships have shown me I have a weakness for picking the wrong men.

Perhaps next time I needed to let the spirit pick my partner. Spirit is the divine key to our protection. I was beginning to suspect it maybe better to be without a relationship than to be in a wrong one.

The stretching of spirit is what makes the soul sing. In other words we have a chance to grow. Now I can see that Mark was not looking for true love because one time he told me he was old to change his ways. What a weak person in spirit. He was not looking for what I had to offer him, real love on an adult level, but I had to be willing to forgive him for who he was. He was fragile and sick and apparently going to stay that way. I finally realized that if Mark was not going to Heaven with me, I am not going to hell with him. He was hooked on alcohol and I was hooked on him. He was like a rare perfume that excited me on every level. Finally it was Mark who broke off our relationship.

"I hurt you too much and I cannot be myself," he said and that was it.

Once more I was devastated and felt I could never get over it. I had to hold onto my faith more than ever.

Picking up the pieces of my life has not been easy, but I have learned more about personal strength and spiritual growth. My character and personality are much stronger. I was not running down the Little Red Riding Hood path toward destruction. I now look both ways before I hit the road of no return. I approach the road with caution, stop at the stop sign, and look for any deep potholes in sight. Life goes on, but, I do not have to continue making the same mistakes with men. I can keep a sharp eye out for stray wolves in the world. If I see a red flag, like addiction, or dishonesty, I can choose to walk away or stay clear.

If I had not ventured onto my bumpy road, I would not be who I am today. I've lived to tell others how I survived the hungry wolfs and the deep potholes of my life. If I choose to stay, I need to do it with my eyes open and know that I can not change anyone else. Relationships take commitment and courage.

White Feather also taught me that the first step in getting out of a pothole is to admit that you're in one. Ignoring the pothole, like I tried to ignore with Gary and Mark's addictions, will not make them go away. Controlling, manipulating, and trying to fix the situation also did not work. The pothole only gets larger. The only way to smooth out a pothole is to fill it with the spiritual equivalent of gravel, cement; that is faith, joy and harmony.

To find the right ingredients for change, it's important to seek guidance, perhaps, from a counselor, a wise parent or from a friend, a minister, or a spiritual teacher, or an inspirational, book. If you lift your thoughts to a spiritual level in other words think more positive thoughts, then your life will change for the better and you could climb out of the pothole that you've been stuck in. If, however, you continue to stare at the pothole, interact with it or try to fix it, the pothole at best stays the same and at worse expands. If you stay in the light maintain your faith you'll fill in the pothole!

Get involved in helping others and the doors of opportunity will swing wide open for you. It's your decision whether you move forward or slide backward. You have to get out of yourself and look to another avenue of helping others. Your potholes will gradually slide away if you take the focus off yourself and find someone that is in dire straits. Go to a hospital or write a letter to a soldier in Iraq. These actions will automatically take your mind off yourself and you will feel contentment inside of you. Take a risk on an individual in a business venture. Do an astonishing act you have never done before but step out in faith. The reward will be freedom from your pothole because you are thinking correctly.

Potholes are not just relationships. They are any problems that can sink you into despair, like your son doesn't do what you ask him to do; you fear the loss of your job or position. Then, you go to the doctor and the doctor tells you, you're sicker than you thought. What are you going to do with these potholes? Sink into the muck and mire, burying you deeper into the potholes?

Margaret fell into a major pothole with her son and she was scared to death that he would not come through for her. She permitted her son to borrow a large sum of money from her. As collateral he promised that he'd take a mortgage out on his house and reimburse her, but he was giving excuses for not following through.

She had bills and other financial responsibilities, but she believed in her son's word. If he didn't return the money, it would shatter the image of her son, and she would never be able to trust him again. After I heard the story, I offered to do some healing prayer for her financial potholes. Then it came to me to tell her to have her attorney draw up a contract for the loan which included interest on her money.

She took a deep breath and hesitating said, "after all he is my son."

I reminded her this was not an excuse for his poor attitude of making you wait for your check. I continued the prayers for her and I encouraged her highest good be served, and encouraged Margaret to do the same.

She went to her attorney and had the contract drawn up. Several weeks went by when I saw Margaret at the post office. She told me,

"That she had not received any money,"

"Faith is the answer," I said.

"You have to skip over your potholes and have great faith." I urged her to trust in her prayers that only the best and the highest would evolve in this situation. Then, I surprised us further when I heard myself say,

"Margaret, you'll get your check in the mail plus interest in three days," I said.

Her face lit up and finally she said,

"Are you sure?" she asked.

"White Feather just told me and she is never wrong." I left with a knowing smile on my face.

Three days went by and Margaret was looking for me all over town when she finally found me at the ranch. She yelled out her car window holding the check with interest in her hand.

"Jean, I received my check just as you told me I would," she said with a big happy smile on her lovely face.

"Good, I am happy for you. I never doubted it for a minute," I answered. A slow, pleased smile formed on my face but inside I was joyous. It made me happy to know it worked out just as I told it would but it was White Feather that helped and gave me the answer. I thank White Feather.

Again we witnessed the power of faith overcoming the facts of the situation. Margaret discovered as long as her energies were focused on the problem the pothole grew larger, but when she turned to prayer and meditation the road grows smooth.

What happened to Margaret is just another example of what can happen when we admit to having a pothole problem. Ask for help, listen for guidance and then, fill the pothole with prayer, faith and meditation. When you believe and have faith and start to follow your spiritual path, then healing and wisdom seeks through the pothole and you get the right guidance for your problems. As Jesus said in the Bible, *"All things are possible to him that believes"* From Mark 9:23.

Potholes can be the liniment of life if you see them as schooling. I have learned many hard lessons and my potholes are now smooth because I didn't quit. I believe in a spiritual connection and in keeping my inner voice strong through prayer and meditation they have never failed me. If I had given up in the cross-roads of my life, the wolf would have won and I would have lost. But I kept going like the energizer bunny, and kept telling myself, 'I deserve a richer and more rewarding life.'

Here is another excellent example of how I pushed through a deep pothole of mine. I had to rid myself of my past with the wolf and clear my credit report and that was not easy. Going to see a certified accountant in regards to cleaning my credit report, she gave me information and without charging anything. What a great and helpful spirit she is. I worked on my credit report for a month but it was finally cleared of the wolf' bad credit. I found a caring car salesmen and I bought a beautiful used car from him.

"There are not many people who are as strong as you are," he said.

If I would have felt beaten down my used car would not be sitting in my driveway. I became a stronger person from this experience.

If I had not started becoming the tigress, the wolf, would have not have given me one red hot dime, but this time I was the one who kept on growling until I got what the court allowed. The wolf better not pull my whiskers. The wolf, does not like to part with money, only if he is persuaded by

Adam hauling him back to court. If I had quit I knew in my heart that I would not be where I am on my spiritual journey.

I had to remember that I could be in my vehicle and I might hit a big rock on the road and spin out of control. Traps and potholes might be lurking all along the way. It was necessary to travel at a slower speed and study the map to see where I wanted to go, and not just dive into another heart filled emotional rock road.

Now I'm finished on this destructive path. I'm capable of taking care of myself, and I am never going down that rock-strewn path again.

Although my potholes have names like Gary and Mark, and the most devastating one of all, Hungry Wolf, who had a death grip on me. Potholes come in variety of shapes and issues, and no matter how big a problem or overwhelming the issue, the principles are the same. Look inside your heart and be honest with yourself. Are your potholes little one's that you just choose to ignore or are they big one's that you are hiding from, perhaps tripping over?

Here is some insight into what to do with your potholes. First of all make sure that you want to get rid of them and be happy. Now here are a few principles to help you when you look at your problems. Do not look at the donut, look at the solution. We spend too much time going over and over the same problems.

We need to spend time working on the solution.

What event would change the circumstances, improve the situation? One of my spiritual principles is put your attention toward whatever is upsetting you, then put the pothole in prayer and let go. Prayer will also calm your emotions and you will feel more at peace. When you have a positive attitude then the answer or solution will come. Trust your faith and patiently wait for God. The answers result from having the right attitude, prayer, and waiting for God. That is it in a nutshell.

Endow your relationship pothole with prayer, meditation, friendship and therapy. No matter what the pothole—financial, career, health, or relationship, the pothole needs to be filled with a spiritual attitude. Because potholes are painful, people often want to fill them with addictions like drugs, alcohol, food, or spending, other means to numb one's self, but you will never heal a pothole with addictions. You have to step up and come to the plate and realize where you are in your life. You have to admit that you are in a pothole and then, ask God for help. God will supply that love and support no matter what age you are. You can come out of your pothole. Believe it and it will happen. Pray for the situation because prayers are very powerful.

Everyone has potholes. It's what one does with them that make the difference. Most of us were trained to focus on problems that come up. Then we find a solution and then do something about it. Take the right action to fix a pothole with a foundation of prayer and meditation because you get to the truth of the situation. No matter how deep the pothole is it may look impossible when it looks like there is no way out. God has every intention to bring the good into your life. God is in your favor.

Some people think God will not help them because they have been bad and the pothole is enormous, or they think that they are not good enough to be forgiven or that they are too old and God is not there for them. Any excuse will do, but not with God, he is the way, the truth, and the light. The truth is, God provides, let him shoulder your burdens. Ask in prayer and no matter how bottomless your potholes are or how hopeless you might feel, they will be influenced by your prayers. Remember prayers are compelling.

Most of all I needed to heal that part of me that felt like a throw a way woman. I had to spend time seeing my worth. In my heart I knew this healing would come if I did not give up and continued to believe that my faith would get me through. Too climb out of my bondage and be free to love and start over. I felt stronger compelling and powerful my tigress was moving me forward on to a higher spiritual path. I was taking that path and not be stuck in the past. I was not going to let my past ruin my future.

Potholes will clear up through soul coverage when you use faith. Live your life in prayer and have faith in that power. He knows we do not always do the right thing but he always gives us a chance to change our mind and do what is right. There is always a choice and when you make the right choice

God gives us our divine resolution. No problem is without a solution from God! He wants to clear up our potholes and he always comes through with His love and grace.

An old Indian is teaching his grandson about life. "A fight is going on inside me," he said to the boy. "It is a terrible fight and it is between two wolves."

One is evil—he is anger, envy, sorrow, regret, arrogance, self-pity, resentment, inferiority, lies, false pride, superiority, and ego.

The other is good—he is joy, peace, love hope, serenity, humility, kindness, benevolence, empathy, generosity, truth, compassion, and faith.

"This same fight is going on inside you and inside every other person, too."

The grandson thought about it for a minute and then asked his grandfather,

"Which wolf will win?"

The old Cherokee simply replied, "The one you feed."

—Captain

Chapter Eleven

The Spiritual Quest

"To grasp God in all thing—this is the sign of your new birth."

—Meister Eckhart

I was reading the Sunday San Francisco Examiner when I saw an advertisement describing a bed and breakfast on the Navajo Reservation in Monument Valley, Utah. I was attracted to the place when I learned that guests are invited to stay in a traditional Navajo Hogan. I felt like I needed to go there but didn't know why. I went into meditation hoping to receive guidance why I felt an attraction to the Navajo Indian reservation.

I closed my eyes, went into meditation and I heard White Feather speak. "You are going to Monument Valley to stay in a Hogan." That was enough encouragement for me. I was excited with the prospect of an adventure and I wondered if I was going on some kind of mission or spiritual quest.

I called Mark and asked him,

"Would you like to take a road trip to Utah and Arizona and visit a Navajo reservation?"

"Yes," was his immediate reply.

I was shocked but happy by his reaction. In my heart I had heard White Feather correctly and that Mark also felt an inner guidance to accompany me on this journey.

The next day I made reservations for us. We were to leave in a few days, on April 14th and arrive April 18th. Without delay, I started calling my clients and asked them to focus their energy and consciousness on April 18th at 3:00 P.M. I did not know why I was doing this. Then, I realized that is the day I planned to do prayer and meditation work, plus a visualization of energy for each one of my clients. I know that powerful healing spirits who live on the reservation and doing prayer work while I'm there would add tremendously to the power of the prayer. When energy comes together and consciousness meets, great power results. To do prayer work for others while I'm there would be a privilege.

A few nights before we left I woke up in the night and suddenly found myself in deep meditation. I saw three Native American Indian spirits in my room. One was an Indian elder. He was a large man with gray streaked black hair of medium length, penetrating brown eyes and a smile that was warm and pleasant. The other two Indians were tall and slim and much younger and had their black hair in ponytails. The whole group smiled at me affectionately. They looked at each other and did not say a word, but I felt they were waiting for me in Utah and Arizona.

The next day I called Charles and told him about the visit from the Native American Indian spirits.

He told me to get,

"Get a piece of paper and write down a description of my visitors," Then, he wanted me to put the paper in an envelope and put it away for safe keeping.

"This way they will know that you saw them," Charles said.

I followed his instructions and tucked the envelope away in my purse.

Mark and I packed the van for our trip. I was excited just wondering what spiritual mystery lay ahead. I was also happy to leave my troubles with the wolf behind. I figured if I was outside his turf he wouldn't be much trouble to me. I was divorced from him, but the financial settlement was not final and the wolf liked to hang on and draw blood.

At the start of our adventure, we spent the first night in Reno, Nevada and the second night in Kingman, Arizona. The next day, we drove to Sedona, Arizona, which is famous for the healing power of its mystical red rock formations. This is particularly true of Bell Rock, Cathedral Rock and Boynton Canyon. This is one of the reasons why I wanted to visit Arizona and experience their mystery. The other reason was because White Feather suggested I go.

Inside me, through deep meditation, I heard White Feather articulate to me,

"This trip will be a spiritual quest on many levels." she said.

I knew that I too, was going to receive a gift of healing power and energy. The power I was going to receive would also give me healing energy and strength to help my clients heal once I hold them in prayer and in the light.

The drive through Oak Creek Canyon stretches out for twelve miles then you enter Sedona. Different shaped rock formations rose up from the desert floor. Each one can represent a different healing. One formation made me think of Rocky Road ice cream and another reminded me of full bosomed women ready to be discovered in their heavy, spotted gowns. It was amazing for me to see these unusually vibrant rocks. At any minute I felt they could come alive and walk down the canyon and hold a conversation with me. That's how authentic they felt.

Mark and I stopped and took some pictures of the canyon. It was an exceptionally spiritual place and my heart sang with joy. The spirituality of this area captured my soul forever. I closed my eyes and wondered if anything else in this world could be so splendid, and my soul whispered, this is where I want to be. I felt alive and peaceful, all at the same time. Only God could have put together such a panoramic wealth of luminous color and depth.

Without a doubt, this scene would be in my heart forever. Taking a mental heart-picture, I quickly tucked it away in the back of my mind. 'Thank you Father for all your love,' I said to God out loud. A cold shiver swept over my body as I knew this was a mystical place of magical healing power. That realization shook me to my very soul.

Mark and I found a camp ground situated near the river and only a block from town. We unpacked and made camp. I looked up and saw the dramatic red rocks of Sedona high above the clouds. I was captivated by the towering red rocks and the feeling of peace that swept over my spirit.

Mark took a walk by the river while I went shopping. Sedona is a small, charming town, and I spent a couple of hours going through different shops. The people are very friendly, which to me is very unusual, but refreshing. Later Mark came to find me and we went back to camp.

As evening approached, the stars appeared slowly, shyly, one by one. They looked like each one was hanging on a silver string and I could play them like a harp. They were so close to me I felt I could pull one of the bright stars from the sky and hold it close to my heart and make a wish. I did, I made a wish. I wished for peace on earth. All at once I was engulfed in a symphony of a magical star-shining canopy of star light. As we looked up at the stars, and the camp fire was crackling beside us, I could feel the warmth come through my entire body. A mystical feeling fell upon me and I felt at peace. I took a breath of fresh night air and felt that at last I was home in spirit.

The next day, we packed up and went sight seeing. I went to climb into the van and just for a moment I thought I saw the footprints of the wolf. That mangy old creature was following me. I blinked my eyes and the footprints were gone. I couldn't believe it. I thought I had left that crazy old wolf behind and here he was haunting me in the middle of my quest. I felt happier than I had for a long time and then, poof, his footprints appeared on the healing red dust of Sedona. The footprints dropped me out of my bliss and into wolf reality.

I kept what I'd seen to myself since I didn't want to talk about him. Mark and I went in search of the energy vortexes in and around Sedona. These vortexes interested me the most because of my work in the healing arts. A vortex is a place where the earth's electromagnetic fields are strong. Spiritually, many believe that a vortex is the intersection between the spiritual realm and the physical. The Sedona power spots have long been sites for meditation, healing and religious ceremonies. For many, Sedona is a spiritual Mecca.

There are four major power spots in the Sedona area; Bell Rock, Cathedral Rock, Airport Vortex and Boynton Canyon. Power spots are electric or masculine energy vortexes. Electric vortexes are places where the earth releases energy, creating negative ions. These are favorite areas for people wishing for a rejuvenating break from the stresses of their daily routines. Bell Rock is also seen as a focal point for those interested in extraterrestrial visitations.

When I climbed Bell Rock I experienced a profound realization. I knew without a doubt that energy healing is right here on earth, and we can feel it within our bodies. All one has to do is open up their hearts to that powerful force. While I walked up Bell Rock I could feel the pull of the rock's energy. My feet were almost held to the surface by this force. I opened my heart and the splendor of this rock shot right through me like a bullet. I knew that all my charkas (body vortexes that convert God's vibrations or energy into body energy) were cleansed. My spiritual energy source was charged with renewed power by the time I climbed down from Bell Rock, I just knew it. I also knew White Feather had guided me to this magical place. A complete healing of my mind, body and spirit had taken place. The healing was like a humming sound surrounding my body and it shook me to my core. It reminded me of a car that had been elegantly tuned up.

I sat on a rock and poured the Arizona dirt from my shoes, thinking to myself how lucky I was to be able to hear from within. I did a deep meditation, and felt at peace. All of our answers are within us and I knew then that I was on my true spiritual path from the signs that I had felt in Sedona. I felt that my life had a specific purpose to help people heal and this journey reinforced my true gift. We visited all four vortexes before we traveled on to Monument Valley which we reached in the evening.

A huge sand storm ensued. The wind and sand whirled around the van. I thought I saw the wolf again in the strong wind, but I think it was my imagination. Either way I realized I was spending far too much time dwelling on this. Starting to panic but I pushed him out of my mind. We had to get to a place to stay but the only hotel was full so we had to stay in the van over night. No fun, it was a rough night. Finally dawn came and I got up early to get a cup of coffee. Mark came into the restaurant later and we ordered breakfast. Our next stop would be the Navajo Indian Reservation.

We arrived at the reservation at 8:00 A.M. I felt I was coming home. There was an energy surging through my body that was so powerful, unusual, that I didn't know what I was feeling. Was it in my DNA? Was I a Navajo in my past life? Was White Feather connected to this place, somehow? I knew for some reason there was a purpose for me being here but I had not discovered it yet.

I was going to experience the traditional Navajo house for the first time. I was curious about this strange looking house. I had never seen anything that looked like a Hogan but it was so unique and simple I knew it would be an enjoyable experience. When you first look at a Hogan the distinct shape catches the eye. It is a multi-sided house made out of bright red Arizona dirt that is more round than square. Standing under an immense blue sky, the Hogan has a doorway facing east. This traditional dwelling fits the land well, blending in with its surroundings. It also fits the lives of those who call it home. When you grow up as a Navajo, I am sure you remember the fire crackling and the warmth and sense of well-being that lives within those walls.

As we came into the reservation, and drove close to the Hogan, we saw a small older Navajo man cleaning out the place we were to stay in. He had short silver and black hair with warm friendly eyes. We looked at each other and I knew immediately that we were one in spirit. He had the smile of a fox and the grace of a deer as he pulled different objects in and out of the Hogan to prepare it for us.

Rolling down the van's window I yelled to the man,

"You don't have to hurry, take your time," I told him with a smile.

He gave me another smile and opened the door to the Hogan and quickly disappeared.

Almost immediately another Navajo man came out to greet us.

"I'm Ray, it's is nice to meet both of you," he said.

Ray was of medium build, with short black hair, and kind brown eyes. He shook hands with Mark and gave me a gentle smile. We told Ray we were going to explore Monument Valley and that we would be back at 1: 00 P.M.

We crossed Monument Valley and came to the only gift store in the town of Mexican Hat. We stopped the van, stretched our legs and went inside to view the Native American crafts for sale. We stayed a short time and then drove through the rest of Mexican Hat. Mexican Hat, which was named for a rock formation that's in the shape of a hat. Mexican Hat consists of a few small huts along a winding canyon. I noticed them as we crossed a small bridge and turned around to go back to the Navajo reservation.

As we entered the Navajo Bed and Breakfast once more Ray came out from his small hut to tell us our Hogan was ready. The older Indian, Gary, I later learned was Ray's father. He approached us slowly.

"I am going to gather up some wood for a sweat lodge," he said in a kind voice.

Mark offered to help and they both jumped in a gray truck and I watched as they drove down a dirt road. Oh, my there he goes again, running off, I thought as I took my hand off my hip. The wind came up and the sand whirled around the white van as I stood there wondering what to do next.

Ray approached me, pointing to the Hogan.

"Just drive the van over to the Hogan and unload your things," he said with a radiant smile on his face.

As I pulled up to the structure I felt like nature was once again welcoming me home. Climbing out of the van, I sensed an inner peace and joy in my spirit.

Entering the Hogan, I noticed a round stove stood in the center of the room. Up against the wall was a small table with bottled water and a bowl to wash our face and hands. The table also held a plate of fresh fruit. Beyond the metal stove, on the ground there lay a bed covered with a white bear rug. Neatly piled on the bearskin were Native American Indian blankets. Above the white bear skin rug was a white flour sack that had been nailed to the log over the bed.

The word Hogan means home for the Native American Indian. The Hogan is often built of logs and is earth covered. It provides a snug shelter against spring winds, summer heat and winter cold. It represents the Navajo Indian from birth to old age, as it provides the setting for all stages of life.

I unloaded the first suitcase. Ray knocked on the door and came in. He told me that a Navajo Indian Shaman had blessed this Hogan in 1988. I had no doubt that White Feather had sent me to this special blessed Hogan so I could do my prayers and meditation for my clients.

The weather changed rapidly while Mark and I were at the Hogan. It rained and the wind blew, sand all around us. The Hogan was cold until I started a fire in the stove. There was a wooden fire poker to tend the fire and a talisman to ensure against misfortune. I continued unpacking and made up the bed on the bearskin rug. There was no mattress but padding made with downing, and it was very soft and comfortable. The last blanket was pure wool and it held the pattern of multi-colored diamonds.

Mark joined the older man Gary in the sweat lodge. The sweat lodge is one of the most powerful healing atmospheres that a person can experience while staying at an Indian reservation. The Native American Indians believe it is a part of the Great Spirit or Creator itself. The sweat lodge embodies the concept of the circle, sacred in all American Indian cultures, as with others around the world.

The history of the sweat lodge structure symbolizes the combined strength of five special powers, earth for support, stone for stamina, fire for heat, water for cleansing and wood for the rib of man and heat. A huge fire is started outside the lodge where stones are cooked until they are red hot. Then the stones are moved from the fire to the inside of the lodge and placed in a circle keeping the heat inside of the stones. All those attending, enter the lodge and a blanket is pulled over the entrance.

This was Mark's first sweat lodge adventure. Mark and Gary chanted before entering the sweat lodge. Then they entered the lodge. Mark sat with Gary inside the dark hot womb of the sweat lodge. They sat facing the center pile of steaming rocks offering prayer and healing herbs to the Creator. They talked about their childhood.

While Mark and Gary were still in the sweat lodge I finished unpacking and I brought out my white candles for prayer and meditation. I would not have known what to do, but I was guided by White Feather. Placing the white candles on the red dirt I wanted to be one with the land and closer to nature. There is strength in the Navajo red dirt. I lit the prayer candles, making a circle around myself, and began to see the colors of red, gold and blue flashing in front of my third eye. This was very powerful. I prayed for my friends and clients; Jenna, Kelley, Charles, Tina, Joy, Meredith, White Feather and myself. I also prayed for Mark who needed more faith in himself.

Later, Mark told me he heard voices, Gary told him it was the winds. But, Mark knew what he had heard. Mark would not tell me what the voices told him. He was always so secretive but I guess that was the Native American Indian in him.

I asked White Feather to be with me. I asked her to cleanse the impurities in Mark's mind, body and spirit. I asked for help for each of my friends and clients. I asked for love, guidance, prosperity and additional hope and faith for the future. I asked for White Feather's healing ranch and chapel to evolve. I prayed for White Feather's book to be extremely successful so others can learn their spiritual lessons. I remembered that the Native American Indians believe we are only here to love and serve. I also called upon my angels.

White Feather started chanting, and I heard,

"I am pleased you are here," she said in her soft voice.

I had cold goose bumps that ran down my back as she continued,

"Jean, you have served well, you followed the path to Arizona, not knowing why. That shows complete trust in me as your guide. Your spiritual quest will be granted, which is everything you want: ranch, chapel, center and horses if you continue your faith," she continued,

I thought I was about to faint. My whole body was shacking from being with White Feather.

I was listening with every ounce of strength in my body.

"The spiritual path is not easy, but it is the only path that is fulfilling and rewarding and where you can learn your purpose. Keep your faith and reach for the stars. It will all materialize in your life according to God's plan for you. Keep your thoughts in Heaven and believe in yourself and your spiritual connection with your spiritual guide," she told me,

"I do White Feather," I said.

White Feather continued,

"No matter what it looks like in the outside world, keep yourself going no matter what is said or who says it. Through you I will teach others to follow the spiritual path of love. You have learned well and I will give you more healing ways in due time. Just believe and move on knowing the truth for who you are. I have never let you down and never will," she told me.

I was stunned as I had never heard White Feather give me that much imminent in sight and inspiration at one time. I was in awe and grateful. I felt dizzy so I reached for one of the poles, for strength, when she spoke again.

"Jean, you are loved beyond your understanding. You are giving Mark a new beginning. He will either accept or reject it. It's up to him," she said.

"This has not gone unnoticed with the spiritual counsel. All is well in your world. Never let go of your spiritual guide and friend," she concluded.

I knew I was hearing the truth and receiving a blessing. As I came back from meditation to physical reality, I was still sitting in the circle I had made around me. I looked up and there was Mark.

He had opened the door to the Hogan and stepped in.

"I just got back from the sweat lodge and I feel great," he said.

As I was looking at him he looked almost like an angel. I saw white light radiating from his aura. He looked magnificent, healthy, alert and alive in spirit.

"The sweat lodge experience was more than I could ever dream of," he said. Then, he thanked me.

"I would have never done this, except for you, I never forget this unusual experience," he confessed and gave me a big smile.

As I blew out my candles, Mark was still smiling at me.

"Shall we go for a walk and look at the Indian ponies?" he said.

"That sounds like fun," I said.

Mark lifted me up out of the circle and we walked outside. I looked at the crystal blue sky with its rolling clouds. The purple mountains seemed to be made of sand. I knew within my soul that a healing, on every level, had taken place in our hearts. I took Mark's hand and we strolled toward the horses in the corral. They looked up as if to say, 'It is about time the both of you come to see us,'

"Hello, you two," I said as they gave us the horses nod. The horses were pintos; some were black and white and a few were brown spotted.

Mark and I continued to walk toward the mountain. We circled the Navajo village and then walked back toward the red Hogan. It was nearing dusk and the wind and sand were both beginning to blow around us. When we arrived back at the Hogan, Ray came over with a tray of Navajo food, consisting of pita bread, soup and fruit.

"This is dinner," Ray said, as he handed me the tray of food.

The three of us sat down on the ground and Ray stayed to have a conversation with us. Mark had already prepared some abalone that we had brought with us. We shared our meal with Ray and gave him the abalone shells to use for making jewelry. The Navajos treasured the shells.

After dinner Ray looked at me and asked,

"Jean, what kind of work do you do?"

"I am a healer and I give healing massages," I responded.

He surprised me when he responded by asking me,

"Jean, would you do a healing massage on my mother, Jessie?"

"Ray, I would be honored," I said.

"Tomorrow at the ceremonial room I will have Jessie, my mother with me and I will come and get you before the two of you leave," he replied.

He turned around and looked at Mark and with a big grin on his face.

"See you tomorrow." he said.

I didn't realize until the next day that the Native American Indians planned to do a ceremony as one part of the ritual for us and his mother.

At the Navajo religion center, rituals are preformed by shamans following a system of intuitive and sympathetic (healing) magic. All Navajo rituals have certain aims in mind: restoring health, securing food, and insuring survival. In the Navajo universe, two classes of personal forces are recognized: human beings and the holy people or supernatural beings.

Ceremonies are aimed to restore a proper balance between the good and evil that exists in the world. Navajos do not believe that people can eliminate evil entirely. That evil must be controlled so that beauty and goodness can prevail. For Ray to invite us into the ceremonial room was a great honor. I accepted the spiritual invitation with deep gratitude.

After our dinner we went outside into the night air to look at the stars and as before, I felt like I could reach out and touch them. The wind and sand started to blow, so we had to go back inside the Hogan but not before we got a glimpse of the stars.

Early the next morning at early light, Ray knocked at our door and told us breakfast was ready. We enjoyed soup, Indian bread and hot tea.

Ray came inside the Hogan and sat down on the ground, his eyes fixed on mine.

"Jean, would you please come with me and I will take you and Mark to the Ceremonial room where my mother is waiting for you," he said.

We followed Ray to another red Hogan, but it was much bigger inside. I felt honored to be inside, as the Hogan was breathtakingly striking and it held much Indian culture. He led us to where his family was waiting. Ray's girlfriend and both his father and mother were there. As I approached her, Ray told me her name, was Helen. She was a large Navajo woman, who was looking at me with dark brown eyes and smiling. I spoke softly to her. She did not speak English but she knew from my mannerisms that I was here to help her. Smiling, as I put my hands on her back. I felt White Feather's energy move through me as I slowly worked down her spine. She stooped over in the chair, groaned and leaned into my hands. From there I held her and talked in a soft loving voice,

"White Feather is here to give you relief of your pain," I told her.

I gently touched her body and started doing a light massage in many different areas, as she had many cold spots which indicted a lot of blockages in her body. Her healing was already taking place as I could feel it. When I was finished, she turned around to look at me and she put her brown hands into mine. She had a big smile on her face as if to say, 'finally I had some relief of my pain.'

"When I get back home," I said to Ray,

"I will send you a letter telling you how to take care of your mother's arthritis."

At this point, Ray brought in his mother's hand made jewelry. I was given a piece of jewelry as an offering for the healing. I chose a necklace, strung with seeds I didn't recognize a cross colored with a revolver's blue steel. The necklace had been blessed to ward off bad dreams.

We left the ceremonial room and walked back to the Hogan to pack the van. Ray and his father came over to us before we left. They hugged us,

"We hope to see you both again," they said.

"Maybe one day," I said, while having faith that I would. As I climbed into the van I gave thanks for this healing spiritual quest and blessed the Navajo Reservation. As we drove down the dirt road, which once again was blowing dirt in our faces, we opened the window and waved good-bye. I wondered if I ever would ever visit the reservation again, I hoped in my soul that I would and my faith would lead me back to the reservation. This enchanted experience touched my heart.

As a result of my quest I felt more spiritually uplifted and rewarded. My heart felt full because I had captivated the healing energy and completed my mission.

"A cheerful heart is a good medicine."

—*Proverbs 17:22*

Chapter Twelve

"I Don't Want To Hear It"

"Joy comes in the morning"

—White Feather

Mark and I drove straight home. We were carried home with the renewed energy we had received from the reservation.

However, I did not see the three Native American Indians who came into my room the night before I left on my quest. However, I felt they followed Mark and me throughout our trip. Maybe they just wanted to keep us safe, which they did. I guess I was not ready to meet them and they knew this, but I was glad to have their company, because it made me feel protected on our trip.

As we approached Fort Bragg I knew something was going on with Mark because when I tried to talk to him he clammed up.

"What's wrong?" I asked.

"I just want to get you home," he said angrily.

I wondered what had happened. Then, I remembered the conversation, with the pink patties. I figured that Mark was holding a chip on his shoulder. When we stopped the van at my front door, Mark took my suitcases out of the van and walked up my steps and waited for me to open the door.

Once I opened the door, he brushed past me with the suitcases and came into the middle of my front room and threw the suitcases down on top of each other. I knew then he was mad as hell.

"I have to go," he said in a rough tone. He took two steps and out the front door, then he took off and jumped into his car. 'Same old Mark I thought,' as I watched him run away. He never wanted to face anything. Then I realized what was wrong.

On our drive home we had an uncomfortable conversation that was anything but friendly. We had been driving for many hours and our conversation led to the past. He started telling me about the time when he was in the military and was wounded and hospitalized. He was taken care of by a cute nurse. Why is he telling me this? I wondered. Then he went on to say that he told the nurse,

"I bet I can tell you what color your panties are?" and she said, "Oh really, what color are they?"

When she bent over to take his temperature he told her, "Pink,"

"Why in the hell am I hearing this? I exploded.

"I don't want to hear this," I yelled.

"In fact, pull over at that motel. I'm getting out of this van. I'm getting my own room!" I said.

I marched into the motel and the guy told me,

"There are no vacancies and every motel in town is full," he said.

I looked at him as if he had two heads and I walked out and stared at the van knowing I had to climb back into the van with this crazy guy. We slept in the van that night and we did not speak to each other until morning. We found a restaurant and got ourselves some coffee and drove another twelve hours. Even though we didn't mention the pink panties again, the fight was still brewing. Now, I was angry all over again. No good-bye or nothing, but that was Mark. He was a man of few words when it came to talking over any problems or misunderstandings. Anything uncomfortable he did not want to discuss. I remember it well.

Once he was gone, I got into my car and drove toward a local restaurant. On Main Street, I saw Charles with his thumb sticking out hitching a ride. I stopped short, pulled over and he came over to the car.

"What are you doing here? How did you know I was home?" I said.

He smiled his usual knowing smile.

"How was your trip? Did you see the Native American Indian spirits?" he asked.

"No," I said.

He just stood looking at me for a moment.

"It's over," he said.

"I know, but, I don't want to hear it," I was actually upset and started to cry.

"I'm leaving and going out to eat," I told him. He waved good-bye and did not say a word. I know why he had come in the first place, to soften the blow.

After the restaurant I went home to unpack. I checked the answering machine and found quite a few interesting telephone calls. Most calls were from my clients who I had prayed for while in the Hogan. Paris said she could feel my spiritual work while in the Hogan.

"I quit taking the medication because it was altering my personality," she said. Her healing was accomplished, and she was happy and grateful. A client in San Jose had gotten back with her boyfriend after a year apart. She thanked White Feather for bringing them back together. She was now engaged, and another healing resolved.

Another client of mine had wanted a computer, but could not afford one. One of her clients that owed her one hundred and fifty dollars just happened to call her that night saying she had the money and on the same night another friend called to inform her that she had a computer for her at approximately that amount. Another prayer answered. Two other clients called to say they were feeling much better physically and emotionally.

I was happy to hear that their prayers were answered. The trip was successful on the spiritual level and manifested on the physical. In my heart I felt that Mark was at a turning point but I did not know what he was going to choose. He would either choose a more enhanced rewarding life or he would go back to his old ways which would have him repeating the same behavior over and over.

On the other hand, I knew I had advanced on my path, as the phone calls were confirmation of the work I did. As a result of my quest, I felt more uplifted and rewarded. My heart felt full because I had captivated the energy at the reservation and had completed my mission.

"Though they are so great, so glorious, so pure, so wonderful, that the very sight of them (if we were allowed to see them) would strike us to the earth, as it did the prophet Daniel," holy and righteous as he was, yet they are our fellow-servants and our fellow-workers, and they carefully watch over and defend even the humblest of us."

—Cardinal Newman

Chapter Thirteen

Angels Our Heavenly Host

"Millions of spiritual creatures walk the earth unseen,
both when we wake and when we sleep,"—John Milton,

—Paradise Lost, IV

In the cold bleak winter of December 1999, I was weary in spirit. Mark, the man I had been dating, had run away from our relationship again. When he left he did not tell me what was wrong or why he left. It was a mystery to me but I suspect it could have been the last argument we had. This type of behavior is very cruel. It hurt my soul and my feelings. It was as if he put a knife in my heart and shredded it. The pain was excruciating. My heart was torn in two. I needed help immediately, not physical but spiritual.

In desperation I searched for answers to help heal my heart. I searched everywhere, praying and asking for guidance in my life. In meditation, I heard,

'The relationship is not quite over,' nonetheless on the physical level, nothing was happening.

It was a soft voice and I know it was White Feather she was there to protect me like always. In the Bible it reads, *"Do not judge by appearance, but judge with right judgment."* From John 7:24.

I fought to keep depression from taking over and deplete my joyful spirit. If it had not been for my dear friend's and my faith, I could have become depressed and stayed that way. Falling into a depressed state was not going to help me, or answer the questions that were in my heart. Why did Mark run away? Was this fair in the game of love? Why didn't I have a loving and compatible relationship? Mark loved me in his own way and I loved him. I had to figure out some other higher avenue. Yet spending time on such stupid behavior was silly since it was a cop out.

The one thing I knew about Mark is that he did not like to deal with the reality of how a relationship works. Communication is necessary if one is to have a loving relationship that lasts and becomes filled with more love. Mark would rather run than talk. I feel now he was afraid of making a deeper commitment. This is what it really is all about.

White Feather usually lets me make my own mistakes about people, so I was surprised when she told me to leave Mark and to move forward on my path. She tried to tell me a long time ago but I would not listen. Sometimes White Feather does not mince words. White Feather knew I had to find out who I was. Some of my purpose was becoming clear, but not all of it. White Feather I realized, was protecting me from more hurt with Mark. She wanted me to have the best man and she clearly felt it was not Mark. She never gave me the specifics of why she felt this way, but I do know she felt this. Eventually I would learn the truth about Mark from White Feather but knowing her, she had her own timing.

One cold rainy day I decided that since Mark would not talk to me, I'd seek help from others. I could not stand the thought of talking to White Feather about my problem because she knew I still wanted to hang on to him. Still hoping for a miracle to heal our troubled relationship, I just could not let go.

I turned to the angels. I believed in guardian angels and I sought Heavenly guidance. Guardian angels can give inner guidance and since angels are messengers from, Heaven I would enlist their help with my troubled love life. A celestial companion is what I needed at this very moment in my life. At a crossroad, and I needed a boost. Now, I just needed to reach them.

Some years ago at the ranch my friend Danielle and I talked to the angels. We had a feeling that we could do it and that the angels would hear us. I realize now that White Feather opened the door to our talking to the angels, because she wanted us to know that spiritual help comes in many ways. We believed in angels and felt that we could talk to them even if we didn't see them. So, we asked them questions and then write down the answers or what we heard. We felt that we were really communication with them. The angels communicated with us through an intuitive feeling in our gut. It was not White Feather's voice, but still it was a healing presence. Experiences like this strengthened my faith in angels. We did this for years. Their answers always calmed us and we could feel their loving energy run through our souls.

We asked the angels to help us with our heartaches and anguish. Then we asked where our future is heading. Would either of us marry again? We both felt we would get married to the right men. This experience strengthened my faith in angels.

Thinking about Mark, I knew he wasn't sitting around over come with grief. He had drugs and alcohol to numb any pain from our break-up Opening my heart to the angels and White Feather I tried to raise my consciousness to a higher level.

Healing I knew would come, but it would take time, as time heals all wounds. Heartache is just things of this earth, but in the higher realms it did not exist. Except right now it felt like it would take a million years to get over Mark. I did not hold back like he did. He was experienced and he'd just throw a shield over his heart and when needed, chock down some beers to cover his feeling for anyone. After all I was just another woman and they were not worth much to him. He could replace me in a couple of months or sooner. That was how shallow he was. This made me cringe inside because of how much I had loved him.

I needed to know more about angels, so I searched for a book that could shed light on the topic. This whispering in my head I realized could be my guardian angel or White Feather, and I knew in my soul the angels would help me over come depression. Mixed with emotional pain it was hard to tell whose voice it was. White Feather knew I was with my guardian angel. I had asked White Feather if this was all right with her,

"We are both here with you and are surrounding you with Heavenly light. Do not worry who is with you, just know that we are here," she said.

That was White Feather and her voice was almost like singing. I could never forget that song!

A willing heart is needed in order to receive answers from angels. So, I bought white candles every night, I prayed and meditated. I made myself do it whether I wanted to or not. I decided to reach the angels; I needed to do these things. I needed to raise my consciousness to a higher level. This went on for weeks without anything really happening, until one day my answer arrived. Praying my heart out for a month, a letter had arrived from a man who said he was an angel prophet. He called himself, 'As Ariel the Angel Prophet.' Then I thought, why not? Here I had received an answer to my prayers but I was suspicious, so I didn't send for the information. His advertisement seemed too commercial. But finally, I changed my mind and sent away for the packet anyway.

In a few weeks, at the end of December, I received the envelope. It was extraordinary. When I touched the paper its light blue vibrations of love and colors of pink, purple, and gold were radiating from it. In my soul I knew this packet was full of warmth and kindness. It contained just what I had prayed for personally typed pages, with information about guidance from angels. What I happily discovered was that angels were already working miracles in my life. In my mind's eye I saw the angels in the sky above my house, each one sitting on a soft white puffy cloud, waving to me.

The angel packet also included a pamphlet explaining that, As Ariel Prophet is an apostle of God, who has been blessed with the gift of the spirit known As Angel Prophet. Angel Prophet reveals miracles that may occur in your life as a result of revelations from the Angel. The Ariel Prophet directs you on the proper blessed path.

As Ariel wrote,

"When someone asks what a miracle is?" I answer them,

'For those who believe in God, no explanation is necessary, and for those who do not believe in God, no explanation is possible.'

Direct instructions on how to initiate specific prayers for specific situations were also included. I learned the names of angels who are currently protecting me. Angels might talk to you through your intuition, your gut feelings, or they can show up in a human form to save you. They speak to us through our gut instinct. This is a prophecy from a higher level of thought. This information represents the words of God as revealed to As Ariel the Angel prophet. This information was treated with the respect it deserved. The words are sacred if you believe.

It was told to me that one of my angels would reveal the blessed path that I was to follow in the next year. This information lets me enter into a personal relationship with angels. Those powerful angels hear our prayers, and if we ask properly, they will see to the fulfillment of our prayers. Remember this only happens if you have the faith and believe in God. As the Bible states, *"Faith is the assurance of things hoped for, the conviction of things not seen."* From Hebrew 11:01.

I took the sacred packet in my hands and read every word that As Ariel had sent me. I applied each instruction on angel prayers to my life. I was conscientious and diligent in my effort to undertake a new avenue of learning. Not only that, I applied the angel prayers to my everyday existence. In my heart I knew that if I persisted, I would see subtle changes in me. I believed my life was about to change and improve. I picked up the sacred angel pages and held them close to my heart. Regarding my relationship, I knew that an answer to my prayers would appear. This was the beginning of love and miracles for me, and grateful tears ran down my face. White Feather was watching over me and saw what was going on in my life. She was happy that I was receiving the right answers.

These are a few paragraphs I would like to share from the packet sent to me by As Ariel:

LOVE

There are numerous miracles of love on your blessed path during the next year. These miracles will come in the areas of friendship, family and romance. Jean, your holy angel of love is Rahmiel. Please do not confuse love with lust. Rahmiel will fill your next twelve months with an abundance of true perfect love if you will let her. Rahmiel is quite accessible. To make any request of her simply hold your sacred love icon and pray: *My loving Rahmiel, carry this prayer to Heaven and bring me back my desire. O God, I love thee above all things, with my whole heart and soul because thou are all good and worthy of all love. I love my neighbor as myself for the love of thee. I forgive all who have injured me, and I ask pardon of all that I have injured.* Ariel the Angel prophet informed me after reciting this prayer, "Jean, ask Rahmiel for exactly what it is that you desire. If you want assistance in romance just ask Rahmiel. Jean, please do not give up on romance. It is never too late for love. For improved friendships ask for help and be specific. If you desire new friends say so. If you wish to renew old friendships you merely need to ask. There are many friendships that lay ahead on your blessed path, even one that is more important than any you have experienced before. You will find this to be true in the next few months."

Rahmiel did answer me when I asked her about Mark! She told me,

"Let the relationship go for right now. Don't try and make it work. I will help you heal your heart. Don't try and fix it. If the relationship is meant to be then you well be together again."

That's exactly what I heard. Even so, when Mark wanted to try again on the relationship, I went for it. It still did not work because there were no changes. Mark did not want to change and he got very mad if I suggested he do so. Our relationship was choking me to death so I had to let it go. It took me four years to get over it our relationship but I finally did. I over came my heartache, I could again think clearly, and realized we just could not make it together. Also I recognize God never gives us a mountain we can not climb over but it took every ounce of courage I had in me to reach the top of the mountain.

The most recent angel experience I had was when a client of mine was on White Feather's healing massage table. I saw gold light all around him which told me that another angel was with us. After he left I went into my kitchen where I noticed something flicker by my window. I thought it was my cat, but when I looked closer, I saw white feathers. For a quick second I saw a glimpse of an angel. I just stood in my kitchen with a big smile came on my face. I knew it was not White Feather, but one of her angel friends. White Feather had already left when my client got up from her table. To me this visit was confirmation that we are doing powerful work together.

During this time I was visited by a magnificent vision of an angel behind plate of chiseled glass. In the center of this image was a long stemmed rose. The angel had on a white gown with light shimmering forth surrounding her. It was at the ranch and I had just returned to my apartment. I was going to lie down on my bed, for a few minutes. I looked at her lovely face and radiant smile, and the halo above her head was gold. Her light was illuminating out so much it shown through the round plate glass. I was overwhelmed. Within two minutes the angel was gone, but I knew this vision would never be gone from my memory. I went over and lay on my bed, so I could receive her rays of healing light. The warm feeling was penetrating my soul, and I responded with a smile. I can still remember the light and love of her, showering me with faith. Again, this showed me that I'm doing the right work and on the right path.

I believe that an angel in human form delivered that packet into my mailbox because it was an answer to my prayers. The angels knew I would receive the correct answers sought regarding Mark and that a healing would result. Although I did after that see that I am now at peace due to the information I received from the Angel prophet and his healing packet.

White Feather encouraged me on my search for answers through the angels. But what I know now is if I would have gotten the wrong information she would have stepped in. That's the way she is, an angel of love and mercy because she understood my aching heart and she was always with me no matter how many angels I had.

Angels are all ways with you, no matter what the circumstances. Here is a wonderful example:

Once during a winter storm my electricity had been out for five days. My house is all electric and I was so cold I was getting very upset. I was covered from head to toe with blankets sitting on my bed at 3:00 A.M in the morning. I started praying and finally I said out loud,

"Why do I have to go through this cold condition?" I did not think I could stand it another minute when suddenly a bright angel appeared above my head. The light was startling, looking up at the light a yellowish glow was around this very tall angel. I sat there in the middle of my bed and stared for a minute then I yelled out,

"I need help! Please turn on my electricity right now," I said. The very minute I asked the angel my electric came on. Just like that.

"Thank you so much." as tears of thankfulness ran down my face. This is one miracle that I will never forget.

Our angels are here and we should believe in them and know they always have our best interest at heart. All we have to do is believe. White Feather and my guardian angel guided me with their loving ways gently, tenderly as they showed me the way to peace and harmony in my life. Angeles are our Heavenly hosts and we are so fortunate to have their protection while we are here on earth. God and our angels are all we need to get through what life throws at us. Take a deep breath and look above, they are there, angles our Heavenly hosts.

"Live your life in prayer."

—John Paul II

Chapter Fourteen

White Feather's Menu to Prayer

"This is a menu to prayer for beginners to advance. Starts with the first step the way to you're spiritual path. It starts with you."

—Author

White Feather had told me to write several chapters on prayer and as you compare them I want you to remember that these are the tools that can save your life. Prayers are an exercise of faith.

White Feather told me,

"Give this menu as a guide for healing and for the human race to rescue themselves in times of crisis, which seems to be all the time."

That is how much White Feather cares and loves people. Then I heard a gentle laugh as she continued to explain that these chapters are the main part of the book, the most important and inspirational. These chapters will help you work through your challenges. As we learn in metaphysical teachings, *Grace is one wing of the bird; your effort is the other wing.*

There will always be physical challenges in life but these chapters will soften any blow or any situation that anyone is dealing with. Prayer will give you hope and additional faith. You are moving in a dance of light through receiving more faith and love. Heavenly messengers are always around you.

I knew that White Feather was right about this because I could remember the turmoil's I have been in and how through my faith, things turned around for my highest good. The tools she taught me had saved my life, and I had used them to ward off the energy of the Wolf.

The following information is what White Feather channeled to me and how she simplified this knowledge for others. I have also included my experience using this knowledge to deal with the wolf's games. She asked that the chapters be presented in the following order:

The Creamy Foundation—chapter is for the reader that has read little or nothing about prayer. This chapter will encourage the reader to visualize the new information they are given. White Feather's teaching will stimulate the reader to use their vivid imagination to see the creamy foundation of a cake batter. Then the reader will have the knowledge of how prayer and the energy of prayer work together in the universe. It is also a spiritual baby-step for the beginner in prayer and how to pray correctly.

1. The Prayer—is a chapter is for those who have studied prayer, but still need to remind themselves to continue to pray and take action through prayer. It also has elements to calm anxiety and put faith and hope in our hearts for our future. We must stay prayed up because this pushes us forward on our spiritual path.

2. The Seascape—is a chapter is for those readers who need to think and feel what they are reading. This chapter teaches us how to be calm in an emotional storm. It puts the reader in a healing environment and gives them the basic foundation of why we pray. When the reader practices prayer and meditation through this visualization, their mind, body and spirit are comforted and at peace.

3. Meditation—The Real Voice shows the reader how meditation calms the mind and soul. Prayer is when we talk to God and meditation is where we receive messages and answers to our prayer. As I have said, "They go together like peaches and cream."

4. Amazing Grace—is a chapter filled with answered prayers. God always answers prayers. This is of course in God's own timing and when the time is right the answer will be astonishing because God is supernatural and he works in mysterious ways.

"The most significant prayer you can say is," Thank you."

—White Feather

Chapter Fifteen

The Creamy Foundation of Prayer

"The following chapter describes how you can shape your prayer and then visualize the creamy foundation of your prayer. This will give your prayer substance and power."

—White Feather

After the incident at a local restaurant I refused to meet with the wolf. However, this did not stop him. The wolf's footprints continued to show up in all areas of my life, continued to track me down I know a wolf will starve itself to death before making a mistake in the wild. As I grew in spiritual strength and understanding, the wolf hounded me with an increased intensity. It was as if he feared the changes he saw in me. On one hand he wanted me to be self-supporting and independent on the other hand he wanted to take it all away from me.

I sought higher ground to keep me sane in all these major challenges. I listened and practiced what White Feather taught me and I studied the metaphysical teachings of Dr. Ernest Holmes, author of the Science of Mind, and founder of the Church of Religious Science. This teaching expanded my thought to a higher consciousness and I grew personally on every level; mind, body and spirit. But, the wolf, who mates for life, continued to hound me in every possible way. He was not finished with me he wanted his teeth burred in my skin.

The Hungry Wolf wanted to smell blood.

Finally, I was forced to ask White Feather for help with my fears of the wolf. I know that fear can't hurt you unless you surrender to it but I wanted encouragement and White Feather was always there for me.

"White Feather, how do I pray more efficiently to keep the wolf away?" I asked.

White Feather didn't get a chance to answer before I was over taken with an urge for a piece of chocolate cake. I knew I was hungry for something to soothe my raw nerves. The Hungry Wolf was really getting to me. Having heard about my work with White Feather sometimes he'd call me with discouraging negative in-put. He refused to pay my support without belly aching about it and he now was so angry, I finally had to quit seeing him. He'd show up at restaurants or events that I attended and would force me to listen to him, threatening to make a scene unless I put up with the wolf. I was stressed out about money and getting the wolf out of my life.

"Don't think about eating that cake. Instead, take that cake batter and turn it into a *creamy foundation of prayer,*" That's where your answers lie," White Feather said.

"Visualize a *creamy foundation.* Why should I do that?" I asked.

"What did you say?" I said.

She continued,

"This powerful batter has every ingredient of healing, for your highest good. See a creamy foundation with all the elements in it such as love, health, prosperity, and healing," she continued,

"See the lumps, bumps in the batter, which are your fears and doubts about your situation, smoothed out. See your fears replaced with faith. Replace your worry about the wolf with an image of yourself opening your mail box and finding a big fat check," she said. That made me smile.

She continued,

"When we pray, our prayers start to take shape and they build a magnetic energy connection which is the cream of the prayer. Concentrate on clearing your mind and heart. See yourself with the energy of bright light forming in the universe. See yourself following this light for spiritual growth and enlighten-ment.

She continued,

Remember that the drive of the universe is always higher consciousness. The more awareness you have, the more you will experience a loving and healthy life. In your mind say, I see myself feeling strong and healthy. I see my body looking the way I want it to look. I see myself moving with ease in a flexible manner. I take my positive image into prayer," she said.

I was very surprised to hear White Feather tell me this much all at once, since she usually gave it to me like a spoonful of medicine, one spoon at a time.

For example, if I had an illness like cancer I am not going to take my condition or poor health in prayer—that's the lumps. I take my positive image into prayer. Instead I am going to see myself as completely healthy, that's the smooth prayer batter. We have the power to heal ourselves if we have the faith to believe.

When I do this is I know my prayers are being heard and formed and will be answered in accordance to God's divine timing. See yourself with more hope and inspiration—a *creamy foundation* developing in exactly the right way with all the lumps whipped out of the batter. When all the bumps and lumps, are gone you know your prayer will happen. You have generated the right energy power and illumination for your *"creamy foundation."*

I used the information White Feather gave me. I began to see a creamy chocolate cake batter filled with images of prosperity. I had a fat wallet with thousand dollar bills in it. My bills were being paid and I saw myself calm, knowing that God was taking care of me. I saw the Hungry Wolf writing out a check for me and putting it in the mail for me, however, I did not limit my prosperity to him. I literality saw hundreds of thousands of dollars flying toward me from all multiple sources.

I felt a calmness come over me as I practiced this form of prayer. This calmness laid a foundation for good things to come into my life. I grew less stressed and more trusting. I practiced this prayer and learned how to smooth the lumps in the batter. In other words, I was able to take the wolf out of my consciousness. I had to look at myself in a different light. I was not a snail to be stepped on rather I had to see myself as a tigress to be dealt with. I was just starting to change from the humble Little Red Riding Hood to a new cub tigress.

White Feather taught me to look at your prayer like I was making the best creamy cake batter. You put all the right elements into this batter or formula. Another example, if you are having a disagreement in a relationship, instead of playing the argument over and over again in your mind, you can see yourself with this person in a happier situation. You are laughing and talking easily together. Put all the right elements into this batter, or formula.

You look a little closer and *see* a creamy smooth, (no lumps), consistency, for the combined components, which is happiness, fun, laughter and love between each other. The mix is as smooth as vanilla ice-cream on top of your chocolate cake and you can taste it going slowly down your throat. Yummy! When you taste this amazing batter, it fills your soul. Then you know your prayer is in God's hands and your cake has risen to perfection.

When you bake your cake and look at the cake in the oven, you can see it rise and start to take form. The cake starts to smell so good and Heavenly. In that moment that's when your prayer starts to take hold. That's when you know you have prayed and used all the right ingredients.

Now, this is when you let your prayer go. You do not have to go over and over your prayers. If you do go over and over them, you're really telling God I don't believe you heard me and I want to make sure you did. This is a fear voice, not a believing voice. Pray in good faith, pray diligently, and pray believing. Your job is to create the creamy batter.

Remember, White Feather reminds me to not take the facts or situation as I know them into prayer because God knows them too. The facts are the lumps in the batter and we don't want any lumps in our cream. God already knows the cold hard facts. Take into prayer the positive. The object of prayer is to change the facts and conditions. Visualize, what you believe, not taking the facts into prayer. God already knows your car is broken down and that you are out of money. God already knew that the wolf was hounding me and that I was stressed about money.

My spiritual commitment was to pray until I could see a smooth cake batter of affluence flowing toward me and the wolf was removed from my life. My work was to believe my prayer had already been answered and thank God for my prosperity. It seemed like the last minute God and White Feather always stepped in whether it be new clients for healing massage or Adam finding a way to get my checks from the wolf or a client sending a check for prayer. I was always protected because I had no doubt about prayer. That is the key to unlocking the door to prosperity. Pray in good faith, pray diligently, and pray believing.

My effort in prayer was to pray until I could see a smooth cake batter of money flowing toward me and the wolf removed from my life. My work was to believe my prayer had already been answered and thank God for my prosperity.

Everything is possible through God because He is supernatural. Just remember God works in mysterious ways and we do not know how He will answer your prayer. God is in charge of your cake. You need to take it out of the oven. Just smell the aroma and feel the power of your prayer in and around you and the energy in the universe working for you. There is no hardship or anything that God cannot solve. You have to wait upon the Lord to answer your prayers and believe that he will. He is always listening and loves us beyond our understanding. We do not have to know everything. Sometimes we get too nosey. God is teaching patience and love. Look to the good and see what happens. Be aware it will happen in a positive way. God is love and he loves your batter and the cake you made. Divine timing is in Gods' hands for only he knows the whole picture and purpose for your life. Remember you are praying to a supernatural being. He has great power. Be patient.

Nothing is more powerful than prayer. It changes the hard facts of life. When I talk about prayer, I am also talking about training your mind to trust a Higher Power. I am talking about concentrating and using your energy in a positive way. Without a mind trained in prayer you are like loose cannon. You could be drowning in negative stuff. You're not building the right foundation in prayer. Your thoughts are all over the place. Instead of thinking about the solution you are thinking about the problem.

A trained mind thinks about the solution and stays on the highest levels.

Prayer is an implement of the highest value. I am giving you a sample of the fundamentals of prayer. Now, make your own special cake batter and create for yourself a new energy, a new life for yourself. It takes commitment and courage, to see where we are in our lives and not cover our true feelings.

Learning prayer will change your whole life in a very positive way. It will change the way you see yourself and your situation. It will change your sorrows, your pain and limitations. It will give you hope of any improved life through learning how to create the *creamy foundation of prayer*. We will use this spiritual treatment (prayer) for life to change ourselves and enhance our life. Only prayer can change the human spirit and everyone close to you will get the benefit.

Wait until you "see" the result of your *creamy foundation of prayer*. This spiritual connection can change your life. Journeying into a new thought process and energy will amaze you, astound and over whelm you and bless you. Please hold on to the seat of your pants, you are going to experience the ride of a lifetime.

The way you make your formula for your cake depends on you. But I can tell that unless you start believing in prayer and spirit, nothing in your life will change or improve. It will be the same old rut. The vibrations of your soul need to be changed by changing your attitude and having more faith. No one can do it for you. It's up to you to dig in and get that batter going.

Making your creamy foundation of prayer is something that you should practice everyday in order to keep the enthusiasm and energy going. Learning to pray is like everything else in life. People have to want it like it's their last breath. Be motivated. The more you pray the better you become at it. You have everything to gain and nothing to lose. Some people have to be in crisis, hit the wall with old thoughts and behavior, before they are willing to change.

As the Buddha says,

"Each has to walk and find the way themselves. There is no one who can enlighten another being."

In other words if a person wants to keep his blinders on, there is no way you can change that fact but you can pray for them and never give up.

The right cake batter and your finished cake will bring you your heart's desire and compassion for others. Do not wait until you are pushed up against the wall or some major catastrophe happens. The practice of your prayer can be perfect. It is totally up to you. Serve God with your whole heart. It's worth your greatest effort.

This is how I used my creamy foundation prayer for a client of mine. A client of mine brought a friend of hers to see me. Her name is Crystal and she looked very depressed.

"What is wrong with you?" I asked. Crystal was very withdrawn and in a lot of pain.

After two years,

"John, my boyfriend, left me with out telling me why? He only said that he changed his mind. I am suffering," she said.

"I am sorry to hear this. We can pray for the situation to heal and know that if you both are to be together again things will turn around," I said.

"I think that this is fine with me. I am looking forward to my healing massage," After the healing was done from White Feather, Crystal spoke up,

"I feel so much better and my heart does not hurt as much," she said.

"I am so glad and I'll keep praying that the right thing will happen for the both of you," I said.

"Thank you, and I will too."

A year went by and I did not hear from her. She lived out of town. One day out of the blue, she calls me,

"Jean, I have been helping John with his mother and we ran into each other and he asked me out on a date. It was wonderful better than the past dates we have had. He then, asked me to marry him and the answer was yes. He gave me a lovely wedding ring and I am so happy. I feel it has a lot to do with the healing from White Feather and our prayers," she said.

"What wonderful news. I am so happy for the both of you. Thank you for calling and telling me. I appreciate it when my work is valued," I said.

I thanked White Feather for her gift of the creamy foundation and reflected on the following Bible verse. *"All things, whatever ye shall ask in prayer, believing, ye shall receive."* From Matthew 21:22. You notice there is no doubt or lumps in this verse—just a strong belief system. Then I heard, *"Ask, and it will be given to you; seek and you will find; knock and it will be opened to you."* From Luke 11:09.

We need to see the cream and energy as smooth as silk and flowing into our life. If our cream is not smooth but lumpy it is not coming from God. We need to know the cream of our prayer is an instrument of God. Try and always come from a position of prayer and keep that cream blending. This will gives you inward power and strength and divine answers to your life.

"What lies behind us and what lies before us are
tiny matters compared to what lies within us."

—Ralph Waldo Emerson

Chapter Sixteen

Prayer

"For I know the plans I have for you, says the Lord, plan welfare and not for evil, to gave you a future and a hope. Then you will call upon me and come and pray to me, and I will hear you. You will seek me and find me, when you seek me with you're heart, I will be found by you, saith the Lord."

—Jeremiah 29:11-12-13

Prayer is quite simple. The hard part is getting our mind to associate with the right mental picture. White Feather states the following;

1.   Prayer is when we talk to God; and this puts us in alignment with Him.

2.   Meditation is when we listen and are more aware of the truth.

White Feather says that prayer and meditation go together like peaches and cream. White Feather knows that prayer is as natural as breathing. She wants us to pray daily, so we can improve our life. Prayer will lift us out of ourselves and into our spirit and heal our soul. It is what helps us to overcome negative thoughts, and change our negatives (-) to a positive (+). Affirmative action is what prayer does.

God invented prayer so that we will come to Him and continue talking to Him. He wants us to get to know Him through our prayers. The more you know God and trust him the easier it is to pray and believe in your prayers and keep your faith strong. White Feather wants us to be happy when we pray because you are going to get the help you seek.

Prayer is a choice and a life style. You don't just pray when you are in the midst of danger or loss. You pray everyday so that you strengthen your connection with the divine. Thank God for his loving support. Kept God in your heart and bless Him. Choose to pray and stay focused on Him for he knows all our fears, heartaches, and sorrows. Uncertainly breeds fear but prayer is more powerful. God will strengthen and uplift you and bless us. God will not make us part of the problem, but part of a Heavenly solution.

If you feel your prayer is not answered right away. Do not give up. Keep your faith alive in pray. Nothing is more important than to continue our prayer life. Continue to pray if you are dealing with something that might not have lifted, like depression, or any other major problem keep praying. God is testing you, he will not forsake you. Prayer is powerful and you can rely on prayer. I kept my prayers strong in dealing with the dangers of the wolf.

Be persistent in prayer. Search for answers through prayer, God will guide you and give you the right intention for your life. If a purpose is what you are looking for, God has the answer. All you should do is continued to pray until you learn the answer and let your heart be, 'open' to it. Believe what you hear. When you soul is in the Lost and Found Department find the way out through prayer. God is our source not you, we just have to follow the yellow brick road down our path to enlighten spirit. It all starts with you.

You are in God's favor. Elevate your spirit. As we draw nearer to God, he draws a million times nearer to you. God always has a plan for our life. Plan A, fails he will have a greater plan B. When one door closes God will open another door or window. God is working behind the scene. He's painting you a rainbow. He is for you and not against you, and He will strengthen you in your hour of need. You might ask yourself,

"How can a human being fight the devil?" Only through prayer can we survive the arrows of the devil. Grab your bow and arrow and start shooting powerful loving arrows from God's bow. God will hit the mark. Never fear for God is with you all the time and nothing is impossible with God. But with out faith it's impossible to please God.

When we chose to have fear in us we do dreadful things or put off going to the doctor because we are afraid of the results of your tests. You run away because you feel you cannot stand up to the situation of your relationships. What ever it is do not let fear over come you, put it in prayer and you will see changes that will enhance your life.

About the time you are ready to give up here comes God with his super-natural power and something wonderful that you least expected happens. Don't give up on your miracle before it happens. I have seen ordinary people, through prayer, do ordinary things for God and become very successful.

We may not comprehend why some of our prayers are not responded to immediately. That is a mystery to humans. We have to have patience and wait for God for our answers, sometimes the silent years seem to take forever. God is doing a great work in you and you are learning many lessons. God is working on your spirit in many ways. You are being prepared for greater status in life because the silent years are teaching you many new things. Be prepared for many different changes of tremendous healing, or improved health, a new car, a greater job, more understanding in your personal relationships with your family. God will come through.

White Feather reminded me of how simple it is to pray because God is always listening. This reminded me I had to pray with conviction of the highest truth and pray with great faith if I wanted things to change in my life. All the good was there for me. Nothing is more important than prayer and I know prayer will lift me to the highest level and that is when soul is lifted into the spirit world.

We are promised, *"If we ask anything according to his will, he will hear us; and if we know and had no doubt that he hears us, we know we have the petitions that we desire from him."* From John 5:14-05.

Here is a good example about waiting for God. I had a client who is just learning how to pray. She sat down to pray her very first prayer and it was answered immediately. She thought this is great. The second prayer was not answered right away. A couple of days later she called me,

"I must be doing something wrong?" she said.

"It's up to God and his timing when prayer is answered, you can't push God." I said.

The object is to let God be in charge of your prayer. We do not have control over any prayer. When we continue to pray and show God that we have faith and believe in him things turn around for the good. Now look for the greatness of His power to move you forward on your spiritual path and the blessings that come out of your prayer when you keep your faith in Him.

If you feel your prayer is not answered right away do not give up. God always has a reason as to when prayers are answered. Trust God and continue to pray. If you are praying for something that might not have lifted, like depression, or any other problem keep praying. Live your life in prayer because your good deeds are your highest prayer. Keep God in your heart and bless Him. Prayer is powerful and you can rely on prayer. Keep your faith alive in prayer, because sometimes you have to get out of your own way in order to have spiritual enlighten-ment.

That is what I had to do when the wolf was chasing me into every conceivable dark corner. I forced myself to stay focused in prayer morning, noon and night. I would not let go of God's love. The veil of sin was lifted and the truth had been revealed. I had to push that wolf aside and go into prayer with a clear mind believing God and White Feather were protecting me. Also because of prayer my character had been strengthened. One Bible verse *"I can do all things in him who strengthens me."* From Philippians 4:13. This continued to run through my mind like a mantra.

When we pray, we often tell God about our problems. Instead of focusing on what we do want, we tell Him what we don't want. We must stay positive in prayer. White Feather reminds me to leave the actual facts and conditions of a problem out of prayer. They are not the truth. White Feather tells me to take positive images, positive facts, and conditions into prayer. She reminds me to leave the negative out of prayer. Then take positive action, as our actions reflect our belief. What you want to take into prayer is a positive affirmation.

For example, if you want to purchase a new car, see yourself having all the money you need to pay for it and then, see yourself driving it home. What you do not want to do is see yourself driving a second rate car and paying for it with maxed out credit cards. Be positive in prayer and know that God will bring the right car into your life.

When you bring negative into prayer, you push and block out positive flow of prayer. Give God a chance, have some patience the response will be meaningful. Patience is probably another lesson for you; I know it was for me. Be inspired in prayer be bold. White Feather often reminds me to pray. She reminds me do not negate my prayers. Be positive all times in prayer.

"God is listening and always responds," she says.

Our prayers are the foundation that proceeds ahead of us on our spiritual path of light. If I did not have God, and faith in White Feather and the angels, my time on earth would have been shortened because I would have given up. Thank God and White Feather that there's a loving spirit to protect us. There is nothing more profound and powerful then a band of angels helping us in times of great need. This shows us we are loved beyond measure. This is why it is so important to stay prayed up.

While the wolf kept bullying, threatening, and pushing me back to court, I kept my faith and prayed. I continued to pray and meditate. This saved me. Nothing is more powerful than prayer. Through prayer I was guided to the right thing. He was determined that he was not going to pay me one dime. In fact, he felt I owed him millions. I had made up my mind that this time I was the winner and he could shout and scream all he wanted too. I was determined to get back a portion of what he had taken from me. The wolf was not going to be satisfied until he got what he wanted a good juicy, piece of my flesh for his dinner.

He knew how to hunt his prey but this time I was not going to be his prize. I had grown a backbone instead of a wish-bone. I was no longer going to keep running; instead I took control and fought my ex. in the battlefield of the court system.

After my divorce, when the wolf put my house into foreclosure, I was forced to move. That almost devastated me because I really loved my house. However, I had a small barn that was still on the property. I needed the barn moved to where my mare was living. The attorneys for the owner of the house were a pack of ravenous wolves and would not let me move the barn.

"The barn is hooked on to the house therefore, you cannot move it," he said, with an angry voice, I shuttered when I heard his voice. That was a lie because the barn was on skids and could be moved.

I was very upset by his behavior. So I called my friend who is also a minister and asked her to pray for me.

"Jean, do not take the facts into prayer. God already knows what the facts are. Pray for what you want to happen and visualize the barn where you want it," she said.

So, I did exactly what she told me to do.

A couple of weeks later his attorney called me and said,

"Ms. Little Red Riding Hood, we will give you two weeks to move the barn." he said in a stern voice. I moved the barn off the old property and on to the new. Misty Moonlight and I were able to enjoy its new spot for five years. I thanked God, White Feather and my friend for helping me with prayer. My prayer was definitely answered.

When you pray, believing in your own prayer: Any negative will be changed to—a positive thought. Learn to think, on a higher level, when you pray, by focusing on what you like to have happen. Then let your prayer go and put God in charge of the prayer. Try and not go over and over your prayer because you are telling God I have fear and do not trust you. The prayer will manifest if it is God's will for your life and if the prayer is in divine timing.

Be sure to thank God for your answered prayers because you know there will always be something to pray for in your life. It's not a good idea to go down the road of life and continue asking God for answers with out thanking him for what you have. Prayer is not built on what you own or how much money you have or do not have or even how many wolves you have in your life. Prayer does not have anything to do with education or the lack of it. Prayer is built on faith and love and commitments to God.

The Heavenly realms know about wolves in sheep's clothing, that is what I had to remind myself. God knew what was going on and White Feather was looking out after me too. That is what kept me going, knowing, and believing I was going to rise above it, and I did. This was my opportunity to grow in spirit and my challenges were enormous but I always heard, "God never gives you more than you can handle."

I now believe that's true. That does not make it any easier to survive my challenges but I did use my faith and trust in God. It is important to keep your prayers going especially if you do not see anything happening or receive any answers. I knew the answers would come and tomorrow could be harvest time. I knew that was when God was testing my faith. I knew the tables were turning on the wolf and I was not going to run away. With God's help I was going to win these court battles.

White Feather encourages me to put my trust in God. She says,

"God has the answer to life's greatest challenges. Keep in mind it is a privilege to pray. God always answers prayer. When God does not respond to your prayers, it is because you are not sincere and you gave up too soon on believing in prayer. We have to keep the energy going in prayer. Sometimes, the answers are not what we were looking for, or in the time line we requested, but the prayer is answered," she said.

The object is to let God be in charge of your prayer. We do not have control over any prayer. Most people just want to have a fast fix, but this is not how prayer works. We should remember, to be calm within is to know God. The power of love within you is the presence of God.

Occasionally, when we pray God tells us to do something else we have not done for a long time. Our actions reflect our belief system. For example, take action, contact someone, write letters or call a new friend. This is when it's important to do what we know we are guided to do and not change what God wants us to do. The answer may not come in words, but in a feeling in one's gut.

The key is to take the right action on what you hear from your angel; she is nudging you in your gut and giving you a message. You can pray until you are blue in the face, but unless you take the right action your prayer is kicked out of the box and nothing will change. Also ask for guidance when you pray so you take the right action. I then thought about what William Randall Hurst said, *'Action is life.'* I know how to pray and take action is what sums up prayer and changes our lives for the highest good for all.

When I say action I mean the right action to change your way of thinking especially if you are negative and living in fear. For example, if in prayer you were told, *'Do not gamble any more or take drugs,'* but you continue to do these things, then your life will not change. God always has a reason for asking you to do something. You are asking for difficulty in your life. I had a client who need to quit gambling and she didn't until she lost everything.

My client and I had been talking about continuing her old addictive habits and I gave her a warning.

"You can not make up for your past mistakes or the money you have lost," I told her. I encouraged her to move on with her life in the right way. Trust in God and believe if you had prosperity once you can have it again. God works for us, not against us. God is in our favor and is working behind the scenes. As far as I know my client took the right action and turned her life around. Now she is more productive and a much happier person. She is back with her family and learned a very valuable lesson in life.

Another Bible verse popped into my head, *"God will restore the years the locust has taken."* From Joel 2:25.

In order to pray it is important to focus and clear one's mind and go into silent prayer. It's good to start praying at night when there are fewer distractions.

Deep prayer does work the more you pray, the better you will become. In learning to pray it's important to clear your mind and go into silence. This is your time to get to know God. During this time you can concentrate your thoughts upon God. Avoid the constant company of other people.

People are like sponges. If they are not on a spiritual path they can take everything out of you and sap up your energy. They want you to stay on their level. These people need help and pray that they get it. Be a leader and not a follower of negative thoughts, think higher spiritual thoughts. Remember, you are what you think.

Each prayer does work for our highest good. The more you pray, the better you will become at praying. You will feel comfortable, relaxed and know that prayer is your friend. Do not give up. Your soul knows, prayer and meditation are the most Heavenly tools we have. Prayer and our faith will get us through the hardships of life. Stay in prayer the help is coming; harvest time is near. Just because you don't see your prayer answered does not mean that it won't be. What is good for you is on its way. Give God a chance. Have patience wait for God he knows the diving timing for our prayers to be answered.

Just keep in mind, your faith will get you through the adversity of life and bring to us our purpose and our true gift. Keep your faith high on your list.

"So we do not lose heart. Though our outer nature is wasting away, our inner nature is being renewed everyday. For this slight momentary affliction is preparing for us an eternal weight of glory beyond all comparison, because we look not to the things that are seen but to the things that are unseen: for the things that are seen are transient, but the things that are unseen are eternal." From 2 Corinthians 16:17-18 .

Learning to rise about the physical is not easy but it can be done. Focus on the spiritual not the physical world. As Jesus said,

"Rise about the appearances of this world."

Take into account to pray for yourself, first. Don't feel guilty. Before you can help anyone else, you have to help yourself by strengthening your own faith. Other wise, your prayers will not come from the right place in spirit. You are the one asking for help. You are learning to have a prayerful mind, a trained mind in spiritual principles. You are developing a mind that thinks about God and that can get the right guidance in your life, a mind that sees only the good coming in. Later on, when you are confident in your prayers, then you can pray for others. *"The prayer of a good person has a powerful effect."* From James 5:16.

There are two prayers I really feel that are important: one is the Lord's Prayer (Matthew 6:09-13). and the 23rd Psalm. When you are down and troubled and you need something to believe in turn to Psalm 23. This beloved biblical passage has helped and comforted millions of people in the face of life's problems, difficulties and tragedies. This prayer has everything you want in it, everything you need. It has protection, solace, and food for the soul. It can speak to Jews and Christians or anyone in need of hope and encouragement. You have to bear in mind that believing, is the power of Psalms 23.

The ancient Hebrew poetry, believed to have been written by Israel's King David, is so soothing you can make it part of your daily life and will help you learn how to pray by clearing your heart and mind and give you comfort. Here is this loving and comforting prayer please, take it into your soul and know God loves you and is listing to you reciting his prayer.

The 23rd PSALM

The Lord is my shepherd;

I shall not want. He maketh me to lie down

In green pastures, He leadeth me beside still waters.

He restoreth my soul. He leadeth

me in the paths of righteousness

For his name's sake.

Yea, though I walk through the

valley of the shadow of death,

I will fear no evil;

For Thou art with me; thy rod

and thy staff they comfort me

Thou preparest a table before me

In the presence of mine enemy

Thou anointest my head with oil;

My cup runneth over.

Surely goodness and mercy

shall follow me

all the days of my life:

and I will dwell in

the house of the Lord forever. Amen

White Feather knows that no matter how deep ones sorrow or pain you will find comfort in this prominent prayer. Please, say it aloud several times a day and you will find the peace and hope you have been looking for. Let the words flow over you and listen to their meaning. This power comes from knowing that in spite of all the violence in the world and because of hope that you feel, it's through God's grace that we can love again or forgive.

After you have read this healing prayer, think of the interpretation and the compassionate words in this prayer. The love God has for us, we must remember that prayer is the answer to any of our life challenges. This is why this prayer was given to us, it has everything we need. In other words, the prayer is saying, '*Take it to the Lord in prayer,*' you will find love and be comforted and free from worry and anxiety. Be devoted to God because we are his beloved.

For instance, there was a young man hell bent for destruction, he drank, smoked, and slept with other women while he was married. When his wife got pregnant, they had a little girl who, he loved more than anyone. The little girl was five-years-old and when she got sick with a fever this man was told she would not survive. "I'm sorry," the doctor told him. Sometimes we have to be at the end of our rope before we learn our lessons in our life. The man opened the door to his daughter's room and got down on his knees and prayed for the first time in his life. He recited The Lord's Prayer from his childhood and he did a simple prayer of his own. When he looked into his little girl's face and he saw a white light over her head. It was an angel touching the little girl. He looked at the angel with love and awe, said, "If you save my little girl I will give it all up." The angel looked at the man, and then touched the girl and the fever left her. It was a miracle of love. This man has not drunk, gallivanted around and only sleeps with his wife, just like he promised the angel.

You can see how fast the man gave up his old habits and turned to God when he saw the miracle of his little girl. He knew in his heart that without faith and change his little girl would no longer be with him. Most of the time our lessons are tough but with God's help, He can get through the hard times. *"Tough time's never last but tough people do."* Doctor Robert Schuller wrote these famous words many years ago and I remembered them and used this saying when I was down and it always helped me climb back up into the light.

One more way to look at prayer is the complete act of the human spirit, touching all the faculties; intellectual, emotional, spiritual, even physically. God is an expression of what and who we are.

Soul seeks to know itself. The new awaits us and our soul is hungry for growth and newness. The heart is thirsty and wants to be devoted to prayer. Fill that parched soul with love and devotion and be honest with your prayer to God, because he knows your heart.

My prayer has been answered in many ways through the years and it's always a mystery on how my prayers are answered. I have received guidance and opportunities through out my life. When I was at the darkest hour, the dawn it (prayer) showed through. I received protection. When ever I travel, I ask for White Feather's protection on the road, I also remind my friends and clients to pray to her for safe travel.

I'm concluding, this section with two more prayers because I've found that it takes some people awhile to develop the right thoughts in prayer, so it can be helpful to have some prayers to recite.

Here is an affirmation from Dr. Ernest Holmes, founder of the Church of Religious Science and author of The Science of Mind.

Command my Soul

Spirit within me, commands my Soul to do thy bidding;

Compel me to follow the course of truth and wisdom.

Control my inward thoughts and my outward ways.

And make me to understand Thy laws.

Command my Soul to turn to Thee for guidance and light:

To turn to thee for wisdom and knowledge,

Let the paths of my life be made straight and sure;

Let the journey of my Soul find its completion in Thee.

Command my Soul to do Thy bidding.

I put my heart and soul in prayer and this saved me from the hateful wolf. He could huff and puff all he wanted but I was not running away. I knew my prayers were being answered and as Lazarus rose from the dead I would raise above the wolf scenario. As the Bible states, *"Pray at all times in the spirit, with all prayer and supplication."* From Ephesians 6:18.

In the summery of this significant chapter everyone can become skilled at how to pray. I know that this powerful chapter of White Feather has taught the reader a valuable lesson in learning to focus and put your open mind and heart on your prayer. That is what a skilled mind in prayer is all about. We are spiritual beings with a lot of prayer power, power to change our lives for the better and help those around us, when we are in harmony with our higher selves and God.

"The love of God is passionate. He pursues each
of us even when we know it not."

—William Wordsworth

Chapter Seventeen

Meditation—The Real Voice

"Only God knows you're heart."

—Myrtle Walker

"Trust God to reveal the desires of your heart."

—Nicole Walters

The reason I meditate is to get to the truth and its power. In meditation, the noises of outside world and the chatter of my mind fade into the background and I am able to hear the voice of my Higher Power. White Feather says,

"Meditation is the soul's answer to who we are and we must listen to who that is." Our life is more valuable because we are connected to our own internal power. Meditation nourishes and enriches our everyday life and our relationships with others. Our life in general is more valuable because we are connected to our internal power.

Meditation is a spiritual practice which trains our mind to focus on contemplation, to go inward, and hear our real voice of tranquility and calmness. This ability to listen guides us to inner peace. Let your life be a mirror into the spiritual world.

During deep meditation an alignment of mind, body, and spirit occurs placing each aspect of the self into a state of well-being. Meditation and our hearts will connect us with our highest source of energy power within. Meditation helps us connect to the answers that await our questions.

Meditation is the most direct way to come to grips with our daily life and receive guidance in our affairs. It will also help us learn become more self-aware, strengthen your intuition, and enhance your creativity.

Contemplation will also increase your ability to have more perception of what is going on around you. In other words, you can feel the connection to your Higher Power. Meditate in faith. You will also relive stress and constant worry. Give your problem to God, he has big shoulders. You will be at peace. You will grow, learn, and you will be healthier through meditation.

Meditation techniques have helped people with HIV, cancer, and in coping with fatigue, anxiety, headaches, heart trouble and daily stress. Most disease is caused by not thinking correctly and not doing prayer and meditation. In meditation you will feel hope and a feeling of personal connection to the right source of healing. Maybe your life is in pieces, let go of your boundaries and be at peace. Through a bridge of love and harmony calmness will prevail.

At first I did not understand the advantages of meditation, so White Feather asked me to start a meditation class so we could see the bigger picture of our life. She knew that this experience would heal me and bring me the benefits of meditation. I had been thinking about joining a meditation class, but White Feather has guided me to have my own. I invited several clients to join me. She told me if I would do this she would attend and would guide us in how to meditate. We met for four years and the beginners learned how to meditate. The intermediate improved their techniques and the advanced developed more awareness. I improved by teaching others the value of stillness which brought me peace of mind.

White Feather taught her healing meditation in a sequence of baby-steps. The first baby-step, which we practiced in my class, White Feather wanted us to learn was how to be still. Without still-ness and quiet we could not listen. To get to this quiet White Feather asked us to close our eyes and sit quietly. No form of escape, such as television or radio was used. No one in my class had ever sat in silence before. It seemed like a strange thing to do, but in time it became more natural. My class and I practiced this together week after week. Sometimes I would lead the class in a chant to clear our monkey mind. The minds that tell us to pick-up the clothes at the cleaners fix lunch or start dinner need to be quieted.

Occasionally, White Feather asked me to lead the group in guided meditation, but this was only after we sat in the silence. To be still in your mind, body and spirit, is a breath-taking experience. No one can do this for you. Only you can learn to do your own meditation. It is a private source for healing.

I also practiced this utter stillness when I was alone. I learned that silence is our friend. People try to avoid it because they are afraid they will hear something they don't want to hear. I realized that silence does the opposite of this. It brings you comfort. Sometimes I drove out to the ocean or woods, or any place that is quiet and peaceful, and I sit and listened. When I went into the silence, White Feather knew I was at peace.

This is definitely the way to train the mind to learn meditation. Practicing meditation was like learning the scales to play a piano. I had to be methodically dedicated.

I still do this almost everyday. This spiritual practice is to teach you to learn of your soft inner spiritual voice and how to recognize it. So I continue to sit still and listen because I wanted to learn this powerful skill and devotion. Will it be worth the effort? To become skilled at meditation is worth everything I learned. I still go into the silence and do a deep meditation. Meditation is a lifetime reflection on your true voice.

White Feather did not give us another baby-step until she felt we knew what it was to sit in the silence and let it become our friend. She encouraged us to wrap ourselves around the friendship of meditation and cradle it with all our heart. Meditation is not just to be used when the mood strikes us. Meditation is to be absorbed everyday so it becomes a part of our normal life like breathing.

Early one morning in meditation, I heard White Feather say,

"Jean, you are now ready for the next step in learning to meditate?"

I laughed and said,

"Are you sure?"

"That's right, Jean," White Feather laughed and responded,

"It's very good, Jean, to be lighthearted. Now take a deep breath and relax. Please close your eyes. The second step is to learn to recognize the energy of your inner voice and hear her guidance." she said.

Gradually, I began to hear a whisper of a voice in the silence. The voice was very soft at first, but then it became clearer! This voice told me 'To keep practicing meditation so that I will hear the truth.' I knew then, that this was my inner voice from White Feather. Meditation was pulling me out of myself into the light of God.

White Feather wanted us to learn meditation immediately but she knew you had to practice. Practice makes perfect. She wanted us to hear our inner voice that she had helped us develop in our study together. White Feather wanted us to realize that meditation is a powerful key to our spiritual growth. Through meditation, my mind and heart had connected to the universal source of my own strength. Once we knew how to guide our minds, White Feather guided us to hear our true inner voice. I finally thought I recognized this soft whisper of my inner voice. I continued in silence, and my inner voice became very clear. It grew stronger. I knew it was my authentic inner voice because it was so unmistakable direct at first, it sounded like a soft radio signal. It was the inner voice of my heart. I realized that I had several voices. One is my everyday voice that talks to people and does everyday chores and the other voice is a beloved inner voice of truth coming from my heart. I felt like I now have a conscious awareness of these two voices. That is the trained voice of meditation and it was worth striving for.

Suddenly everything made sense. I had been gifted with divine understanding. I knew I was in the right conscious awareness and what awaited me was love and peace.

White Feather told me to take this wise voice into my heart and my mind,

"Now you are in genuine deep meditation where truthful guidance is found,"

She continued,

"Aren't you glad you did not give up on practicing meditation? You now have a divine guidance of truth that will help you through out your life as long as you continue to achieve meditation," she said.

In that moment, I understood fully what she was telling me. The spirit of my meditation gave me a healing, which came though meditation and act of forgiveness. This empowered me. It truly made sense to me now and I was getting the spirituality of meditation.

Also I realized it is a choice to master meditation and learn to sit quietly in silence. This was for my spiritual development and guidance. It also helped release my stress and kept me calm. What a spiritual blessing!

The final step I was to learn was when to take the right action. White Feather taught me to be silent, and then listen to my voice, then taking action on what I heard. She taught me to let the absolute silence be my friend and following that I was able to hear my inner voice. I next need to learn to take suitable action in my life.

She told me,

"You can meditate and meditate until you are blue in the face, but if you do not take the appropriate action noting new will happen," White Feather further says,

"The sprit says, 'act' it is almost liked a movie director who yells 'Action!'

It's up to us to follow the right guidance and know things will work out. This is because we have used our Heavenly tools of prayer and meditation, we become wiser and this saves us from making mistakes.

You are starting to become responsive and aware through meditation and are learning to focus your thoughts on the divine. You are training your mind for more spiritual growth. Meditation will refresh, center, calm and free your spirit within. You have embarked on a great adventure in search of inner peace, love and truth. You are using healing energy and peace for yourself and everyone in the world.

In meditation, White Feather told me,

"Jean, you are going to do my healing massage and write my book."

As I said in an earlier chapter, I thought she was nuts. It was like someone telling me I was going to visit outer space and the aliens were going to write my story. However, meditation changed my life and I have been willing adhere to her directions.

Some people are lazy. They want the answers, but do not want to do the spiritual effort. Answers do not come out of the blue. People do not want to sit in meditation for even five minutes because they think it is a waste of time. It's not. It is a gift from God. It is a way to make peace with ourselves and calm down from the outside world. Like anything else, the more you practice, the better you become. I want you to know meditation is a lifetime practice, not a one night stand.

One night after class Rona told me,

"Jean, I finally get it," Rona said.

I can see the advantages of meditation and how much it helps to relive my stress in my life. It if had not been for meditation, I would not have had the guidance to enter a car drawing. After entering the car drawing I received some money from an unexpected source to help buy a new car,"

"Thank you Jean, for having this class," she said.

"You're more than welcome. I think everyone in class received something out of the meditation class that's the reason White Feather told me to have it." I said.

She put her arms around me and gave me a hug. That was just a great feeling, almost as if my heart were bursting. I was grateful that I was teaching meditation.

When you feel more at peace in meditation, the closer you are to God. God hears your meditation and moves a million times nearer to you. The peace of meditation is the language of God. When you find God in your meditation first you will see Him in all your splendid pursuits of life, in true friends, and in the right thoughts. You will be at peace and it will demonstrate in your life. Our spirit wants to lift us to a Higher Power.

Through meditation you can accomplish this by reaching out to God and by transferring our fears through meditation. Then you come to God in contemplation and know He is listing to your meditation and will act in response. Stay in meditation to achieve peace and this will teach you how to share your love with others. Plant your seed of faith through meditation. You will have a spiritual renewal.

I have found it helpful to meditate at the same time each day. I like to meditate in the morning before the day begins. The body, mind, and spirit actually anticipate this scheduled time. Therefore, one should establish a daily meditation time. If you're a beginner to meditation five to ten minutes is a good span of time to meditate. If you're more advanced set aside twenty minutes. You are learning to know God through meditation. Now you have found a great source of wisdom. Meditation is the sacred key to inner peace and truth. Nothing will bring out the truth about your life faster than meditation. This is where the real healing begins. Meditation will take you where you want to go. God, through meditation, can take you to places you never dreamed of going. Give that some thought, what else can give you hope for a brighter future. It starts with you and your determination to move forward in your life.

White Feather gave me the following guidance instructions for meditation to use for myself and others.

Close your eyes, rest your hands easily on your lap, and open your heart. Feel your body and consciously soften any obvious tension. Let go of any habitual thought or plan in your mind. Bring your attention to your breathing. Take a deep breath. Feel the movement of the chest, or the rise and fall of the belly. Let your breath be natural. Relax into each breath. Feel the movement and the soft sensation of each breath, in and out. Listen to your heartbeat with each breath. You can affirm "in with the new," as you breath in and "out with the old," as you exhale.

After a few breaths your mind may wander, especially if you are beginner. Then think of your next breath. Mindfully acknowledge where you have gone with a soft word in the back of your mind. Know that you have to come to center, quiet the mind and be at peace. Take another breath and relax. Then know that you are here to learn meditation and to maintain a clear mind. You must want to learn the truth and be guided. Keep in mind what you are doing and why. Stay focused on your breath. Be at peace with yourself as your next breaths hear the wind in your nostrils and your lungs expanding slowly. Know that it's "in with the new," as you breathe in, and "out with the old," as you exhale. Be calm and tranquil.

Relax into the next breath. When your breath becomes soft, let your attention become gentle and careful as the breath itself. Listen to your heartbeat. Follow the rhythm. Take a soft breath and begin to hear the rhythm of your heart which is soft and gentle. It's the same soft rhythm, one breath in and one breath out. As you listen to your heartbeats you will forget what was in your mind and concentrate on emptying your heart of torment and old wounds so you can start to heal. You will feel the calm energy flow of meditation throughout your entire body. Keep in mind the value of what and why you are learning to meditate. Your soul already knows. Listen to your own heart because all the answers are within. There are no answers in the external. Amen.

Meditation practitioners believe that there is a direct correlation between one's breath and one's state of mind. Meditation can put you in touch with your inner guide, allowing the bodies own inner wisdom or your true voice to be heard.

The reason White Feather had me follow the meditation chapter with forgiveness is everyone has something they need to forgive of other persons, including themselves. There is always Heaven or Hell on our shoulders, and it's up to us to discipline our minds through meditation and seek the truth for ourselves and make the right choice. No one can do this for you. It is up to you to seek your own truth. I tried to reach people on their own terms so they could get the feeling and the wonderment of this practice but it did not work. Meditation also helps us lift our faith in the right direction and awakens our inner voice. What meditation does is make people more aware of what they need to forgive. I know this chapter will help guide you to that healing place.

If you bought my book, "The Hungry Heart," you can receive White Feather's healing CD by simply paying $7.00 plus shipping ($1.11) and handling. Order through my Post Office Box 356,

Fort Bragg, California 95437. It's healing music for the soul. It was channeled through White Feather and is special harp music for healing. Thank you for reading White Feather's words and listing to her healing song. My website, Angel-Ranch.org. is pending but should be out soon.

"In order to learn from the past you must forgive it."

—A Rabbi

Chapter Eighteen

Forgiveness—A Slippery Slope

"If you don't forgive your past you cannot move forward toward your future.
The gateway to forgiveness must be in the divine."

—White Feather

White Feather asked me to follow the meditation chapter with a chapter on forgiveness. Meditation and forgiveness are closely connected because they both make people more aware of whom they need to forgive. What if needing forgiveness stands in the interim between where we are right now and what we are striving to achieve as you reach for the stars.

When I sit in the silence and I hear the truth, my highest good is revealed. I see this as an effort from God to heal my heart. When the truth is reveled, it is like a boil that is hidden in the body and now surfaces on the exterior so that it can be seen. We have to be thankful for the experience of forgiveness. Resentment is an example of this and sometimes you don't even know it's there until you are in a meditation. For example, I was setting in meditation one day when the face of this woman I knew came to mind. I knew that she was resenting me, so I had began to resent her.

At that moment, I asked to be released from the pain for this resentment and every time I thought of her, I would do a meditation and pray about it. With time, I healed my resentment through forgiveness. I did not want to be held back on my spiritual path. I'm not sure what happened to her, but I know through forgiveness I am free.

When we forgive and forget, we are really forgiving ourselves and letting go of our anguish. I have suffered much in human relationships. I have had a rocky road with men and my potholes have been deep. Everyone is different, but when is it time to trust someone who has hurt us deeply? Not all humans are trust worthy. Some can be sheep in wolves' clothing. I know because I have found a few, and I should have just kept on going but, oh no I had to try again. A verse from the Bible, *"Then Peter came up to him and said, 'Lord, how often shall my brother sin against me, and I forgive him?'* Then Jesus answers, *"As many as seventy times seven."* From Matthew 18:21.

Before we can forgive someone, we have to know what forgiveness means. Forgiveness is a simple act of the heart, a movement to let go of the pain and heartache. Everyone is haunted by our past. We all had difficult times, and when we remember that scary event, it reminds us of our past burden of resentment and outrage that we carried. With one hand the past moves us forward with the other hand it holds us back. Let it go and a sense of freedom will occur. In its place, you will feel relieved, and a smile will spreads across your face. Feelings of enlightenment, compassion, and happiness prevail because spiritual forgiveness is powerful.

One member of my meditation group kept having trouble with her mother butting into her personal life. I suggested that she ask in meditation, why her mother was doing this. At the next meeting she told me, she had learned that her mother was lonely and that helping me solve my problems was her mother's way of making contact. This knowledge made it possible for my friend to forgive her mother for meddling. Once she forgave her, she was willing to find other ways for the two of them to be together.

A client's husband walked out on her without telling her why.

When she came to see me I said,

"It might be a little soon to discuss this, but when you feel you can forgive him, it will help you. You also need to forgive yourself for the anger you feel toward your husband." I suggested she ask for forgiveness and move on. She wasn't sure she was ready to let go of the anger, but she did want to be free of the pain, so she agreed to pray for the willingness to forgive him. She came back to see me a few weeks later and she looked like a new person. The pain and sorrow had lifted from her shoulders and face.

She shared with me, that she had awakened one morning and knew she was willing to forgive him for leaving her, so she did. Later he contacted her and told her that he had been confused in their relationship. He explained that he had been receiving mixed signals from her and wasn't sure she really loved him. The forgiveness effort that she had done opened the door for him to come back and talk candidly with her. They are now back together and act like newlyweds. Thank you Jean and White Feather.

The only way I know to finally forgive is to go deep into your heart though meditation and see the truth of why you're carrying this resentment around. The Buddhist believes that our attachment brings us our greatest pain and that through compassion and forgiveness we can let it go. To forgive someone is your compassion trying to immerge to the surface. These two spiritual practices go hand-in-hand, when we develop these principles you immediately get something of immense value and the results, is peace of mind.

Forgiveness is a great instrument of God. Adversity and forgiveness can be a stepping-stone to something fresh and new in your life. Sometimes it is how we act under stress in our life that determines our character. Sometimes our struggles can lead us to higher ground by making us look at ourselves and know a change has to occur within us. The decision you make in an instant defines your true character. The way Paul stated this in the Bible was, "*I can do all things in him who strengthens me.*" From Philippians 4:13.

If you carry a chip on your shoulder it will only hurt you and your shoulders will get mighty sore from holding the load. The person your sore at, has already moved on with their life. Your past can be very seductive because we are a reflection of our days gone by. Let all hurt and pain go into forgiveness and release it. You will feel lighthearted and boost up and stronger spiritually because you finally did the right thing and took the right action.

Within three minutes of the time you put your feet on the floor in the morning you have decide how your day is going. Start everyday fresh. A new beginning is yours. Be grateful that God loves you so much, anything is possible.

One of the greatest gifts of spiritual life is forgiveness. Forgiveness enables us to release our pain or anger, to let them go, and more forward in our life. We need to let go or to forgive, so we can become free in our spirit. When we ask God to forgive, then we are forgiven. It will happen that fast if we want it too. It starts with you. Do not give into doubt or fear because they are of the enemy. The devil knows our weakness and depends on us to let go of our faith. If we hold to fear in our hearts we are not trusting God. You are sending a message to God that says,

"I do not want you to come through me, and God knows our uncertainties."

White Feather once asked me to imagine that I was in jail, with cruel bars all around me and there is no way out, but only through the door of forgiveness. Imagine then, that one door is the door to your heart and that a person you are unwilling to forgive is sitting right in front of the door and the only way through the door is to forgive this person. You feel you are trapped. White Feather told me that if I am holding resentment toward myself or someone else, then I am sitting inside my self-made prison bars. We can not find forgiveness until we let go of our anger and grudges. So in meditation, you say or do whatever you need, to become willing to forgive that person that stands between you and your freedom.

In willingness, you find yourself thinking something like the following:

I have forgiven myself for being so stubborn and hurting others. I forgive the whole situation and any misunderstandings. I ask God for my own forgiveness. I release through prayer all my anger, doubt, and fear. I know life without love is no life at all. I know I am forgiven because I feel a different view has come into my heart about everything that has been hurting me. I feel no anger, pain, or sadness for anyone. I only feel love and forgiveness and kindness. I feel free of the guilt that I have carried on my shoulder for so long.

I know the future will be lighter because I understand my heart. Thank you, God, for helping me forgive others as well as my-self. I want to live my life in prayer. Amen.

Those heartfelt words will open the door to absolution and free your mind of uncertainty, trepidation, and fear. You have walked through that door and now you are released from suffering, burdens, and bondage. You know the joy of peace and true forgiveness and you will never have to look back on your past. You now have a new passageway to your life and you feel wonderful where it really counts. You now know the path and walk the path. There are no yesterdays, only today, and this very moment that counts. You can't use the past to fill what missing in the present so let go of the past mistakes forgiveness is a good place to start. Forgiveness is absolution of the soul. A new beginning is now yours try and use to your best advantage.

On May 13, 1981, on a sunny day, Pope John Paul 11 was visiting St. Peter's, in Rome. He reached down to pick up a little girl when in the crowd a shot rang out. The Pope slumped over. There was moment of stillness in the air, yet people were running around wanting to know if the Pope was dead or alive. Evil was loose. The Pope was hit at point blank range and rushed to the hospital for surgery. Well, he survived and never stopped his work. The police caught the man who shot the Pope, and the little girl is grown up now. People refer to her as the woman who saved the Pope. If the Pope had not reached down to pick up the little girl, the bullet would have hit the Pope's heart.

A few years later the Pope went to visit the man and forgave him. Then he prayed for him. This is true forgiveness on the highest level. He faced the man who tried to take his life. That takes genuine courage.

One of my favorite exact quotes comes from Eleanor Roosevelt.

'Every time you meet a situation, though you think at the time it is an impossibility, and you go through the tortures of the damned, once you have met it, and lived through it, you find that forever after you are freer than you were before.'

Here are some issues about unforgiving:

"Oh, you are not ready to forgive that person? You want to hang onto not forgiving a little longer? You are not ready to forgive? You want to wear yourself out and feel the pain and burden forever? You would rather keep on hurting? You are not hurting the person you are angry at, they have moved on with their life. Instead you are being held back. Yes, keep holding on to your anger and pain."

Instead of letting go, you keep things mixed up in your life. You are playing right into the devil's hands.

"I have you now," he says.

Remember the devil is a twisted liar. In contrast to this, you could choose forgiveness and be free of emotional upheaval and move forward with confidence on your spiritual path. God is waiting for you to make the right decision and unburden yourself. Your greatest adversity or hard times can be your greatest asset because when you are pushed against the wall of anguish, sorrow or fear we do something about it. Sometimes it's how we act during stress in our life that builds our character it deepens our hearts. Let all the hurt and pain go in forgiveness.

The choice is yours.

Forgiveness can take years or seconds. It's up to you how long forgiveness takes. Forgiveness goes through many stages of grief, rage, sorrow, fear, hatred and confusion. We can pick up all these stages or none of these stages, but most people pick at least one or more, because they cannot shake it off. Our grief is buried deep inside our heart and if you let yourself feel the pain you carry, it will come as a relief, for your soul because you are feeling your pain and not burying it deeper in your heart.

You can look inside your heart and decide if you want to live with a burden of unforgiving the rest of your life. This unwillingness to forgive keeps you from advancing on your spiritual path and getting ahead in your life.

Sometimes, a person can commit the most horrendous act against us, yet it will be the pain of the insult that causes our heart to open up and provide opportunity for healing. And then we can choose healing or bitterness. From time to time people use indifference when dealing with grief as a cover-up for their true feeling. Let these burdens go quickly in your heart and spirit and you will feel the results right away. Remember, because you forgive someone or are forgiven, this does not mean you have to like that person. It also does not mean you have to forget what the person did. It does mean, however your heart is now open to a new avenue for a richer life. One of my favorite Bible verses just came to me. *"If anyone is in Christ, he is a new creation; old things have passed away; behold, all things have become new."* From 2 Corinthians 5:70. This verse is what forgiveness is about, we let go of our old thinking and become new in our life because God in his mercy forgave us and we in our grace forgive.

Forgiveness cannot be forced. It can not be artificial. You are learning mindfulness, a practice that unites a new awareness in yourself, a new beginning, and you have learned to have a trained mind. You are living in the moment and are present right now. Your life will turn around when you forgive or let go of your past, your spirit will be blessed because you are standing on higher ground.

The following are practices in meditation we can do to help ourselves to let go of our pain and suffering.

The following meditation will help you forgive others. Say this affirmation out loud because it will be stronger for you because words have power.

"Sit silently in meditation. Visualize a person who has harmed you in some way. See them sitting across from you. Next visualize the person's Higher Self. Then tell their Higher Self how you feel about them. Express all the anger, resentment and frustration you have toward the person and then think I'm going to release all these feelings. I'm choosing to clear and cleanse my soul. I am going to have a better feeling about you. I release you." Amen.

One reason we do this in meditation, is that the other person may not be willing at this point to cooperate with you.

"Visualize yourself free of this painful situation and the burden released for your spirit. Then think, Thank you, God, for forgiving me for holding on to my anger for the past, my poor choices, my attachments or any misunderstandings I've had in my life. I release myself and this person through a healing spirit." Amen.

Don't let yourself be trapped in the past because of some poor choices you made. You'll never go forward looking back. Don't stay focused on your past mistakes. The past is the past and we cannot live in the past. You have to shake off the past and move forward to your bright future. Examine your heart and clear yourself through forgiveness. The act of forgiving is a powerful tool to erase our past errors. At some point you have to forgive, because suffering is caused by the misuse of free will. Time does not always heal our wounds unless we pray or allow it. You can not just slide by in life unless you want to get nowhere. You can think, I don't give a hoot, but inside you do.

Visualize yourself as that person who is free of the situation and the burden being released in spirit. Then say,

"Thank you God, for helping me to let go of my poor choices and attachments of the past, or any misunderstandings, I've had in my life. I release myself and this person through healing spirit." Amen. Say this affirmation until you take the right action. Keep praying so your forgiveness will come from your heart, so you can release yourself of any bondage.

I had to learn to rule over my emotional attachments. God does not hold grudges against us. He forgives us in a second. Humans are the ones that hold grudges. God is loving and forgiving. I am not saying that you can go around and keep doing the same ungodly things. We have to change our attitude in our heart because God has a greater plan in store for us. He does not want you to be on a destructive path. That is not what forgiveness from God is all about. We must strive to develop our spiritual path and ask for guidance everyday and move forward on our path God has in mind.

The best way to move forward is through forgiveness of any hurtful situation. Now let spirit take over and you will feel a powerful spark of newness in your soul, a feeling of freedom from yesteryear. You do not want to be stuck in the past. The stress of thinking about the harmful situation will be gone, because forgiveness is a great healing instrument of God. God has a way out of making good things come out of bad experience. Let the old go so the new can come in.

Through suffering, I have grown spiritually and this growth has given me the ability to help others with deep bleeding wounds. It took every bit of courage get over my divorce. My forgiveness of the

Hungry Wolf has taken years but finally I am healed. I have no contempt for the wolf. I feel relieved and happy that my healing has truly taken place in my spirit. Some of my healing was taking place as I wrote this book. It was seven years of a lengthy hard journey that I never intend to travel again along that winding dark road. Thank you God and White Feather for my complete healing and the valuable lessons I learned along the way of my own self-discovery. I am a stronger person because of my journey with the wolf.

Once you have forgiven completely, and your compassionate heart opens you will see a big difference in yourself, as well as, your life. You will be kinder and more considerate to people. Remember you will never change what you indulge, but through the act of forgiveness you open your heart to new level of compassion. When you feel rejected and your bruised soul can heal through forgiveness. Now, you are completely free maybe for the first time in years. Now you can shake off the sadness and chuckle and feel lighthearted.

In concluding this forgiveness chapter I would like to end this chapter with a powerful Bible verse. Jesus said,

"Therefore I tell you, whatever you ask in prayer, believe that you will receive it, and you will, And whenever you stand praying, forgive, if you have anything against any one; so that your Father also who is in Heaven may forgive you your trespasses." From Mark 11:24-25.

To error is human, to forgive divine. We want to forgive each other and when we do we can fly from the lift of each others wings

"Everything else can wait, but our search for God cannot wait."

—Paramahansa Yogananda

Chapter Nineteen

Amazing Grace

"And the Lord restored the fortunes of Job, when he had prayed for his friends; and the Lord gave Job twice as much as he had before."

—Job 42:10

White Feather answers all kinds of prayers. She has saved my life in numerous ways to many to tell. I learned years ago to take White Feather with me on my travels and to tell my clients to take her with them, too. All we have to do is say White Feather 'help' and she is there in less than a second. Over and over again, she's put her hand between me and imminent danger.

My friend, Sundance and I were traveling to a ranch where she trains horses. The ranch was about eighty miles away and we needed to drive part of the way on a very steep narrow road that comes dangerously close to the edge of the cliff. The ocean laid thousands of feet below. There is absolutely no room to pull over for any reason. I took the time to pray to God and White Feather for our safety as we drove to the ranch.

We had a lot of fun at the ranch and on the way home we started down the steep mountain. About two miles down the road we spotted a huge truck on the other side of the road coming toward us. He was pulling an aluminum silver trailer and the road was too narrow for it, so the truck moved over to our side of the road. In a split second, he hit the driver's side of our sport's car. At that moment there was metal all a around us. The impact pushed us over to the ocean side of the road. We were left with only one wheel on the road as I looked out at the ocean, I knew I was going to die. It all happened in an instant. I've never been so frightened. I cried out to God in prayer, 'I surrender,' I said. I thought I am going to die and I am not ready. I thought of my animals and their care.

My whole life flashed before my mind. Then, I heard a thud on the door on my side of car. This was the ocean side of the car where there was absolutely nothing to bump up against. Miraculously that's when we were pushed or lifted to the other side of the road. We landed in a ravine and the truck just kept going.

Sundance and I were in shock. Sundance put her head on the steering wheel and I leaned back in my seat. Our hands were shaking. We grabbed each other and cried like babies. We both gave our thanks to God and White Feather for saving us that near fatal day. I knew White Feather had pushed the car over to the side of the road and saved our lives. There was no doubt in my heart that she protected us. She knew it was not our time to leave mother earth. Our spiritual light had to keep shining because our purpose for our life was not complete. We had work to accomplish and that is why we were spared. There are no accidents, only miracles.

It took my editor, Lorie, a while to understand this but more than one life saving incident has convinced her.

Lorie and I were doing some work on the book, when we were done she said,

"I am going away for the week-end," she said.

I quickly replied,

"Do you want me to pray for your safety?" I said.

"Yes," she said as she got in her car, waved good-bye and yelled out her car window,

"I love you." she said with a sweet smile on her face.

I stood in my doorway and held her in the light of prayer. I asked for her safety and sent White Feather with her.

The week-end went by and Monday rolled around and Lorie called me.

"Jean, I have to see you today. Please, make time for me," she said in and anxious voice.

I looked at my schedule and told her to come in at 3:00 P.M. that day. When she arrived, I opened my door to Lorie. Her dark hair was tousled and disheveled. I looked at her and I saw that she was upset.

"What happened?" I asked her.

"Jean, I nearly died last week-end!" she said. Chills ran up and down my spine.

"Tell me," I said.

I saw fear was present in her dark blue eyes.

"I was driving on Highway 128 to San Francisco. I went to pass a huge logging truck, didn't realize how fast he was going until I started to pass him. I pushed my foot down on the accelerator so I could quickly pass him. I was just about to pull in front of him when I saw a car which had been hidden by the truck in front of him. This was scary enough but then I saw a car coming toward me from the opposite direction. I didn't realize how small a space I was trying to pull into. I cried out,

"God, I don't have room," When I looked in my rear view mirror, it was as if the truck was in slow motion. Something incredible and bigger than his breaks held the logging truck back. It took a powerful force to slow that size truck that quickly. A human being couldn't do it. I knew a greater force was at work," she said. Then out of breath from telling me her story she continued,

"I barely squeezed into the space," she said.

"When I got the chance I pulled over to the side of the road as soon as I could. I remembered my last conversation with you where you said you would pray for my safety. Jean, I am grateful to be here," she said.

I looked at Lorie and put my hand on hers,

"Lorie, I am glad you are safe," I said.

As we bent our heads to pray, we closed our eyes,

"Thank you God and White Feather for all you do for us everyday. Thank you for keeping us safe wherever our life takes us," I said. Lorie put her arms around me,

"Thank you Jean, for everything and especially for your powerful prayer," she said.

"Your welcome, I am glad you're still here." and I meant that from the bottom of my heart.

White Feather had been there to stop the truck because of the many times she had saved my life on the Highway. I know in my heart that this, near fatal accident made Lorie more of a spiritual believer.

White Feather often reminds me to pray. She reminds me do not negate my prayers. Be positive all times in prayer. God is listening and always responds, she says. Remember our prayers proceed ahead of us on our spiritual path.

White Feather answers all my prayers big and small. There are no limits in. She helps me with the smallest little thing like finding an ear ring or she can save lives as in the above examples.

When it came to working on her book White Feather found the right editors, cover artist, graphic artist, CD producer and publisher.

My relationship with White Feather, like any relationships, it has its ups and downs. There are many levels to my friendship with White Feather. There have been times when White Feather and I disagree and she insists that I see things her way. She does not give up in her kind way she kept reminding me that I have left something undone. Finding my editor was one of these experiences.

I looked all over for the right editor for this book. I needed an experienced editor with an appreciation of spiritual material and she needed to be reasonably priced and willing to trade for some of the work. I was having no luck and was feeling overwhelmed. As a last resort I asked White Feather and she told me to go down to the print shop a block away and ask the woman who does my typing if she knew anybody. I did this and was given Lorie's name. She worked several hours for me. I knew she was the perfect person for the job, but she had already told me that she was very busy and that most of her time was committed to another project. When I approached her about doing more work for me she declined. I was disappointed and tried to talk her into continuing the work, but she again declined. At this point I would have given up, but White Feather kept at me.

"You call that girl up and tell her she needs to work with you as much as you need her," she said.

"White Feather, I can't do that. She does not want the job and she is not interested in trading for a massage. I've already asked her," I said.

However, White Feather would not back off, so, shaking in my boots, I called this editor up and told her what White Feather said. For whatever reason she listened and ended up coming over for a massage. Lorie has moved to another area but we are still friends.

Only White Feather and God could have made this happen.

Now I knew my book had a chance to help others and be a success.

God wants us to keep the prayer and energy going. What is important to God is our communication with him. Then, when energy is in alignment with God's will, the prayer will be answered according to God's will. Not our will for He knows best. You cannot manipulate God and you should never try and change prayer. Your prayer is in God's hands and his purpose will be done for your life. Prayer is the beginning of every good thing for your life. Go for it and you will never be sorry.

A very extraordinary miracle happened one late afternoon when my editor and I were watching the horse race at the Belmont Stakes on June 11th, 2005. We were sitting in my front room doing some work on my book when all of a sudden I got up.

"Lorie, the Belmont is about to begin," I said as I walked toward my bedroom to turn on my television.

"White Feather just told me,

"I have to watch the race and pray for the safety of the horses," I told her.

My editor looked at me like I was crazy. We had scheduled this time to work on the book and here I was interrupting us to watch a horse race.

"My friend used to own a race horse, with the same bloodline as Afleet Alex," I continued. Lorie followed me into the bedroom. We both sat down on my bed and I turned on the race. The horses were approaching the starting gate. When the race began I got a gut instinct that told me to get on my knees and pray for the horse's safety.

"I do not know why I am doing this, but White Feather is guiding me," I told Lorie. Then I started chanting and praying as the horses came down the track. Lorie joined me in prayer. All was going well and Afleet Alex was a nose ahead of the other horses when he collided slightly with another horse, sending him to his knees, almost touching his nose to the dirt. He stumbled with jockey Jeremy Rose hanging on for dear life. I was praying and praying. We kept praying asking for safety for all the horses and jockeys. We might not have been the only ones praying, but I know why we were praying.

Afleet Alex and his jockey gathered themselves, regaining their momentum. They then won the race. Lorie and I took a look and we were in awe of what just happened.

"That was unbelievable," she said.

"That horse was going down. He and his jockey would have been trampled." The trainer credited the athleticism of Afleet Alex and the jockey Jeremy Rose he adverted a disastrous spill.

"It was a combination of things—and a lot of luck, too," the trainer said.

As I watched replays of the collision I saw Afleet Alex's nose was about 4-6 inches from the ground traveling at forty miles per hour.

This was a victory for Afleet Alex and a miracle from answered prayer because I had asked White Feather to be there. It also reveals that when we see things that need prayer, we can not wait for somebody else to take the responsibility. We need to do it.

It was a miracle from White Feather. Afleet Alex and his jockey won the race.

"That was unbelievable, that horse was going down he and the jockey would have been trampled." she said.

In August of 2005 Hurricane Katrina struck the Golf Coast and New Orleans life stopped as humans knew it. The people were gripped by despair and lawlessness. It was the worst national disaster that ever hit the United States. I was praying for everyone and asking White Feather to unravel all the government blockages to be removed so people could receive the help they desperately needed. A couple of day's later help began to reach those in need. Movie stars were going to the south they were opening up their pockets and giving what was desperately needed.

I prayed for all the animals. I was in harmony with White Feather. At one point on the television news I saw a Golden retriever stuck on a porch. I prayed all night with White Feather asking her to save all animals and that Golden retriever dog. The next day the media featured a pet rescue which showed the Golden retriever getting into the boat and later getting a bath and licking the water. He was having a lot of fun. I thanked all the angels and White Feather for hearing my prayers and answering them.

Then eight dolphins were pushed out into the oceans that were from the aquarium and did not know how to take care of themselves in the cold water. The trainers that had raised the dolphins were out trying to save all of them. So I have been praying with White Feather asking her to please help save them. The trainers were going out to the ocean they found every dolphin and saved them. I thanked all the angels and White Feather for hearing my prayers and answering them. This again showed me how quickly prayer will be answered.

Even though I knew that White Feather answers my prayers, I do not like to bother her with my little stuff. What I know now is that White Feather wants to be there for me. She doesn't know big or small about prayer. White Feather listens to my prayer and answers them.

One rainy day, I stopped to buy groceries. When I reached for my twenty-dollar bill to pay the bill it was missing. I looked down by my feet thinking it had fallen out but it was not there.

I looked everywhere in the store, but no luck. I racked my brain trying to figure out what happened to it and I began to beat myself up for me losing the money. I paid for my groceries with a check.

Suddenly, I heard from White Feather,

"Go back to the service station,"

Before I stopped at the grocery store I had gone to buy gas. I turned my car around and drove to the service station. It had started raining again. I pulled up to the pump I had used and rolled down my window. There it was right in front of me. I saw stuck to the cement step, near the gas pump, my twenty-dollar bill. I opened my car door and reached out to where the money lay soaked with rain.

As I retrieved it old familiar voice of White Feather spoke,

"And you don't think I am here for you. I am always with you, especially when you need me the most," she said.

"White Feather, I needed the money. Thank you." I responded.

She once again put her angel power on the problem and came through with flying twenty-dollar bill. I was grateful.

Another time White Feather came to my rescue, was the day I was all dressed up wearing a Native American skirt, blouse and a pair of stunning hand made earrings a client had given to me. I went to the grocery store and when I finished shopping, as I sat in the front seat of my car, I noticed one earring was missing! I started to panic. Where was the earring? I went back into the store and walked up and down the isles.

I asked everyone in the store,

"Did anyone turn in a turquoise earring?" I asked.

'No one,' had seen it. I continued looking for the earring, but it eluded me. I was thinking two conflicting thoughts. I'll never find my earring yet I knew it is within my reach to find it.

I went outside the store and looked in and under my car. I still saw no earring. At that point I was desperate. I was standing in front of my car when I remembered to ask White Feather for help.

"Where is my turquoise earring?" She responded with,

"About time you asked me, I'm the last one you turn to. Go back into the grocery store and go to the milk case,"

She continued,

I shrugged my shoulders and walked to the milk case.

"Jean, look under the black tile." she said.

I looked down at the squares of black and white tile. One of the black tiles was loose. I bent down and picked up the tile. I couldn't believe my eyes. In the corner of the tile was my turquoise earring! I stood up with the earring in my hand. It was so amazing to me to think White Feather cares enough about me to even find my lost earring. I was in awe. Those earrings were from a special friend and White Feather knew how much they meant to me. As these earrings dangle from my ears, I recall how often White Feather has come to my rescue.

To embark upon and tackle everyday life I have come to the conclusion that without my spirit guide, White Feather, I would not make it one minute on this planet. She has given me hope and inspiration at times, when all I felt was despair. White Feather inspires me everyday of my life. She even motivated me to write her book. I have had many wonderful people in my life but they come and go, where as, White Feather is steady, bringing humor to much needed situations. When I get up in the morning I say to myself, 'I am good to go.' That is the spirit of White Feather. She is very practical, yet uplifting in her quest to help the human spirit.

When I met White Feather I was stuck in my comfort zone and did not want to make changes in my life. Then I realized without change I could not grow in my emotions or my spiritual life. I knew change would come anyway so why not prepare myself with White Feather direction. I learned to have an even balance in my life. My existence is fuller and richer due to my faith and White Feather's guidance.

In other words, I had to move forward if I was going to have a richer and more rewarding life.

Little Red Riding Hood is gone forever. I have advanced past my Little Red Riding hood days, had threw away the cape and hood. I am much more independent and more motivated. I have learned to have my own thoughts and not be so dependent on others. This is answered prayer.

"Few are those who see with their own eyes and feel with their own hearts."

—Albert Einstein

Chapter Twenty

Sea Scape Prayer

"When the well's dry, we know the worth of water."

—Benjamin Franklin

I asked White Feather what we have to offer a person that is different on the subject of prayer and meditation.

"Jean, go somewhere that is quiet, so you can hear my voice," she said.

"Is the ocean okay?" I asked.

"That's the perfect place, I will be with you by the ocean," she affirmed.

I drove my car toward the ocean, which was only a short distance from where I live. I decided to go to the cliffs to look out and see the full spectrum of the seashore and God's spectacular creation. So, I turned left into the first beach parking lot and parked the car. I rolled down my car window and smelled the salty wind that was touching my face. I looked out at the ocean and felt the tenderness of peace. I got out of my car and walked to the cliffs. The ocean's, healing waves were pounding on the rocks and the surf of the ocean was gently moving back and forth like a graceful, precise ballet dancer.

I thought about prayer and how White Feather taught me to pray. As I looked at the sea and smelled that fresh air my mind came alive with inspiration. I knew that White Feather was guiding me to the exact place she wanted me to be. Everything was more vibrant and it was so invigorating to the soul. The waves were breaking. Then, the ocean mood changed. The ocean grew rougher and the wind pushed the waves even higher to the blue sky above. The wind became stronger causing the white water to ripple like a fan. I felt like the spray was going to kiss my face. The waves hit the black rocks hard and I heard the splash against the rocks. I got out of my car and walked to the edge of the cliff. The waves sounded like they were communicating to each other. I knew there was a storm in the air. Then, I remembered why I was here. It hit me like a led balloon. White Feather was going to teach me about the storms of life, and that only, through prayer could anyone survive. She also taught me to read Bible verses for encouragement pointing clearly to the fact that the Bible is our survival kit.

Prayer does prepare you for the storms of life, the good bad and the ugly.

"Are you ready to learn?" White Feather said as I stood by the cliff.

"Yes, White Feather," I said.

"Jean, close your eyes. What do you see?" she asked.

"What do you mean?" I asked.

"Can you picture in your mind and heart the white water dancing on the tip top of the waves gleaming in the sunlight?"

"Yes," I said.

"This is how you ready yourself to pray. Clear your mind of any clutter and allow a positive image to come to mind,"

"Yes," I replied.

I had to think about this for at least a minute. I took a deep breath of the salt air which was so refreshing and God must be here, I thought, because this was Heaven on earth.

"The ocean is always changing and renewing and cleansing and replenishing just as we do through prayer. You are only a thought away from prayer. That is your greatest assist. Put your mind in Heaven and believe," she continued,

"Listen to those waves coming in and going out. That is the way prayer and your thoughts work. Put the good positive stuff in and get rid of old negative thoughts. Say it like this,

"Prayer in, junk out," she said.

I had to laugh at that one. I opened my eyes. The sea was really rough like many situations in my life. The wind blew hard and powerful.

White Feather, says,

"Prayer and faith must be like the wind out in the universe free from all negative thoughts. The wind blows to clear our minds and protect us. Just like faith you cannot see faith but it is there for you." I thought when I pray my mind is in Heaven and it is.

"I will try my best to learn and practice prayer," I said.

She continued,

"Jean, the gleaming sun gives the ocean protection like prayer gives you. Prayer changes and improves any situation. Stay prayed up. This is what prayer is all about. It gives you hope, strength and joy. Like the ocean gives humans," she said.

Now this was powerful and I accepted it and I was still amazed at her. I knew in my soul that White Feather was unsurpassed because she always gave her complete love and support.

White Feather left for a moment, but I knew she would be back before I left. I enjoyed the rocks and the waves. The ocean was still doing her dance of healing. My focus landed on the black rocks. The rocks are solid like prayer I thought. When we know and affirm in prayer, that is, when the light and energy are correct and that is the strength of your prayer taking form. The energy is coming together for you're pray which makes the prayer more powerful.

To pray and take action is what sums up prayer and changes our lives for the highest good of all. Prayer like the ocean goes out and comes back to us when we need it the most.

A good example of a solid prayer is when I prayed for a check to be in the mail and it shows up the next day. That is because I had no doubt about the energy and universal law. I am not saying that what I want shows up the next day. I am saying that it can show up but on the other hand it could be a couple of days. My focus is that it is coming and it did. A great Bible verse came to me, *"What things so ever ye desire, when ye pray, believe that ye will receive them, and ye shall have them."* From Mark 11:24.

Another great Bible verse came to me because I was filled with the spirit.

"Every one then who hears these words of mine and does them will be like a wise man who built his house upon the rock; and the rain fell, and the floods came, and the winds blew and beat upon that house, but it did not fall, because it had been founded on the rock. And every one who hears these words of mine and does not do them will be like a foolish man who built his house upon the sand and the rain fell, and the floods came, the winds blew and beat against that house, and it fell; and great was the fall of it." From Matthew 7:24-25.

"Yes, build your life on the rock of God's foundation and all will be well in your life and world, nothing is more important than prayer," White Feather said.

The sun was still shining, and the wind still blowing, the sea was still pounding against the black rocks. Right there in front of me was the answer to White Feather's prayer and her teaching me how to pray more efficiently. I took another deep breath of that healing air. It smelled so good. I always pray for guidance and insight.

The rock is my foundation and my life is like the ocean whose waves are strong and deep. This is because prayer is strong and unfathomable and inspiring to motivate me. I am not building my life on the sand which is washy and full of holes because my prayer is strong and powerful. I am as good as the prayer I seek and the answers that will come. The salt air cleanses my body like the power of prayer and the sun heals my wounds that are still in my heart. The power of prayer is like the rhythm of the ocean, bringing in the good and letting go of the old.

I always pray for guidance and awareness. The sea air was so crisp and clean. I took another deep breath of that healing air. It smelled so good. Prayer teaches us to have faith to believe in the truth of God and yourself as a soul, not as a human. When I pray, I use spirit and higher thoughts. I pray my mind is in Heaven, which is using higher thoughts or spiritual principles but we have to go one step further and do something. Sitting around wishing does not get it. We have to put power beneath our wings. I looked up and there were sea gulls flying about me they could not fly unless they had air. We cannot fly unless we have prayer and faith beneath us.

I closed my eyes again in meditation and contemplation. When I opened my eyes as I looked out to the sea, there was not a cloud to be seen and the sky was blue gray. I thought, clouds, are like my problems. They will stay away if I use prayer, instead of my fears.

Then, White Feather said,

"Jean, put what you are seeing together in your mind like a Seascape painting. Now, frame the picture in your heart and you will be able to recall the power of prayer by the sea."

I closed my eyes and framed the ocean, the spray, rocks, and the sky into a Seascape that I carry with me within my heart. I realized that no matter where I am in this world and what was going on in my life, God and White Feather are with me. By recalling the Seascape scene, I will automatically clear my mind of negative thoughts and fill it with the light and vision of God. I learned what White Feather wanted me to know about prayer that day.

As I got back into my car it was moving from the wind hitting the frame and I realized it was time to leave. I had learned what White Feather wanted me to know about prayer. White Feather had given this knowledge to me and to others because we need more faith now then ever before. The world is suffering so we need to stay prayed up. Please use this prayer lesson to your best interest and share it with others. I remembered her telling me while I was praying.

Prayer is the power of the ocean; the salt air cleans my body, the sun and spirit healing any wounds I might still have in my heart. The rock is my foundation in God and White Feather. In breathing the fresh air I took into my lungs, which cleans my soul and White Feather was within my spirit. After all she comes and goes like the wind. Just like the wind I know she was there and I could hear her, but could not see her. I thought this was also how faith worked like the wind. I could sense it but could not see faith but I know it was working for me out here by the ocean.

Before I left she came back to say a few more words,

"Jean, keep praying it brings you to where I live into your world. Stay prayed up." she said.

I knew that prayer brings us to Heaven and this is what was needed. That is why White Feather brought this lesson about prayer and the ocean if I could understand if there is another way to look at prayer and how it can be learned. Anyone that wants to learn about prayer, can, that is White Feather's goal.

To pray and take action is what changes our lives for the highest good of all. Prayer, like the ocean, goes out and comes back to us when we need it the most. White Feather asked me to compare prayer to something beautiful because prayer is beautiful.

Then I heard a ruffle of feathers,

"I am your beloved angel. Never give up. Always keep hope in your heart. It's coming all the good for your life. Your life is changing and you are moving forward. Keep your faith in prayer and believe," she said.

"White Feather, thank you for your instructing me on a deeper level of prayer," I told her. I heard a gentle laugh. Boom, she was gone. White Feather floats in and out of my life like the wind.

Prayer will inspire and guide me the rest of my life to help others learn the power of prayer, a unique tool of. I had learned more about prayer by going to the ocean. The ocean had captivated my soul just like prayer captivated my heart. I had no doubt that I had heard everything White Feather had to say on the Seascape it was so uncomplicated and simple and full of love.

Right before I drove off, White Feather came back again.

Jean, memorize this, *"What I desire is aliened with spirit and is on its way. Oh, God is in me and is powerful and working for me. I might not have it now but tomorrow is harvest time. This prayer is powerful and rewarding,"* she said.

My life is a true adventure like the ocean and the waves, strong and deep. Prayer is like the ocean very powerful and like the ocean it moves in its own way. Prayer is the power of the ocean the salt air cleaning my body, the sun and spirit healing any wound I might still have in my heart. The rock was my foundation in God and White Feather. Prayer will guide and inspire me the rest of my life and to help others learn the power of prayer a unique tool of.

Now I could return home and write about Seascape prayer a healing journey.

"Try not to become a man of success but rather try to become a man of value."

—Albert Einstein

Chapter Twenty-One

Outstanding Attorney

"My attorney came from prayer and he is one of the greatest men I've ever met."

—Author

When White Feather said we were going to take care of the Hungry Wolf she meant it. I continued working on igniting my tigress inside and feeling her power. With White Feather's continued support I began to look for an attorney. One day White Feather came to me and told me it was time to get an attorney now. She had one in mind, but she didn't give me the name. Instead, she told me to call my minister friend and ask her to pray with me regarding the right attorney.

I called my friend Danielle and told her I had seen an ad in the local paper for two new attorneys in the area.

"You pray with me, too. It will make the prayer stronger," she said. A couple of days later she called back.

"I think Adam, this Legal Beagle is your man," she said.

"What do you think?" she asked me.

"I agree with you. I will call him next week," I responded and I did.

Adam did not want to take my case. He explained that he could not afford the time and the effort it took to take a financial settlement that had not been to court.

I could not believe that he was turning my case down. After all, he was my declaration of prayer.

"Please I need you. You came through prayer," I pleaded.

As soon as I said the word prayer he hesitated for one second and that is all I needed.

"Oh, please," I said again. He took in a deep breath.

"Oh come in," he said.

I realize now that I had the right words to sway my attorney because of the creamy foundation of prayer that my minister friend and I had prepared. If it was not for the creamy foundation we put in ahead of time, I wouldn't have gotten in the door. I know that just as sure as I know my name.

When I first saw Adam I could not believe my eyes. I was sitting in his waiting room when he came out to introduce himself. For some reason I thought most attorneys were old and grouchy but not this man. He is very handsome and has a great smile. His smile put me on the moon. I was impressed by his presence even before I walked into his office. I was thinking, says the spider to the fly.

We discussed my divorce and financial situation. I did not tell him the whole horrendous story for fear that he would run the other way. I answered only the questions Adam asked of my circumstances. He told me what it would take to go back to court.

Even though I did not give him every detail, I believe he knew that I was pushed beyond my breaking point. I had given up thinking anything with the Hungry Wolf could be resolved. What I really needed to protect me was a steel tank with armored men surrounding me. I also needed a miracle and I received several. The big miracle was getting Adam and having him in my corner.

Over the next year and a half Adam and I worked closely together to comfort each other in the power struggle with the wolf. This battle went on for over seven years while the wolf still wanted to play his usual tricks and growl all the way to the bank. But I was thinking other thought of how I could turn this around in my favor so I could see the wolf desperate after all these years.

It was during the Christmas season that Adam and I became good friends. It is not easy to be alone on any of the holidays, but this year, it was harder than some. I knew they were going to be particularly sad for me. Besides facing a court date with the wolf, I was losing a close friend or at least it felt that way. After ten years of friendship my friend Danielle married and moved out of this area. Although I was happy for her, I felt sad and alone.

I also got mad at White Feather for the first time in our relationship for giving my girlfriend a mate and leaving me here.

I recalled past holidays when I was with a man sitting around a Christmas tree or out dancing. Now, I was alone in my house, feeling sorry for myself. That's when White Feather flowed into my spirit with such force as to almost knock me off my bed.

"Jean, why are you so blue when I am working for you? Do you think you're going to have a blue Christmas? Well, listen to this," she said as, she broke into song, "Here comes Santa Clause Here comes Santa Clause." I thanked White Feather for her magical Christmas for me because of her my Christmas was perfect. This was a miracle I'd never forget.

Her singing filled my spirit. I immediately felt much better and more relaxed. White Feather then told me to get off the pity pot and work with others. The more I gave, the less lonely I felt. I took a Christmas gift to a man that was in a convalescent hospital. Playing Santa Clause cheered me up. It freed my spirit.

I then sent a Christmas package to Adam thanking him for all the good work he had done for me. He received it with sincere kindness and his telephone call helped me get over the holiday blues and my loneliness. Until that telephone call it had not occurred to me that my amazing attorney could be feeling blue too. Knowing this made him more human to me and helped me trust him and that he would handle my case with compassion, as well as power.

"The Dalai Lama has compassion, spiritual depth, kindness, and visions that he offers the world as a healing path."

—*Spiritual Hero of the*
—Science of Mind Magazine

Chapter Twenty-Two

Heart and Soul

"I surrender to the power and presence of God within me."

—Diane Harmony, 5 *Gifts for an Abundant Life*

Someone once asked me, "If God is all powerful and loving why doesn't he stop the suffering in the world?" What I've concluded is that God does not create suffering, but I do believe he allows it.

God will not interfere with our lessons. He lets us suffer the consequences of our own consciousness. If our consciousness is focused on negative painful thoughts we're going to create suffering in our world. Blaming someone or some other power for our suffering prolongs it. We need to look to our own thoughts, and actions. Then, identify the lesson in the situation and seek a means to release the agony. There will always be pain and suffering in this world. It is up to us to rise above it in prayer.

The truth is you can't hang everything on God. God wants us to experience peace and happiness. God hopes we find our way through the suffering to the other side. Author and medical doctor Deepak Chopra, was asked in an interview why a loving God would allow the suffering and deaths of hundreds of thousands of people in the Tsunami of 2004. Chopra explained that this event reflected the state of the world's consciousness and if enough people walk around with chattering, anxious, conflicting thoughts all day long there's bound to be an eruption of some kind. Our minds are chattering because of nervous tension and lack of trust in the world.

Chopra, stressed how important it is for us to take responsibility for our part in a disaster, instead of blaming God or someone else. We can, look in the mirror and not see the chatter of our true self and by not looking we prolong our own agony. We can listen and not hear what's going on in our mind. By not seeing our true self we keep the lie and the illusion going.

The Tsunami of December 26th, 2004 was an international tragedy. The waves were deadly and came without warning. A path of destruction swept Asia and paradise was lost. This destruction touched every race, creed, and religion. Paradise turned deadly.

People were hit hard, but some survived. The survivors began to rebuild their world in the same spirit that saved them. People were brought together through their grief. Their faith and a new hope carried them through each day and night. They cleaned up the rubble; they did not wallow in self-pity. Instead, they found compassion for each other. They picked themselves up, dusted themselves off and went on.

While all the pain and death was being reported I listened to miraculous stories that were told. A story that touches me was of a seven-year-old boy who was saved by his dog. The boy's Dad who was on a hill above the beach saw the colossal waves about to hit the mainland, so he screamed to his family, below "Run, run away," The command was simple, but it presented, his wife, Sangleta, with a dilemma. She only had a second to decide the fate of her sons. She had three sons, and only two arms. She knew she only had the strength to help only two of the boy's. She grabbed the youngest ones and told the oldest son, Dinakaran to run up the hill. Dinakaran had the best chance of out running the tsunami. But instead, Dinakaran didn't follow. He instead, went to the safest place he knew, the small family hut just 40 yards away from the seashore. Fortunately, the family dog had his eyes on the boy. The family dog, Selvakumar, felt the rumbling of the earth under his feet. He looked around to see where his family was. He saw the mother running up the hill with the other two children and he looked for his friend, Dinakaran. He spotted him.

The scruffy yellow dog ducked into the hut after Dinakaran, nipping and nudging him did everything in his canine power to get the boy up the hill.

Sangeeta had no idea of the drama unfolding below. Once she crossed the main road to safety with the other children she collapsed into tears screaming over the loss of her eldest son.

"I heard from others that my house collapsed. I felt sure my child had died," said the 24-year old mother. Sangeeta said she wept for joy when she saw her son walking up to her together with Selvakumar by his side. The dog had saved her son.

"Selvakumar grabbed me by the collar of my shirt. He dragged me out," Dinakaran told everyone. Sangeeta's brother-in-law gave her the puppy following the birth of her second son, when, the brother-in-law died in an accident two year's ago they changed the dog's name to his. Sangeeta said that she believes some special spirit, perhaps her brother-in-law, resides in the young yellow dog.

Blessings can come out of evil because the thing that was hidden and buried deep, can be reveled to heal. People's eyes were opened to the government and what they did not do. I prayed to White Feather that the truth would unravel like a ball of string and it did. What I saw in this tragedy and others is the strength of people and the goodness of humans banding together to help each other. There is nothing more healing to help strengthen our souls. Then I thought of White Feather. Her healing energy has the power and kindness to heal any wound.

The attack of September 11th and the death of thousands of innocent people were tragic beyond words. The night of the attack, White Feather and three angels came to visit me in my bedroom. Great sadness filled the room. White Feather spoke to me,

"Jean, I want you to write a poem about this day. I want you to write of the destruction and corruption to the earth and the suffering of the human soul. The angels and I are on our way to New York to help the many people who are suffering and are in a great pain," White Feather told me.

White Feather knew that the people of New York were in deep shock and they needed the angels more than ever to look over them.

As I began to write the poem I looked at the angels that filled my room and I saw tears running down their faces. I knew these angels were going to help people in ways I could never understand. The following healing poem flowed through me.

> *The angels are our Heavenly messengers.*
>
> *As they soar to New York, they lifted humanity*
>
> *The angels take the suffering and*
>
> *dying and envelope the people in their wings. The*
>
> *angels embrace death as they fly the beloved souls to Heaven.*

When I finished writing the poem White Feather and the angels disappeared. I felt sadness in my heart, yet I knew with White Feather and the angels being in New York, the healing would begin.

I am amazed at the strength in the New York people. In the days that followed the attack, New Yorkers refused to give way to the enemy. The people went back to work and through their faith in God they bonded together and kept going. They worked selfishly keeping their hearts open for their healing. The New Yorkers bonded together and became stronger and loved each other even more because of their sorrow came strength.

That day changed our world. Nothing will ever be quite the same again. The spirit of the New York rose to the occasion. New Yorkers will forgive, in time but it is the forgetting that is the hard thing to do. It is in the letting go of the pain in our hearts is where forgiveness comes from. Our souls need time to release our pain because evil took over that day and spread like wild fire. No one person is to blame. Evil is evil and only through the grace of God and the angels can we survive it. We have to forgive those twisted souls that have hearts as cold as ice.

Prayer, meditation and forgiveness are our way through suffering and torment. They are our rebirth if we look at the situation in the right light. Jesus reminds us to forgive seventy times seven.

Until you completely forgive the people that hurt you, your heart will not be free of your pain and free to love again.

I believe the only way someone finds forgiveness is through God. It has been years I am just beginning to heal from the shock of September 11th and I did not lose a loved one.

I believe God planted a seed for forgiveness in our souls that day so that at some point the human spirit will heal from the catastrophic events.

You might ask yourself, "How can we forget this painful event?" God can help us heal our scars when we remember that painful day. We have to have the spirit of amnesty to forgive our enemy and to pray for the willingness to forgive each other. Here is a Bible verse that tells you what I am relating to "*But love your enemies, and do good, and lend, expecting nothing in return; and your reward will be great, and you will be sons of the Most High; for he is kind to the ungrateful and the selfish. Be merciful, even your Father is merciful.*" From Luke 6:35.

We also want to pray for peace on our planet and the ones that were killed that horrendous day. Through this prayer and forgiveness, a great strength will prevail to help us heal on every level. We must create a way of harmony, peace and love throughout the United States and the world to keep a friendly healing spirit around us. This will protect us from outside evil entering into our own souls and destroying our world.

Evil wants us to fall into despair and let the dark side take over and harden our hearts. Satin wants us to stay wounded and turn away from prayer. He wants us to listen to his lies. The people of New York stepped on satin and pushed him back into his hell hole.

Here is a quote I like: We know there is evil in this world. Do not mess with us we are New Yorkers. "*Evil flourishes when good men do nothing.*"—Edmund Burke.

Out of great tragedy comes our necessity to change and with that comes growth in our spiritual resilience. Our souls have reached out to God for our healing and he has answered. The use of affirmations daily can be helpful to quit the chatter of the mind. Here is a great affirmation that can be said daily:

"I am sending love, peace and forgiveness to the United States of America and its officials. I affirm that we are healed in our mind, body and spirit. I am in God's peace and grace. I pray knowing our deep wounds are healed." Amen.

Then think of White Feather, her healing energy has the power and kindness to heal any bleeding wound. She was there with the band of angels that terrifying day to heal the heart and souls of the people.

In time we must get on with our life and trust again. It is normal to have a devastating reaction to all that happed. To trust is to have faith in our conviction and have self-assurance in ourselves and our administration. We must learn to have buoyancy to keep ourselves going in this time of pain and anguish. We can release our hurting through prayer to God and our angels. Love does renew itself if we do not block this loving energy. We can embrace love because this is the time when we have our angels putting us in the light and putting their white wings of love around us for our protection. In one brief moment, people's lives changed forever and that is what happened that horrendous day.

We sometimes use our own illogical thinking which is not always correct, especially if we are under tremendous heartache and stress. But from your grief you grow in strength. God understands our hearts and knows the pain we feel. He is there for us with his hands outstretched and wants us to be comforted. There will be pain and suffering in this world but we can rise above it. It is really about us and how we apply our faith in God to our daily life. God always inspires and wants us to have the best life he has to offer. Get into that row boat knowing you are being led by a higher power and row yourself to the shore of faith.

I believe the disasters are happening because the world is under assault from foreign countries. The reasons for this; the populace should take more responsibility of taking care of each other. Our earth is precious and we want to help Mother Nature take care of our world. It has to start with us. We are only still here because of God's grace and mercy. The devil is alive and well in our world. God is not weak and he is our provider and will protect us from evil if we ask him too.

Ask yourself, how do I take responsibility for our world situation? I do know I can not sit home in my comfort zone and wring my hands and say,

"Oh, let someone else do it." We have to motivate ourselves to do something and then do it. God will guide you and your purpose will be shown. I could be helping and old lady across the street or a child crying for food and comfort. This will help you to be a better person and improve our world. Put your bucket down whether it is full or empty. You can't wait until your bucket is full before you give. We have to be God's hands, God's eyes, and God's heart. Pray with all your heart for an improved world with more love and understanding for each other. When you see someone that needs help, in some way, help them. That is when you plant good seeds of faith.

We are the children of the most high and God is looking for our prayers for peace for ourselves and the world. When we pray we still our minds. We have great power when we are in prayer. Prayer fights satin. We are creatures of tradition and convention. We have to take the narrow road, not the wide one, as the Bible tells us. After all, the wide road has more wolves and potholes. We must stay on the narrow road to do our best and stay focused on the right thoughts and then we will take the right action in our life and this in turns helps our world.

There are many factors that cause hazardous, terrifying events and vibrations in the world. We have to learn to stay cool and do a healing calm meditation within ourselves. We need to grow in spirit and stop our cluttered and chattered minds. Swiss psychiatrist Carl Jung felt that, at the conscious level our individual minds are separated, but that our unconscious minds merge as one. Mass goodness or disaster can be created at this level.

Some people call this critical mass point the "one hundredth monkey" theory. Many metaphysicians apply this theory to the evolution of human consciousness saying it will take 144,000 people holding a spiritual state through prayer and meditation to create peace and quiet the chatter. Others say the number is 300,000. This is where your help is needed to save the world. We have not been able to get that critical mass yet. We needed people to raise their consciousness levels daily to bring this about.

You have your part in the working of grace. Metaphysical teachings teach you, *"Grace is one wing of the bird; your effort is the other wing."*

"We cannot use a band-aid anymore to cure the world. White Feather told me, We must use our minds, heart and hands," she informed me in her loving way.

I knew that life was fragile and life was to be cherished.

"I love you, you're Perfect, Now Change!"

—Title of a contemporary play

Chapter Twenty-Three

Illusion

"Only a life lived for others is worth living."

—Albert Einstein

"Where in the hell am I?" I said.

I sat straight up in bed and looked around. I looked over to the right and saw someone covered up with a blanket from the head to toe. "God," I thought. I panicked when I realized I was in a stranger's bed. I jumped out of bed. When my feet hit the floor a tremendous pain hit me between my eyes and I was suddenly dizzy. I slowly sat back on the bed and cringed within myself.

"God, what have I done?" I asked myself.

I did not remember one thing about this bed room. I looked down at my clothes which were all wrinkled. I ran my fingers through my messy hair. I felt my face and I know I had cried off all my make-up. I was a mess. I was also fighting a nauseated feeling. Was this a terrible dream? I looked at the person on the bed. I put my hands on the cover and slowly pulled it down away from his face, would I recognize this person? A scary feeling came over me. I saw his face. Yes, I knew him. He was my date from last night.

God, what happened? Did I do anything I would regret later on? I tried to remember. Gradually my memory returned. No, I was okay, I pushed myself up from the bed and went over to the dresser and got down on my knees, I prayed,

"Jesus, please, help me!" God I know you are with me in my anguish.

I lay down on my stomach and stretched myself out like a cross. I cried. My heart was beating so fast I felt like it was going to fly out of my body and I was trembling with fear.

"Please, help me I will never drink like this again, please, forgive me." I think I passed out. The tears were falling down my face and hitting the blue shag carpet. I lay there for at least fifteen minutes when finally I decided to get up.

It was then I heard a soft whisper of a voice within myself,

"Jean, you are okay. However, I want you to keep your promise. If you keep your promise to me your life will not go the way of darkness like others who are not as aware as you are," she said. I wanted to listen to her soft sweet voice forever.

I know now that this was White Feather talking to me. A loving gentleness filled my spirit. I could see a white glow all around me. In my mind's eye, to this day, I can still imagine this picture!

I found out what happened to me that night by piecing together what I remembered with what I could see. I had gone with a date to a party at my girlfriend's apartment. I drank many, many glasses of orange juice and vodka. I blacked out and ended up in bed with my date. At this point in my life I was on a very self-destructive path, but after that night, things changed. I realized how fast drinking habits can steal your soul. I kept my promise and never drank like that again. I realized I was going nowhere and my habit was going to take me over. As I look back over the years and think of all the parties I attended, I am really surprised I kept my word. I really did hear the truth from my spiritual guide White Feather.

You may wonder how I stayed away from the alcohol. It was not easy. I saw everyone else drinking and having a ball (or so it looked) and I wanted to do the same. But, that night always came back to me, and my promise to God. I would ask myself, if the booze was worth my getting into trouble it wasn't. Then I'd remind myself, I can have fun without giving into temptation. Give yourself a chance and remember your promise. Then, I would throw the liquor I held in my hand in a potted plant or in a sink. Anywhere except down my throat.

As the evening progressed I watched the people at the party do some really foolish things under the pretense of having fun. Sometimes their fun got them into real trouble. Was it worth it? I don't think so in fact I knew in my heart that drinking would lead me to destruction.

I knew I was using my faith and my will power. God gave us will power to use, so I went within myself and drew from that power. I knew when I drank my morals went into the toilet. Drinking was not worth it to me. The void and emptiness in my heart could not be filled by drinking. I could not numb myself that way. I did not want any kind of monkey on my back. I knew the more I leaned on drinking the harder it would be to quit. My demon was after me but I knew God is greater and he was with me. I am greater because of my faith in him. The following Bible verse came to me. *"I can do all things in him who strengthens me."* From Philippians 4:13. I had more to lose than to gain. I took the habit by the horns and threw it away. I was not going to lose control anymore.

But, I was tempted again. Earlier in my life I liked the way cold beer slide down my throat. When I was twenty five-years old I was living in Bakersfield, California. I was back into the horse world and I had just bought a Quarter horse. The man that sold her to me was a very nice looking man. One hot summer day he asked me out on a date. We went out on the lake in a rowboat with a couple of six packs of beer. It was so lovely and peaceful on the lake I started to relax. The guy asked me if I wanted a beer. It was so hot I took one. That beer was refreshing and it glided deliciously down my throat. I realized in my soul if I kept drinking this smooth, cool beer, I would never stop. I could become addicted to beer. This hit me like a brick. My spirit told me,

"Jean, this is your last beer, and it was," and I spit out the beer, sitting there like a bump on a log. I was so surprised I just about fell into the lake.

I knew this was the voice of my Higher Self. I knew I could easily become an alcoholic and once I saw this, it was a thing of the past. I grabbed a hold of my faith and will power I knew I needed it now more than ever.

I asked White Feather about addiction. She responded by asking me what came first in my life. "Are you first or are your habits? When we first start a habit of any kind we control the habit, but later on the habit controls us. To lose a bad habit you have to think differently and have a positive mind set. Don't stay stuck in a rut. Get out of your comfort zone. After an individual alters their distractive lifestyle, they can change their life to be more fruitful. Your life can change in a moment for the better but it's up to you. You can replace your abusive habits with motive and purpose. When you do this you will be stronger, healthier, and happier because you are on a higher path."

White Feather has taught me, progress begins with the first step. The determination to change a destructive habit begins with a total desire to give up the old ways and take the first baby step forward. You can do it! The favor of God is yours. This will give you, the strength needed to overcome any weakness. Use your soul coverage.

Our transformation takes place in your soul, if you seek higher spiritual progress, don't be trapped in the old ways and conditioning. Recharge your batteries with hope and faith. A woman was at a conference in Santa Rosa, California a couple of years ago when someone asked, "Where's the smoking area?"

"Nevada," another shouted out. Everyone laughed.

The people at the conference also agreed that 'Smoking is definitely un-cool around here.'

Millions of people are so frustrated with their life that they turn to over-eating, drinking or smoking cigarettes or pot for relief. Their addictions provide them with the illusion, that things are okay. In reality nothing has changed, except that you've fallen more deeply into your addiction. You have become a slave to a destructive habit if you make stupid choices. This is the reason one needs to make the right choices which will gave us better health. If we make these healthy choices we produce a healthier body, mind and a 'cleansed spirit,' because you are on a higher level of consciousness.

Spirit plays a big part in this transformation. The spirit wants to stay clean from any self-destructive habits because it wants to keep growing and learning and for us to become stronger inside. Fight for freedom of your soul. It is worth your biggest effort.

Someone is always noticing what goes on with us. White Feather explained to get over a bad habit you have to use soul coverage. Our soul can be like on open wound. This is where prayer and meditation comes in. It protects us. We protect ourselves with prayer and meditation that is soul coverage. The more we do this work, the more we are covered and protected. Remember it is a privilege to pray. God is always present and angels are aware of what we are doing and thinking. Don't live in a quicksand illusion because your world will come crumbling down around you at some point in your life. Fight for freedom of your soul. White Feather taught me to magnify my God, not my habits

I in turn, have taught and encouraged my clients to give them selves a new start in life. It is your right and spiritual nature to live a clean and productive life, free from compulsive behavior. Do not fool yourself and keep doing the old habit that is the road to destruction. These habits of the body can take your life and throw your health and your self-esteem down a rat hole. Face your addiction. Look at yourself in the mirror and asked yourself what are you dong? Be honest. Put up a fight. The body is weak and will not give in. The body does not want to quit habits, but you can listen to the signs of healing from your heart.

"Use your warrior heart to overcome the enemy of your soul.

God will bring you to victory. Be a victor, not a victim," White Feather said.

When a person hears this whisper, inside their heart crying for help it's time to do something about it. When the body is coughing from smoking and hurting from other destructive habits, the body is waiting for you to come to your senses. The body is weak and your spiritual existence can not stand the stench inside from all your bad habits. You're addiction is an enemy of your soul.

The body is trying to tell you, I can not stand this mess inside. Please, give your body a make-over. I am warning you to clean your body out.

When you hear this voice, it is time to start before it is too late. Your body can no longer serve you. Don't let your physical body get used up by beating it to death with a cigarette.

The soul is lamenting.

"What was the reason you did not listen to me. I warned you. I gave you all kinds of warning signs. Now, the damage will be harder to repair. You lived in a fantasy of illusion and what goes around comes around," Please do not make stupid choices. You only have one body so keep it clean and you will have energy to burn. Live a healthy lifestyle.

The body never forgets how you use or abuse it.

My days of smoking cigarettes were short lived. I was living in Oakland, California and was about twenty-two-years old. I was living with a girlfriend that smoked. This did not brother me or so I thought. We had parties once in a while and it was at that moment, I decided to try a cigarette. Oh, I was thinking I could take or leave these cigarettes. What's the big deal! I did not know I was playing with fire. I started to borrow cigarettes. Boy did those cigarettes start tasting good. One day, I was at grocery store I can still see this image. I had no one to borrow a cigarette from so, I decided to buy my first pack. I picked out a brand and after I had paid for it started opening the pack. I was about to walk out the automatic doors when I saw a brown waste basket in the corner.

Then I heard a loud and clear voice,

"Jean, take those cigarettes and throw them in the waste basket." I stood there and looked around. My hand was getting hot as I looked at my right hand. I looked around for this hidden voice. Where was the voice coming from? This made me a little nervous. I heard this voice again,

"Jean, throw these away right now. If I ever see another cigarette in your mouth you will not live long enough to continue my work," she said.

I know this voice was my angel, and she was protecting me with soul coverage which is a special blend of love and safety. Gee wiz I got caught.

I took that pack of cigarettes and dumped them in the basket. As I was walking out the sliding door of the store I put my hands together in a clapping motion and I was saying to myself,

"No, smoking for Jean. Then I though because I was single who wants to kiss and ash tray."

I know my angel has touched me that day and was on my shoulder.

Thank God, I was listening and did what I was told. This saved me from a destructive habit that I did not have to overcome. I never again bummed a cigarette from anyone nor did I need to. I know this was my spiritual guide White Feather guiding me on my life path. White Feather taught me to magnify my God, not my rotten habits. It is your spiritual nature and right to live a clean and productive life to be free from compulsive habits which take your energy and throw's your health in the gutter.

As White Feather told me last week,

"The body ages to the tune you believe and how you treat it."

I was after one of my clients to quit smoking. Steven had been seeing me for many years, but he wasn't interested in quitting smoking. I started noticing that his lungs were getting tighter and tighter. One time when he came in for a treatment, I mentioned that his lungs were not doing well. I know there was not enough oxygen getting to his lungs. This worried me. I said,

"Looks like your time have come and your clock is ticking. You have to quit smoking."

Steven turned white and lay very still. He just looked at me, but he knew me well enough to know I meant business.

"I don't know about that," he said.

"I know," I said.

"You've been coming here for years and I haven't said anything. Today I was told to tell you that you have to quit smoking, or you are going to be very sick at some point in your life. You're playing with a loaded gun," I said.

After the treatment Steven climbed off the table. He tried to make light of what just happened, but I stared him right in the eyes.

"I mean business," I said. I gave him a big smile because I know he could do it.

About a month later he came back to see me and said he was trying to quit. I gave him another treatment and then continued praying for him. A week later I got a phone call from Steven who told me he had quit smoking and he hoped he could stay quit. His health has improved considerably.

People get these compulsive habits when they are young and keep them the rest of their lives. Then, as you get older and you continue abusing your body with your addiction your body deteriorates quickly. I feel cigarettes or pot are used to cover the heart's feeling. This is like a smoke screen that covers the heart and the soul never has the chance to truly express itself from its pain and sadness. It's just a cover up for emotions. The habit gives a person the illusion that things are better, but in reality nothing moved or changed. In fact the habit is still in control of you, not the other way around.

Some people tell me,

"I can take it or leave it." So why not leave it is what I always think. Get up and take the right action. Your power is in the action. Just be more aware of your health and remember, you will get the benefit of a healthier body and your attitude and self-esteem will improve. You are a person of light. You are becoming your Higher Self. Learn new ways and good habits. Take a beginning meditation class. Look for a good church. Meet new and interesting friends that do not smoke or take drugs. Become active in the right habits and lifestyle. I know you can do it, I have faith in you.

Take the first step and start over. Make it a personal choice to grow in the spirit. Read some healing books. Educate yourself to a different lifestyle. Preservation is the answer. You will be proud of yourself and your family and friends will notice the difference in you. Pat yourself on the back. Hang around dreamers who take action and have a dream of their own. Get a vision of your dream and make it happen.

This is your salvation and a new lifestyle. It's not easy to change a habit. Jesus said, "*Watch and pray that you may not enter into temptation; the spirit indeed is willing, but the flesh is weak.*" Matthew 36:41. Change your programming to healthier habits. Let the Lord touch your life. The choice is up to you.

The good news is people want to quit smoking. There's never been as much help to the smoker as right now. You just have to want to quit and use some of God's will-power and your own. He will lead you to the right place for the help you need. I knew a couple that quit smoking together and they saved what they usually spent on cigarettes, for two years and went to Hawaii instead of spending their money foolishly and harming their health.

White Feather just told me,

"Nothing is more important than your health. Do not abuse it. Your excellent health is a blessing from God," she said.

Your mind is a very powerful tool that can be used for a healthier lifestyle. Most people wait until they are pushed up against a wall and they are about to leave the planet before they are willing to change. Change is a choice. But, when people are trapped in an addiction they don't feel they can change because they are weak or so they think. People have to learn to use their soul courage. What is that? It is your will power.

Depression is also a form of addiction. In a normal human life people have their up and downs and might feel depressed. When you are diagnosis with, "Major Depression Disorder," now that is deep depression where you feel hopeless or hopelessness. The main cause of depression is not enough sleep or enough exercise. Change your sleep pattern and try and get eight hours of sleep. You will not have so many mood swings and you will be happier. Stay in balance with your body. You're not created to be depressed you have to seek the faith inside of you. Let's say you're depressed and sitting around in the dark having a pity party. Get up and open up those drapes and let the sunshine in and don't go out and find people that are depressed like you, find friends that are uplifting and helpful with your situation. Let love touch your life instead of doubt and fear. Walk in the sunlight because God has a new day for you a new beginning on higher ground.

Addiction comes in many forms. Often we are addicted to something before we even know it. This is what happened to me. I became addicted to the abuse of the wolf and the negative feelings I had toward myself. I was stick in a rut and I did not even realize it at the time I was living with the wolf. I had buried my feeling down deep inside of me and I was afraid to let them out with him.

Over time, the wolf's treatment toward me began to crush my good feelings towards myself. What was amazing was I was able to quit alcohol and cigarettes, but years later I was unable to quit the wolf. I was able to quit the alcohol and cigarettes because I still had the control but in the case of the wolf I felt he had the power and the control. The wolf had brains and he had washed my mind. I could not see my way out of the relationship even though I wanted out. I felt trapped but I had read that women do not like to give up on their relationships they hang on the longest and I was one of them.

The wolf told me in many ways that I was worthless and wrong this added to my low self-esteem. I became fearful of him and his verbal abuse was sinking into my skin and soul. I was afraid he would come after me physically because of the Fiasco at the fast food restaurant and then a couple of other times when he pushed me down. After awhile feeling badly about myself became the norm and I was uncomfortable believing anything else. I did not want to admit the truth of my situation. But inside I knew I was going to have to do something about this. I could not fool myself forever.

The wolf took advantage of my addiction to him; he always had a way to stop me from leaving. His screaming kept me from thinking of anything else. He screamed and shouted orders.

"What's for dinner? Don't go out with her. Stay home,"

Then, if my car broke down he would say something like,

"I don't care if your car is broken down. Walk," he'd tell me in his nasty way. I just took it not realizing there was a way out.

Then I realized, evil was a choice. I was in an abusive relationship and I had been reduced to believe I had no choice at all. He wanted to control me and take advantage of my good nature, but I was waking up. I started using my soul coverage and did a lot of prayer and meditation. This calmed me down inside and helped me to realize what was going on. At some point I had to get strong enough to server the cord.

I finally did what people do when they hit bottom in their addiction. I prayed day after day I prayed and finally the angels came. That did it for me what I didn't have the strength to do alone. The angels intervened in my misery and in my addiction. White Feather came and showed me the face of the wolf.

I have known many people who have overcome bad habits. This has shown me that people can quit if they want to. Kerry who was very over weight and under a lot of stress decided to come and see me this afternoon, I then made suggestions to help her with her diet.

"I don't know if I can do it," she replied.

"You will never know if you don't try. You will have to use your will power. Let's take it one day at a time," I said. I sent her to the hospital to talk to the dietitian and for her to make a diet plan for herself. This changed her life. My friend lost two pounds a week just the right amount for women. She stayed on the diet for three months and she looked outstanding. She also had a shine on her face and her attitude was positive toward herself and her life. Another friend of mine was trying to quit coffee and cigarettes.

"Are you determined to accomplish what you start out to do?" I asked her. She said she did more then anything.

I responded,

"Let's start with the coffee. We have to replace the coffee with a good habit. There are certain teas that help clean the body and will help also with cigarettes. You can also get a healing massage from White Feather," I said.

"Sounds like a good plan. I am ready," she said.

"Your diet will have to change and have more protein and no sugar," I told her. She followed my instructions and I also recommended some excellent health books for her to read. Within a month Kerry quit the coffee and cigarettes, because of the spiritual work she did on herself and the help she received from White Feather. Here are some foods instructions that I gave her, that will help with overcoming stress. Eat an all-carbohydrate diet like brown rice, pasta, whole wheat grains also including oatmeal, bulgur, potatoes, bananas and popcorn. You can also add mushrooms, leafy greens, and oranges, enriched or fortified grains. Include Victim B-6, and a B-Complex. She followed my instructions. Within two weeks she felt like a new person. Kerry health improved so much she decided to take walking classes and enjoyed them so much she became a runner. She did not have to do this alone. I was proud of her.

A lot of people think if they have to give up drugs, drinking or smoking their lives will be boring. But the truth is your life will be better because you are going to improve your health and your going to feel healthier and have more energy. No more dragging around half sick all the time. We limit God with our thinking.

A transformation is taking place in your soul, and seeks more spiritual progress. Don't be trapped in the old ways and conditioning. Recharge your batteries with hope and faith. Get a grip and improve your life. It all starts with you.

"A Master blesses calamity, for the Master knows that from the seeds of disaster comes the growth of Self."

—Neale Donald Walsch

Chapter Twenty-Four

The Tigress Is Born

"We, as woman must bring out our tigress."

—White Feather

The wolf and I had not seen each other since that memorable day in the restaurant when he followed me outside screaming at me all the way. This was good for me but not good for the wolf. The wolf was becoming increasingly resentful of my refusing to see him and his having to write me a check.

One day I was standing in line waiting to order coffee when suddenly I felt a man's hand on my shoulder. I turned around and saw the angry wolf by my side. He did not even give me a chance to say 'hello' before he pushed me to the ground and yelled,

"I want you to go to the bank and get some money right now," he growled.

"No, I am not going," I said looking up at him from the ground. From the angry on his face, I realized then I could be in danger. Suddenly the manager of the coffeehouse was running over helping me up.

"Are you all right? Do you want me to call the police?"

"Yes, I do," I said.

"Come inside with me," he said, helping me up.

199

Once inside, the manager phoned the police and as he was hanging up, our attention was drawn to some loud noise outside. We could not believe what we were seeing.

"That man is jumping on the hood of your car."

The manager said in disbelief. I decided it best to not go near him. His arms were bent and his fists clenched in front of him, as he bounced up and down like a professional fighter. The police showed up quickly and came into the fast-food restaurant. Meanwhile the wolf continued bouncing up and down on my car hood. How far would he go? I wondered. When he saw the officer, the wolf jumped off the hood and onto the pavement, but the hood was severely dented.

Leading me outside, the police officer asked,

"Do you want to put this man in jail?"

"Do you want to get a temporary restraining order on him?"

"Yes. Write it up. I am tired of this harassment and I am scared." I said.

Then, White Feather stepped in,

"You're going to learn how to fight back," she said. I then felt that White Feather was disgusted with the wolf's behavior; she had given him plenty of rope and he hung himself. It was a rope of change for him to come across as a better guy. But of course the wolf was still hostile and wanted it all.

This fiasco at the fast food restaurant did me in. I was humiliated and fed up. Something had to change and this time I knew it had to be me. The wolf was not going to leave me alone unless I made him. I knew this was going to be a fight for my survival!

My prayers had been answered and I'd found the right attorney, but I knew this wasn't enough. I knew that Adam would fight for me, but I also knew I needed to stand up for myself. I had to face my fears and the truth about myself.

One day I was talking to myself and I was wringing my hands while saying,

"I can't take care of myself. I can't take care of myself. He took everything but the kitchen sink." I was devastated.

I went on and on burying myself in my victim stance. I finally realized that I had to learn how to fight him. I had to take back my power I had given to him. I remembered, when I was a teenager and a cheer leader in high school we would practice our yells, 'fight, fight,' that is what I had to do, fight for my survival.

"I can hear you two reservations away," White Feather said when she popped in.

"I hear you and I am here. We're going to take care of the wolf once we take care of you," she said.

"How are you going to take care of me?" I asked.

"We're going to find your tigress," she said.

"What tigress?"

"That's what I mean," White Feather said.

"Your tigress is the fire and passion in you and we have to ignite the eternal flame and never let it go out again. You have buried your true self for so long we're going to have to dig deep to get to the fire in you,"

She continued,

"This is a new experience for you to have this feeling again. This is your rebirth to learn how to fight back." she said. White Feather then told me to,

"Go into meditation and think about this and then she would get back to me later."

I thought of how fiery I used to be and how all the fight had been driven out of me. The controlling negative emotional abuse of the wolf had gotten to me. I had lost a part of my true identity and I didn't even know it had happened. I then thought the wolf brain washed me in such a cunning way I did not even know it had happened. What happened to the girl that held the gal up to the shower spout in the gym shower when I was a teenager? Where had that fiery spirit gone? Was I going to let it be stomped out by the wolf? Not any more. I was in a fight for my life. The tigress was ready to stomp, leap and knock the wolf out. The tigress was hungry for the wolf's blood.

When White Feather and I met later that day she said,

"Now, think of the tigress and how she acts. She is powerful and strong. She moves in a slow and deliberate manner. She is acutely aware of every movement around her, ready to pounce at the slightest provocation. She saves her energy for the right moment and waits. She waits methodically for the kill, patient, thoughtful, to pounce at the right time. She controls her anger and her desires which make her powerful," she said.

White Feather continued,

"Now, be the tigress and imagine yourself looking at the Hungry Wolf. He wants to eat you alive and destroy you. You are going to reverse his tactics. You are going to learn how to launch an attack on the wolf by stalking him at a distance," she told me.

I tried to do what White Feather asked. I started to think of the wolf, but grew angry and frustrated when I thought about him. I again listed all the things he took from me and how he did me in. He took me to the cleaners and I resented having to fight for my very existence. Now I had to pull the tigress out of me. I had to let the wolf know he had a tigress by the tail and I was ready to roar.

"I can see what you're thinking,

"You're thinking how sick and tired you are of having someone hound you, those thoughts are making you weak. You look like a wilted Lilly." White Feather said.

I looked at myself through her eyes. I didn't want to admit it but she was right. I had to make a change and transform myself. I spent too many years hounded by the wolf. It was time to face him with teeth bared. I had to learn how to master the art of hunting by crouching down in the grass and wait for the prey to appear. I had to search for the tigress within myself. I had to utilize the fire and anger to my advantage. White Feather asked me to now see the wolf as my prey.

She continued,

"See the wolf and see how he thinks. If he comes toward you be cautious until you see what he does. Then at the right moment make your move. He will back off and that is your time to charge," she said.

My tigress was going to have her dinner. I know now this was the moment!

Over the next few months I practiced this in meditation. With practice learned to think before I leaped. I became more assertive and straight forward in my life. I sought my true self again. I became more centered and balanced. I was no longer focusing on the wolf because of the inner work I was doing. I would think he was staying outside of my presence. I knew that a change in consciousness and in my heart had taken place when dealing with my challenges in a different way. When a problem arose, instead of being quiet and taking it I fought back in a gentle way, not from the emotional level. I'd think about what I wanted to say and then I'd say it.

For example, when Charles did something to push one of my buttons instead of responding like a victim by saying,

"Why are you doing this to me?" I would get in touch with the tigress I waited a few seconds before reacting. I'd think what I was going to say like, "Charles, you can't get away with that," I know what you're up to.

I meditated on the tigress. I started thinking about the way of the tigress, I thought of her graceful power, intention, and physical strength. I focused on the tigress' ability to balance her power. The tigress knows how to balance her power. She never wastes anything. The tigress is cunning and powerful.

I first realized I was changing and becoming reunited with my tigress, was when I had a confrontation with my young neighbor next door. I was inside my house and I heard this bouncing and banging noise. I ran outside my house only to find my neighbor had installed a basketball net. Three young men were standing there talking and one was throwing the ball into the net and when the ball came back it hit the cement with a loud boom. I stepped off my porch and ran over to the group.

"This is not going to work. It's very nerve racking," I told him.

All three turned to look at me.

"Oh, we won't dribble the ball," my neighbor said.

"That will not make a difference, please remove that net," I said.

They all just looked at me like I had three heads.

"I will be back," I said. At that time it took a lot of courage for me to bring out the tigress in me but I had made up my mind. "I was not going to hear that noise at whatever time the kid wanted to play basketball,"

I left and a few days later he was bouncing the ball again. I ran over and he turned around.

"I asked you to remove that basketball net," I said.

"It is past noon I have a right to play," he said.

"I have a right to peace and quiet," I fired back.

"Why not put the basketball net up in front of your house and that way you can use the road," I suggested.

"I'll think about it," he said.

I turned around and left. I went inside my house and called my minister friend,

"Please, pray that my young neighbor takes the basketball net down and puts it in front of his house," I said.

She told me to visualize the net gone and peace and quiet in its place. The next week-end I saw my young neighbor with his truck backed up in his driveway. He was putting the basketball net holder in the back of his truck. I was standing outside and had a smile on my face, and I thanked God and White Feather.

I ran inside called my friend to tell her the good news.

"The basketball has been moved to the front of his house. At least it is not four feet from my front door. Prayer is the power that changes things appropriately in divine timing. Thank you for the prayers," I said. I also knew my tigress had come out to protect me for the intrusion in my house. My tigress was back and next time I ran into the Hungry Wolf, I would be ready.

"Imagination is everything. It is preview of life's coming attractions."

—Albert Einstein

Chapter Twenty-Five

Bankruptcy

"Oh, God is in me and is powerful and working for me—I might
not have it now but tomorrow is harvest time."

—A Healing Prayer

I have always invested in property and never lost any money until I met the wolf. We talked about investing in a new house with property in Fort Bragg, California, because I was tired of living in an apartment. I was willing to sell my home in Modesto, California that I had before I was married. It was almost paid for. I was willing to invest in the down payment for the house here in Fort Bragg, California. I felt it was a good opportunity. Little did I know of the deep pothole I was about to fall into or the hungry devious wolf that I had lived with for eleven years I had not recognized him yet.

My house sold very fast in Modesto, California' and we bought the house in Fort Bragg from the owner contractor. I was so excited about moving into such a nice new place. It was a three bedroom two bath house with an acre of ground off State Highway I. The wolf and I lived in this house for five years until everything went to hell in a hand basket.

The night I left the wolf after that he quite paying the house payment but he was living at the house. I was living with my friend Audrey that I had gone to when I left him. I was sleeping on her couch and nothing was easy. The wolf would not leave the house so I had to go see my attorney and he got an order from court that the wolf only had so long to get out. I think it was less then a month.

Late one foggy night my friend Audrey and I decided to take a ride to see what was going on at my house. We were in front of a police car and as we drove by my house. I noticed when I looked on the porch the wolf was standing on the porch and he saw the police car. He ran to his truck and jumped inside and started his truck and was gone in a flash. I thought that very strange behavior but with the wolf you never knew what he was up to.

The police man was on the road that went past our house.

Later when I get back to Audrey place I called the police to see what was going on. The police man told me,

"There was a disturbance at your neighbor and we came out to see what was going on," he told me.

The wolf had thought the police car was for him because he had to be out of my house in thirty days. Audrey and I laughed our heads off. I went out to the house early the next day and called a lock smith and he came out and I changed all the locks on the house.

That afternoon I moved back into the house. The judge had given me the house in the divorce. It was such a traumatic experience. I found a real estate woman and I tried to sell the house. My house would not sell. I tried to get a person to share the payments that also failed. A friend wanted to buy my house had a terrible car accident and he changed his mind about buying my house. In the end of things the owners reposed the house and put me through bankruptcy and I had to vacate.

The owner-contractor put everything in storage and about a month later their lawyers told me that,

"You have to pay for the moving and storage costs."

I did get the wolf to pay for it which was a miracle the way he was acting. He was living at a motel and paying over $1,000 a month anything to get back at me for leaving. He did not care if I lost it all. I had married a wolf and he was hungry for anything he could get his hands on. He was not concerned if I had to become a homeless person and could starve. He did come through with checks one at a time for my support but I had to beg him for them. This hurt my self-esteem or what I had left of it. I was trying to get over this horrible situation and have some self-respect. I was using my soul coverage and it was helping me a lot.

I was not going to let my animals starve. I was not going to do without food either. I was nothing to him and for the first time I almost hated him but I know that would hold me back but I had to fight my feelings. I was angry and discouraged but I know in my heart somehow I would make it because I had great faith in God and White Feather and I had things to accomplish but I did not know what they were.

To this day I am not over losing my house. After all I had made the down payment and had gotten the wolf and I a lovely place to live. Our home was gone my marriage was gone it was all gone. My life felt like it was dead and how could I come out of this only through my faith that the Bible states, again, *"God will restore the years the locust has taken."* From Joel 2:25.

I had to believe that God and White Feather were watching out for me and someday I would get back everything I lost and more than I ever dreamed of.

It was a new year, a new life, and a new day. I had to get use to being completely alone except for God, White Feather and faith. If not, I think I would have run screaming, uncontrollably, into the black hole of the night.

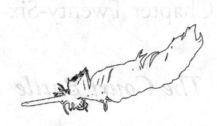

"Time is the measure that man gives to passing events;
The only power in time is what man imparts to it."

—Charles Fillmore, *The Reveling word.*

Chapter Twenty-Six

The Court Battle

"Place yourself in the full center of that flood, then you are without effort impelled to truth, to right and a perfect contentment."

—Emerson's Essays, *"Spiritual Laws."*

It was time for me to face the Hungry Wolf. My Little Red Riding Hood days were over. I knew that behind the face of Grandma was a Big Bad Wolf whose gnarly personality had deceived and betrayed me long enough. Although I was angry at the Hungry Wolf, White Feather taught me how to employ my anger to my advantage. The tigress was in repose waiting for the right moment to pounce.

Adam and I worked long, hard hours to get the information we needed for court. My case was not going to be a piece of cake and we had to be ready for anything the Hungry Wolf might throw our way. It was a great comfort to me to know that Adam was at my side. I did not have to face the Hungry Wolf alone—at least in the courtroom. Adam was not afraid of the Hungry Wolf, but at the same time, he did not underestimate the wolf's ability to maneuver himself into a profitable position.

Before our setting a court date I nearly weakened. I grew tired of the battle between us. I longed for a loving relationship. When I was alone at night I remembered how much I once loved the wolf.

We shared our hopes and dreams, as we planned our future together. Now we hated each other and were embattled.

I grew tired of the stress and pressure of our battle and wanted it to be over. The tigress inside suddenly grew sleepy and longed for a nap. I told Adam that I wanted to settle out of court. He wanted no part of it.

"I don't think this is a good idea. I don't think he will go for it," he said.

"I'm going to give it my best shot. I am meeting with him tomorrow," I answered back.

He realized I had already made up my mind. Adam was not happy about this, but he wished me well and asked me,

"Do not sign anything without me first seeing it," he said.

"I won't," I assured him.

The wolf and I met at an ocean front restaurant in town. We were strangers now and there was no love between us. I quickly saw the truth. Underneath the exterior he presented to the outside world he was still the wolf. I did not order lunch. I was just too nervous. I came prepared to offer him what I thought was a fair deal, but as soon as we sat down and he opened his mouth I knew he was not in the mood for compromise. Angered wisecracks and sarcasm rolled off his lips. I wanted no part of him or any settlement he might offer. He thought if he huffed and puffed enough he could blow the whole court battle away. He whirled angry words at me. I was not going to waste my time with this grouchy and hateful wolf. I wasn't going to let him treat me this way one more minute.

What had I been thinking? The word compromise was not even included in the wolf's vocabulary. He wanted what he wanted when he wanted it as he always did. Nothing had changed in his demure but he was worse. As I examined his face and saw into his soul I thanked White Feather and my angels again for saving me from the clutches of the wolf. All I wanted was to get out of the restaurant and away from this terrible wolf too many memories were floating in my mind.

I got up and told the wolf that I was leaving. All I wanted, then, was to get out of the restaurant. Surprise, surprise the wolf's anger escalated and he started screaming at me. This time he started in on my attorney calling him nasty names and questioning his motives.

"Why do you need an attorney?" he screamed,

"Your attorney is evil and I'll get both of you for this," he yelled.

The hungry wolf's face was twisted with anger and I knew I was in the presence of evil at that moment. I was in a nightmare and I could feel the wolf trying to put his fangs in my throat and claw me to death. I stood there in shock.

"What are you talking about? My attorney is not evil. You must be crazy," I said engaging in his insanity. I was about to explode, but I remembered what White Feather taught me about the cool of the tigress. I knew my tigress would show too soon so I played it cool. She had taught me how to use my anger to my advantage. My tigress was waiting for just the right moment for her kill. The power of the tigress was in my eyes and I was going to slay the wolf.

I jumped into my car, locked the doors and rolled up the window.

"You keep that attorney away from me," he screamed shaking his fist at me.

"He's evil. I'll get a baseball bat and beat his head in," he said.

This scared me. I flashed back to the first time I left him after hearing the growl of the wolf. I again heard that same chilling hateful growl as I drove away.

I called Adam and told him what happened. I even told him that wolf had called him evil and threatened to kill him.

"Please be careful," I said as I started crying.

Adam took my warning seriously. He called the police department so that they would have a record and he promised me he would be careful.

"I knew you could not settle out of court. The wolf thought he could intimidate you like he has in the past, but, you showed him he couldn't. I know you have become stronger and he does not see it or understand the change in you," he told me.

Adam and I were now committed to completing the paper work we had started in order to get a court hearing. I had no idea how much was involved in filing papers for the court. I had to dig up information from my past and remember the abuse I endured again. As painful as this was I was bolstered by the knowledge that I would soon be free of his presence kept me going. My heart filled with joy at the thought of no longer having to hear the wolf's angry words again he used against me.

Finally, the court date arrived. I met my attorney at the courthouse. The only advice he gave me was to say,

"Please, remember don't say that the wolf did this or that, say,

"'I did this and that," he said.

Then he did something that only the very entertaining Adam would do. Adam reached in his pocket and pulled out a child's sheriff badge. I was astonished to see him do this, but what I had come to know about Adam I should have not been surprised because he was a very witty man.

He considers everything before he responds. This is what I had grown to respect and admire in him. I remembered then that the wolf has called Adam evil.

"I have had this sheriff's star since I was eight-years-old when I dug it out of a cereal box. See the writing around the star," he said pointing to the writing,

"This star will protect me from evil," he announced. Next, he pinned it on his deep blue sport coat.

I just looked at him in amazement and a slow smile crossed my face. I like his style, I thought. I marveled at the attorney White Feather had found for me. In my mind the sheriff's badge gave him power to get the Hungry Wolf if it was the last thing we did. I knew we had a tough fight ahead of us but I knew Adam was going to win our case.

I felt ten feet high. We walked into the court room and I sat in a seat beside my attorney. My knees were shaking as I looked at the Hungry Wolf and saw his lips curl and his eyes bulge. I noticed a pile of boxes piled on the wolf's table.

I leaned over and whispered to Adam,

"They're trying to intimidate us with those lousy boxes full of checks, in here,"

"Don't worry. It won't work," he responded.

But it did. I grew angry when I thought of all the times I had met the wolf for lunch in order to get my alimony check. It was black mail. The fear began to move in like the fog. I started to have my doubts about the strength of our case. Then I heard a ruffling of feathers and I knew White Feather was right behind me. I was relieved and blessed.

The bailiff called the court to order. Adam stood up and walked over to where the judge sat.

"You're Honor," he said pointing to the sheriff's star on his lapel. Then, he whirled around on his feet very fast and looked at the Hungry Wolf.

"This sheriff's star will protect me from evil," he said. The judge had a small grin on his face. The Hungry Wolf's face turned white and he burst into loud insults. I knew then, that the badge was the result of the conversation I had had with him regarding the Hungry Wolf's threats.

I was the first to testify. The judge called my name and I was sworn in. Adam questioned me first.

"Jean, how long have you lived in Fort Bragg, California? How long were you married to the Hungry Wolf? When did you get your divorce?" he asked.

I could hardly concentrate on his words because I was wondering about what trick the wolf was going to uncover to win this case. I answered the questions however, as calmly as I could. When Adam was finished he sat down at the table.

Then the wolf's attorney cross-examined me. He came after me with a fierce aggressiveness and a willingness to fight to the death. His strategy was to wear me down and make me mad and he was succeeding. He kept questioning me, over and over and over. At one point the true face of this attorney was revealed to me and I saw a badge standing before me.

In his loud, angry, sarcastic voice Mr. Donnelly asked,

"Why did you meet the wolf for breakfast, lunch, and dinner?" he asked.

Even though I had expected this question, the tone of his voice and his persistent questioning, made me want to fight back. I took a deep breath and remembered what White Feather taught me about keeping my power contained for the right moment.

"That's the only way the wolf would give me my check without a big battle. I asked him many times to mail them and he would not," I said.

The wolf's attorney tried to make it look like we were friends, but I don't believe the judge bough his story. We were not friends we disliked each other with a vengeance.

I answered every question courteously. When the wolf's attorney was finished with me I felt like a tigress. I opened my mouth and inside of me I felt a deep roar run through my whole body.

"That's a lie," the Hungry Wolf yelled and he had a very angry, bitter expression on his face. I thought that is the face of evil.

Mr. Donnelly failed miserably to blow my cool. He continued to ask questions to incite me, but all he managed to do was incite his own client. Now, he had to turn around and caution his client to be quiet after the judge warned the wolf several times that he was in contempt of court.

With an angry look on his face, Mr. Donnelly said,

"I'm finished with you." Like the tigress, I strutted back looking powerful and beautiful. Adam had a smile on his face. I knew that the wolf and Mr. Donnelly were the ones who were finished. The tigress has emerged and I knew it.

It was now the wolf's turn to testify. Adam stood up walked toward the wolf adjusting his lapel to showcase his sheriff's badge in the best light. The wolf was already ruffled up and very angry. This only served to anger him more.

"Mr. Hungry Wolf, how long were you married?" he asked him.

"I think we were married eleven years," he said with a huff.

"Are you still in the construction business and have you paid your taxes?" he asked him.

"I do not have to answer that," the wolf said in an arrogant angry voice.

The judge spoke up,

"Oh, yes you do or you will be in contempt of court," he said, looking directly at the wolf.

If I hadn't been so scary it would have been pathetic to watch. The bloated up wolf barely managed to get through the questions without being thrown in jail. He managed to rack up three contempt charges in the course of the day.

"You may get down," the judge said.

The wolf growled all the way to his seat. He was steaming mad at everyone. When I looked at the wolf I could not believe I was ever married to him or in love with him. It made my stomach turn over and my skin crawl. But, it was now over. My tigress was alive and well.

Adam walked outside with me into the sunlight with his shining badge still on his lapel.

"We will know in thirty days how it went today for the judge to rule," he said. I felt that we had been victorious today.

The wolf had misjudged us. He thought he could get away with murder but he was wrong. He was not going to get away with anything. In fact, we were going to hang on until Adam was satisfied that we had gotten all we could from this savage wolf. Adam and I could smell the blood and we were up to the kill.

As Adam told me once,

"The law will win no matter what the case. That is why I became an attorney," he said.

I showed the Hungry Wolf at last that I had my power back and with my attorney by my side, how can I lose? I was not going to succumb to any screaming from the wolf. He could show me his fangs, but I was not going to show any fear. My tigress in me was stronger than the wolf. It was his turn to tuck his tail between his legs and run for cover.

"I will put you in jail if you do not straighten up," Adam said in a very matter of fact manor not raising one hair on his head. He was extremely cool and professional in his mannerism. I liked this man that had the power and the attorney sheep skin to make the wolf high tail it back to his den. I could hear wolf screams from his hidden den. It was his turn to tuck his tail between his legs.

I was no longer Little Red Riding Hood naively walking to the slaughter. I was the tigress patiently awaiting the right moment to have the wolf for dinner. From that day I was a victor. I felt the beauty of my womanhood and the strength of my tigress. Truth justice and faith were on my side.

*"Don't yawn away your life, but stand slack-jawed in amazement
at the world of possibilities and rise with excitement toward
their realization."*

—Harold Schulweis

PART II
White Feather's Clients

"Love cures people—both the ones who give it, and the ones who receive it."

—Dr. Karl Menninger

Chapter Twenty-Seven

The Power of Healing

"Healing begins with you."

—White Feather

A healing massage from White Feather is exact and perfect for each and every client. The client receives a healing according to their faith. It's all about them. White Feather will take care of any health situation as long as faith and acceptance is present. White Feather never goes beyond one's free will. In the last twelve years that I have been doing White Feather's healing work I have never seen her make a mistake. She always brings my client's their physical healing and enriches their lives with love, hope and faith. White Feather's clients mean a lot to her or she would have not come to help them.

Healing is non-negotiable. It is a formidable challenge for people that have a sense of active power of their own healing power. Healing is, above all, a solo task. White Feather can not heal a person without faith. She can give them a loving massage and try and build up their faith in God, but she will not over-step her boundaries with a human spirit. She will not go past free will. White Feather can assist in healing, but can not heal on behalf of another person without their acceptance in the art of her deep light work.

Most of our diseases stem from our not letting go of our past and not forgiving the people that hurt us deeply. This only puts infection and fear in our bodies and we become sick on every level; mind, body and our spirit. Fear makes us do a lot of hurtful and stupid things we normally would not do and this causes us to be out of alignment with our energy. This in turn causes problems with our health. We must overcome fear with love and with God's love we can overcome whatever our problems are if you take it to God in prayer.

White Feather knows that love and intimacy is the root of what makes us sick or makes us well because our human relationships are our greatest source of love or hate. But out of our emotional pain we can achieve emotional growth. She believes that if she can find the source of our heartache and pain then we can release that pain. What causes our sickness, what brings happiness to our heart and what makes us suffer can lead to our healing. Out of our pain and suffering comes forgiving ourselves and spiritual growth. All these energies are what White Feather sees when a client is on her table. White Feather lifts people's spirits to the highest level which brings on healing of their soul.

White Feather specializes in the area of emotional problems because this is where disease first appears. Uncertainly or difficulty in your emotional feelings can lead to major physical disorders. I know this sounds nuts but you, have to experience White Feather's light before you can really believe in her power. The emotional problems can be lodged in the past or the present. This does not matter to White Feather for she is not judgmental with anyone. What matters is for White Feather to get to the source of the problem, help the client release negative feelings and heal pessimistic energy. I never know what will happen with each treatment. They are all different, but with White Feather I do not have to worry. She is in charge and gives unconditional love and that love is reciprocal and respected by each client. It is all evaluated at the time, of the treatment.

Some people are not honest with themselves, but White Feather does not push them. She encourages the client to release, but she does it through love and patience. White Feather understands the soul of us humans. Some people do not believe in anything and she does not use her healing energy to change that. She understands our human's strength and weakness.

No explanation is possible for the healings I have seen on White Feather's table. I know the light and power is coming from a greater source than me. This is where faith comes into play. White Feather has helped many different people heal serious health problems, such as, cancer, chronic fatigue syndrome, boils, drugs, mental illness, back pain, compulsive addictions, and depression. She gives people the hope and faith to believe they do not have to be tied into a pattern of tragic additions, but they are well in every avenue of their life. It's up to you.

White Feather guides me in the direction she wants me to work with a client. In fact, I let her take over and her hands do the healing. White Feather changes that dark energy into light energy which results in healing. She also gives direction to each client and I write this down on a piece of paper, so the client can take it home to study. She also wants these sacred papers kept in a safe place.

White Feather helps with anguish and opens up a doorway to begin transformation of a client's new life. She leads people toward their own exact spiritual step. She is there when someone desperately needs her. She has given the directions on the benefits of prayer and meditation and the saying, "When the student is ready, the teacher appears." This is where White Feather comes in.

The healing power is already inside everyone. All we have to do is seek it and believe in are own strength. When a client is on White Feather's table she opens the channel for whatever healing they need. She can do this by using her Heavenly power. White Feather changes the negative energy to positive that is where the healing is. Our bodies are alive, pulsating with energy and healing light of our own. White Feather connects her healing lights too our human energy field. Our bodies have a light that extends as far as our outstretched arms and the full length of our bodies. We also have all kinds of energy fields from people that are positive or negative which affects our system. White Feather's energy is pure white and she changes her colors as she heals the client. She gives us a glimpse of transformation and healing our lives which makes us more aware of who we really are as spiritual beings. That's why White Feather has put so much emphasis on prayer and meditation, because these are the tools of her Heavenly trade.

What I noticed is most clients do not realize is that healing needs to continue all of our lives because of the way life is with so much stress and negative vibrations that people carry with them. Sometimes when people need healing they do not realize it and do not seek the help they need. A lot can happen in our life and our world. We must keep our faith now, more than ever. We can either accept White Feather's healing or not it's up to you. She does not push anyone she lets the person decide what they want to do.

Out of our anguish comes forgiving ourselves and other persons who enhances our spiritual growth, White Feather is a gift from God and we can respect and trust her. I know there is not anything more powerful than her healings and love.

"I am free as Spirit. I renounce any sense of being bound by habit,
personal history, experience or circumstance. Wisely using the
law of freedom, I walk free of all that would limit me."

—Rev. Dr. Michael Beckwith, 40 *Day Mind Soul Feast*

Chapter Twenty-Eight

White Feather's Calling Cards

"My calling cards are white feathers and are for healing because I care."

—White Feather

A client of mine recently went though a painful break-up with her husband of many years. Jasmine's husband told her that he no longer loved her and that he had fallen in love with someone else. She was very depressed and when she came to see me she shared how desperately alone she felt.

I told her that she is never alone and that God and his guardian angels were with her. I also reminded her that once she is on White Feather's healing table White Feather continues to look after her.

None of this information seemed to mean anything to her and our work together that day seemed to offer little comfort. After she left I sat down and prayed for her.

A few days later I received a call from Jasmine. I barely recognized her voice because she sounded more alive and happy than I had ever experienced her.

"Jean, I went out to pick up my newspaper and right in front of me on my front step was the most gorgeous white feather. I knew it was from White Feather. I'm really not alone," she said.

"White Feather left that special feather to remind you of her love for you," I told her. There was a moment of silence,

"Finding that White Feather gave me a feeling of comfort that White Feather really loves and cares for me and my life is going to improve."

After we hung up I thanked White Feather, for leaving a white feather which I now know is her calling card.

"Jean, the feathers I leave clients and others are called Spirit Feathers. I leave them to remind people there are angels and love around them and that spirit is with them all the time. They are my sign or calling card," she said.

I remembered back to the different times my clients and friends found white feathers. A really close friend of mine called me one morning and told me,

"I got up early to check on my cat, went into my front room and right in the middle of the room was a white feather," she said.

To her, the feather represented a sign of love and peace. We continued to talk on the phone for a while and then she said,

"Jean, I will never forget this loving experience. Please, thank White Feather for me."

I assured her I would and I did, right then in my spirit.

Then I would run across unbelievers for sometimes this is how White Feather likes to deal with them. One of my clients invited a few friends over to her cabin by the river for the week-end. One of the women she invited was suffering from a lot of family problems and felt depressed. She also had little faith in anything spiritual. My friend and client told this woman about White Feather. They suggested that she schedule a healing massage with me.

"I don't know if I can believe in a Native American Indian called White Feather that communicates with a human being," Margaret said. They had gone for a walk while they discussed their friend's options.

"You don't have to believe," my friend she told her.

"You just need to make an appointment," she said.

"It sounds too far fetched for me." she said.

But, all of a sudden out of the clear blue sky a white feather came floating down right in the middle of the circle. They were all surprised, even my friend had a startled look on her face.

"Well, this could make a believer out of anyone," Margaret said. But, as it turns out the woman did not come to see me. She did not realize that White Feather was letting her know that she could help her. She was not aware of what was really happening on the spiritual level. Sometimes this is the way it is. One has to seek the truth on a higher level.

I play the California Lottery at a liquor store in our town. I have become friends with a woman who usually waits on me. She told me she was having eye surgery. She asked me to,

"Please pray for me," she said. She looked a little scared.

"I will put my spirit guide White Feather with you," I told her. She looked at me and a very sweet smile crossed her face.

"Thank you. That will help me so much. It will get my mind off what the doctor is doing," she said.

What surprised me so much is, she has never been on White Feather's healing table but she still wanted me to comfort her. This special lady has faith of the highest level.

A few weeks later I saw my friend again,

"Jean, when the doctor was performing the surgery I saw a white feather in my eye, then White Feather appeared. It made me feel so good that all my nervousness went away. Thank you for helping me," she said.

"You are quite welcome," I said.

When another client came in for a healing massage she talked about taking a trip to Germany with her husband. I told her I would pray for their safety on their trip.

"That's a good idea, especially since the terrorist attack on the United States. I will feel more secure," she said.

She left and I prayed for them. A couple of weeks later she called me. They were back and had a marvelous trip. She said,

"Jean, while we were in Germany, I found a white feather in the middle of my bed. My husband was going to through it in the garbage. I ran over to him and grabbed the feather away from him and I started hollering at him, are you crazy? This white feather has been blessed and is special. It comes from a spirit called White Feather and it is a blessing to us."

To this day she has kept their White Feather's calling card with her.

I have heard that White Feather leaves her calling card to inspire others. She reminds people that she is watching them and that they need to keep their faith strong.

One of the most profound inspirational stories I was told by a male client was when he took a trip to Sweden. He was going to a healing seminar and he had a healing massage before he left. I told him,

"I would keep him in prayer with White Feather and please take her with him. You might even see a few feathers," I said.

"I will most certainly do that," he replied and he gave me a nice hug then I left his house. About two-weeks later I ran into him in a store and he came over to me,

"Jean, when I was in Sweden I met an attractive woman that I liked and we are going to keep our friendship. It might even go to marriage. But what I want to tell you was when I went out by the ocean to think everything over, I looked out by the seashore and I could not believe my eyes. All along the shore were white feathers; it was one of the most incredible, stunning things I have ever seen. I just kept looking at the white feathers and remembering what we had discussed before I left for my trip.

"That's wonderful," I said

"Your voice and words kept ringing in my ears; and I was overwhelmed with love and thanking you, for your extreme gifts from White Feather. This gave me the encouragement to ask this new woman if we could continue our friendship when we went back to the states and she said, "Yes." White Feather's feathers encouraged me to move on with my life. With that he gave me another hug and winked at me as he left. I had a gentle smile on my face and was thinking White Feather is a gift from God.

My editor, Lorie, and I were reflecting on why White Feather has not left her a white feather?

"Probably because I don't need it," Lorie said.

"Yes," I chimed in.

"She will leave you her feather when you need the encouragement." Then, it occurred to me White Feather's never left me a feather but she will if I ever need one and it will come at the exact right time. Finally I did discover there White Feathers by the ocean. One day when I was down from stress. I looked at my feet and there were three lovely feathers right at my feet. I bent down and picked them up and held them in the palm of my hand with a smile of my face. I lifted them up to whinnied and I knew White Feather had blessed them. I took them back to my car and hung them on my blue crystal car hanger that was hanging on my car mirror.

My editor and I do not understand the time when she will drop her healing feathers for sure. White Feather knows the divine timing to give us the inspiration and encouragement we need for our life. After all, she invented those precious feathers to float down like gentle snow from Heaven because she cares and wants us to have what we need to keep going. White Feather is a healing spirit of the universe and adores us in spite of ourselves. She overlooks our human frailties because she loves us and for our comfort, blesses us with her white feathers.

"If you would reap praise, you must sow the seeds,
gentle words and useful deeds."

—Benjamin Franklin

Chapter Twenty-Nine

The Miracle

"There are miracles happening everyday be patient wait for yours"

—White Feather

One of the most powerful healing massages I have ever done was some years ago. This was a spiritual surgery and nothing I have ever experienced again. If someone would have told me this, I would have looked at them like they were nuts but I can't say that because what I experienced really did happen. My friend Danielle told me of a friend of hers who had gone to everyone in town to get a healing for a problem with her health. She did not embellish on what the problem was and I did not ask. I did think about this person and put her in prayer. I could not figure out why she did not come and try me but that is the way people are. But it did get to me because I know how wonderful White Feather was and her healing was powerful.

One sunny day I decided to take Misty Moonlight for a ride. I saddled her and climbed on her back, taking a trail not far from the barn. As I was riding down the trail I started to sing, 'Mansion over the Hilltop,' and Misty Moonlight always whinnied because she knows in her heart I was singing a Heavenly song. I started to think of my conversation with Danielle and I asked White Feather what was wrong with her friend. I did a meditation and a few strides later I heard White Feather's voice soft and sweet,

"Jean, she has a glitch on her third vertebra, right side."

I stopped Misty Moonlight and sat thinking of what I heard. I realized I had to call Danielle and tell her what White Feather revealed. I had been upset that her friend had gone to everyone but me, and sometimes I wonder about people, but she did not know about White Feather.

Arriving home I called Danielle. When she picked up the phone, I told her the story. She didn't say anything for a few minutes.

"I'll call my friend Sandy and tell her what you told me," she said.

"That would be great." I wanted her to come in for a healing massage and experience White Feather healing work. A few days later I did get a call from Sandy and she asked if she could make and appointment for a healing massage?"

"Yes come in Thursday afternoon," I said.

"Yes, that's a good time. I'll be there," she replied.

Thursday afternoon came and there was a knock on my door. I opened my door and there was Sandy.

"Let's go upstairs, where my table is" I said.

"It nice to see you," she said following me upstairs.

"Let sit down and talk," I suggested.

"What do you want to know?" she asked, curiously.

"How long have you had this problem?" I asked her.

"I have had this problem most of my life. I can't seem to get rid of this stiffness and pain. Danielle told me what you told her. I'm willing to try a healing with White Feather," she said.

"That's good. It will take five treatments to get to your problem. We have to build up our prayers and faith," I told her.

"That's fine. I'm hoping this will get rid of my painful physical problem," she said.

"It will if you have faith to believe," I raised my arm and pointed with my index finger, giving her direction.

"Please go and change your clothes in my bathroom, then come and lay down on my bed. Then let's do a prayer and you should know that you will be healed," I said, helping her onto my bed.

"Just try and relax and see yourself getting well. Breathe deeply and let anything go that could possess you," I said in a whisper as Sandy lay on my bed.

"Jean, I feel this is going to work," she told me.

"I know it will. We must have no doubt about White Feathers love and power," And without a word, breathing deeply myself, I moved my hands several inches above Sandy's somewhat anxious, rigid body. I could feel her start to relax and trust.

"I feel a blockage on your third spinal column vertebra on your right side and your shoulders blades. I know your problem is lodged in your right vertebra," I said.

White Feather came into my spirit and I moved my hands several inches from the exact spot. Next week we will get this glitch out. Our prayers will be very strong.

. We must not doubt White Feathers love and power," I told her, as she got up and gave me a hug.

"What day and time next week?" she asked.

"Let's do the same day and time next week?" I said.

"That's fine. I can do that. See you next week," she said, hugging me again at the door.

"Have a nice week." I shouted, as she waved at me and got into her car.

Weeks had passed, and this healing went on for four more times. Every time the healing energy became stronger. We always prayed and did a meditation. These healing massages were very powerful and healing. The last healing was a miracle. Sandy came in and lay on my bed again.

"Sandy this is the day you will be healed from White Feather. Do you believe that?" I asked her. She just was very quiet before she answered me.

"Yes, I believe White Feather is here and will heal me," she said in a soft voice.

"Yes, she will. Now please go into prayer and I will too. Take a deep breath, slowly in and out and relax. Breathe in the new and let out the old," I told her. I gently put my hands on her and heard White Feather's voice speak to me,

"Put your middle finger on her neck," As I did, immediately I saw her skin separate and open up. Something that looked like a half wallet shell popped up and flew right by me. I jumped back, watching it for a moment before it totally disappeared.

Suddenly Sandy abruptly moved, jumping up, her face twisted in astonishment.

"Jean, it's gone. My God what a miracle," she said.

"I know I saw the glitch. White Feather got rid of the problem," I said.

"I feel so great. I feel wonderful. I never believed completely but I do know that it is true," she said.

"That's right. Thank you Jean and White Feather,"

"You're welcome," I said.

"It was your faith that healed you, with White Feathers help,"

"I will remember this Jean," she said, her eyes still widened.

"All I know is I've never experienced anything like this before. I saw it happen. Your skin opened up like magic. It was a miracle," I said.

"I believe it is too," she said.

"Will you have finished your healing with me,"

"Yes, and it was wonderful," she said.

"It was a great experience, one I'll never forget. White Feathers' healing is so powerful. I just think she's the best," I said.

"Yes, she is," she said.

"We both made a leap of faith."

"No, I will never forget my miracle," she said.

We walked downstairs and as she left I was sincere when I confessed,

"Sandy it was a pleasure having you. Thank you for your faith and thank you for coming and getting you're healing,"

"It was the best I've ever experienced, and I feel wonderful and no more stiffness or pain," she said.

"It was healing and we were excited all at the same time. We got the healing done through White Feather," I said.

"It has been a pleasure to be here. Take care," she said, giving me another hug.

"I'll see you in church." I said.

"Yes, you will, see you soon," I replied. We waved at each other and as I closed the door I knew this was the most astonishing experience, and one that I'd never forget. To see a glitch come out of her body and fly in front of my face was something I had to see to believe. I was so glad now that I had that vision that day on Misty Moonlight. I was glad also that Sandy came in to receive her healing by White Feather. This was a blessing for the both of us and a healing neither one of us would forget.

"We are being renewed everyday. For this slight momentary affliction is preparing for us and eternal weight of glory beyond all comparison, because we look not to the things that are seen but to the things are unseen; for the things that are seen are transient, but the things that are unseen are eternal."

—2—Corinthians 4:16-17-18

Chapter Thirty

Meredith

"Fear not little flock, it is the Father's good pleasure to give you the kingdom."

—Luke 12:32

When I first saw Meredith at a church service, I thought how attractive she was. After the service, Meredith and I introduced ourselves and talked quite a while. We agreed to meet for lunch the next week and we had so much fun our friendship blossomed.

When I left the Hungry Wolf, it was Meredith who offered me an apartment in her barn at her ranch. I moved into the apartment and lived there for approximately three years. Those years were deeply inspiring and Meredith and I grew to be close friends. We flew from each other's wings and were each other's angels.

When my gift of White Feather manifested, Meredith was one of the first people to come out to the ranch where my horse Misty Moonlight was stabled. Meredith asked if White Feather could help her over come her anxiety and her habit of worrying. When she came for her healing massage, White Feather told me to 'Put Meredith on a prayer schedule. She wanted her to pray and meditate at night when she went to bed. White Feather knew this would calm her spirit as well as slow down her heart beat. White Feather gave her the following prayer to recite out loud:

"I am loved, I am needed, and I am wanted. I am keeping my thoughts on a higher level. I look past the appearances of this world. I am loved on the highest level."

Meditation is a state of consciousness and White Feather knew that Meredith needed to develop this consciousness.

White Feather said,

"Tell her to meditate ten to fifteen minutes, morning and night. The more you practice meditations, the easier they will become. It's like breathing and will become very natural," she said.

Meditation will awaken your consciousness because you can't think negative thoughts when you are in prayer if you are negative you're not in prayer. Try and meditate all the time because this keeps out negative thoughts and puts you on a higher level. Do not feel guilty about anything, just relax and let White Feather help you do the work. All is well. White Feather told her to say mentally, I am loved, I am needed, I am healthy, and I have joy in my life. Be happy in the now. She told her to keep thinking positive prayers.

"I know you're in a difficult situation but do not give up. Try to unwind the situation, but do not give into it." I reminded Meredith of several Bible verses: *"Peace I leave with you: my peace I give to you; not as the world gives do I gave to you. Let not your hearts be troubled, neither let them be afraid."* From John 14:27.

"For I know the plans I have for you says the Lord, plans for welfare and not for evil, to give you a future and a hope." From Jeremiah 29:11.

White Feather said,

"You are dealing with too much stress. What we worry about seldom happens. Forget the past. Do not drag excess baggage from your past into your future. This stops you from moving forward on your spiritual path," she said.

"I sought the Lord, and he heard me and delivered me from all my fears." From Psalms 34:04.

Meredith, you have helped many people including myself. Now it's your turn to be taken care of. Try not to be afraid. The angels are protecting you. You have great faith. Enjoy the moment. The future is in the moment. Let things go that are not to be. Meredith, you feed the body now feed the soul. As Jesus said, *"Watch and pray that you may not enter into temptation; the spirit indeed is willing, but the flesh is weak."* From Matthew 26:04.

"For God hath not given us the spirit of fear, but of power and of love and of a sound mind." From 2 Timothy 1:17.

I continued encouraging her,

"Please get on with your life and believe. This is the last part of your life. What is it you want? Believe in yourself and ask for guidance in prayer. I am repeating myself but this is very important and will help you more than anything else you could focus on. You are doing the right thing for your family. Try and not worry about the actions of others. Spend your energy on what's right in the situation. Ask for more inner guidance; take time for more meditation where all the truth is held. The truth never changes."

One reading that White Feather did was with Meredith and it was very powerful. Meredith continued to experience healing with White Feather. Most of it had to do with letting go of the past and living in the present trusting and having faith in her future. Meditation and training her mind to her stay in the present lessened her fears and worry.

When Meredith was trying to depart her physical life and was in the hospital making her transformation from the earth, White Feather had asked me to go to the hospital and see her. White Feather had suggested that I go on Friday around l: 00 P.M.

"Two nurses will be in the hallway and you will have a chance to see her alone," White Feather said.

I left my house that Friday and arrived at the hospital. I was walking down the hallway and two nurses were standing outside of her room exactly like I was told. It always amazes me to this day how I am guided. I slipped into her room, went over to where she was and put my arm around Meredith. She was lying on a pillow in the hospital bed and she was breathing laboriously.

"Meredith, it is Jean. White Feather is with me. Meredith; you have been on your spiritual path and have served well. It is time to leave the earth and become whom you really are. You were an angel while you were on earth and you, will be an angel in Heaven. Please, do not be afraid. White Feather will be with you.

"You can let go now," I said. I knew she could hear me. She took a deep breath and relaxed.

"I love you and always will," I told her as I held her in my arms. I started to be sad but yet since I know where she was going I was happy for her. We had become devoted to each other. She understood my work and accepted the true nature of White Feather healings.

"Heaven is a marvelous place to be going. You are going to have lots of fun and see your family and friends. You will visit White Feather on the reservation. I will join you someday and we will have a great time together as we did on the earth. You will see all the animals we had on earth and it will be a great home coming," I told her with a gentle but gloomy smile on my face. Sad tears ran down my face as I realized my best friend was leaving, but yet I knew I would see her again in the after life. I would miss seeing her almost every day.

The next morning I knew she was a spirit. Her daughter called to tell me she'd passed away in the early morning hours. Meredith was out of her pain and in Heaven and having the time of her life. She is young and gorgeous once again.

Meredith did not leave right away she wanted to make sure everyone she left was okay with her passing. I did feel her around my house, and then after about a few weeks I felt her spiritual energy leave and I knew she was in just where she was to be forever.

Not long ago, a nurse who also helped take care of Meredith stopped me on the street down town and shared an experience she had with Meredith.

"After Meredith passed away, I had a dream where I saw her spiritually. She was so striking with white light all around her," she said

"She was a great spirit," I said responding to this woman.

I also had a dream about her, we were in this white room and she was in a white gown and I was on a massage table, she came up to me and said,

"Jean, I have been assigned to you."

It was then I woke up and knew I had another great angel around me.

As we parted, I knew Meredith was with me and had a loving smile on her face. She had her arms around me as we shared our love. I recalled how much love Meredith gave and how I missed her. I started crying as I left this woman and I remembered all our good times we had while she was here on earth but I know I would see my dear friend again.

Recently, I dreamt of Meredith. We were in this large great house. She was in one of the bedrooms waiting for me to do a healing massage. As I opened the door I was so overwhelmed to see her again and very surprised. She looked elegant still in a white gown. She acted like she had seen me yesterday. She was standing by the bed with a big smile on her lovely face and her spirit was glowing. As I looked at her, our eyes met and our love was so strong that not even death could part us. We were kindred spirits and we had love and compassion for each other in the physical as well as the spiritual. Meredith and I were asking God for this inspiring experience and our memories lived beyond the horizon of time and space.

"Give me beauty in the inward soul; may the outward and the inward man be as one."

—Socrates, Greek philosopher

Chapter Thirty-One

The Spirited One

"My Lord told me a joke and seeing Him laugh has done more for me than any scripture I will ever read."

—Minister Eckhart

I frequented an old fashioned ice cream parlor in town where I lived. This particular afternoon a handsome, tall, lean, young man about thirty three years old waited on us. I had come in with a friend of mine. His brown eyes twinkled with intelligence and playfulness. When he talked to me, his white skin was flawless, and his smile tender, but most importantly, I recognized the love in his heart for others. We both knew each other's souls the moment we met. He leaned over the table and asked, "What would you like to order?"

"I'll have a chocolate soda," I said.

"Okay," he replied.

"What's your name?"

"Jean and yours," I asked.

"Luke," he said.

As Luke and I became more acquainted, we found out we had some things in common.

"What kind of work do you do?" he asked.

"Healing massage," I responded.

"Psychics know each other," he said.

The hair rose on my arms, cold chills ran down my back. I just stared at him.

He made an appointment to see me. He came to see me a couple of days later. He was having trouble with his neck and his stomach hurt him most of the time. White Feather immediately took care of, his stomach. We exchanged spiritual treatments with each other. He gave me a reading and I gave him a healing massage.

"How much pepper do you put on your food?" White Feather had me ask him. Luke just about fell off my massage table and he looked startled.

"I use a lot of pepper everyday," he said.

"You must give it up and let your stomach rest, because pepper is the hardest substance to digest," I told him. After that he had no further problem with his stomach pain.

Luke's treatments were always intense. I always read a few Bible verses before he lie down on my healing table. He would talk about what was happening in his life. In one of the treatments, I told him,

"You will write a screenplay, for older people, to lift their spirits. After you finished the screenplay, you will go to San Francisco and meet a playwright who will help you." Now this depends on if he was willing to meet the challenge. This gift was out there for him but it was up to him to believe in his own gift.

In another treatment, White Feather told me,

"He was going to meet someone for romance. 'Tell him," White Feather told me,

He got so mad at me and jumped off my massage table.

"I do not want to meet anyone," he screamed at me as he ran out my front door. A couple of weeks later he called to say,

"I am sorry. That was fear and I wanted it so much it scared me. I met someone at a party and we liked each other. We are going out on a date Saturday night. I'm very happy.

"Thank you, White Feather," he said.

"You're welcome," I am glad you are feeling so good and are happy.

"Go for it," I said.

During another treatment, Luke told me he felt his dad's presence, he had passed away.

"His dad was trying to choke me," he said.

I asked White Feather to put magenta light around his neck and we did this work for five treatments. He was relieved of his neck pain. Luke later shared with me that in addition to getting his stomach and his neck taken care of he felt more balanced and stronger.

He added that his love life was now out of this world.

"Make this agreement with yourself; I am impeccable with my word. Nurture this seed, and as it grows in your mind, it will generate more seeds of love."

—Don Miguel Ruiz, *The Four Agreements*

Chapter Thirty-Two

Grace

"There are no great things, only small things with great love. Happy are those."

—Mother Teresa

It's always a mystery when someone re-enters your life. Grace and I met years ago because of our love of horses. Grace and I exchanged conversation at our horse trainer's, but we never moved beyond getting acquaint anted. Then we took our horses to different places and we stopped running into each other. One day I was looking at ads in the local newspaper for a place to live, so I dialed the number in the local newspaper, and a woman answered.

"Hi, my name is Jean. I'm looking for a house to rent. I saw your ad in our local newspaper. Would you please tell me something about the house and how much the rent is?" I asked her.

"The house is nice and the rent is six hundred dollars a month," Grace responded,

"That's too much for me at this time," I said.

"I can't take any less," she said. I was about to hang up when she asked,

"Are you the Jean who had the horse that looks like mine?"

"Yes." I am.

"I know who you are," she said.

"You sound upset," I said, sensing that something was wrong.

Grace replied,

"I am upset. After fifteen years my boyfriend and I have split up. I am really suffering from heartache," she said.

"Grace, I am a healer and I can help you overcome your emotional pain through White Feather, my spirit guide. Can you come in for a healing today?" I asked.

Grace repeated,

"Healing massage?"

I softly replied, "Yes,"

"I'd like an appointment." she said.

The appointment was made for 4:00 P.M. that day. After I hung up the phone I started doing prayer and meditation for Grace. I felt within myself that it would help her in time to overcome her heartache.

When I opened my front door, it was if time stood still. Grace stood before me in all her loveliness even thought her heart was breaking. I could see her loving heart beating through all her tears. We just looked at each other and were silent, knowing we were kindred spirits. She climbed on White Feather's healing massage table and received a healing.

"Jean, I've never experienced anything like this, you are truly a healer, and I want to come and see you every week until I am well," Grace said.

I was concerned about her. Grace told me that day that she was depressed and thinking about suicide. A few days later White Feather told me to visit her at her home. White Feather asked me to hold Grace in my arms and rock her like a small baby. While I did this White Feather filled her with pink and magenta light which are the colors of love and healing light. I believe if I had not seen Grace that day that she might have actually taken her life. I am grateful that White Feather intervened.

As we began to learn more about each other Grace began to have more awareness of what happened in her relationship. A relationship is hard to look at in a normal situation, but when you are in heartfelt pain there has to be a surrender or detachment for your heart to heal. This does not come easy. There are no simple answers or solutions to these types of emotional struggles only though prayers are you relived because of your faith in God.

Given time and healing through White Feather, Grace began to heal her soul and started to move on in her life. She would always have memories of her relationship with him but she could remember the good times and let the bad ones go.

The feeling of loneliness of missing a beloved, hurts the heart most of all. We are used to being with that person, caring for that person, and all of a sudden there's a big loss. We are in mourning of the loss of our relationship but really we are mourning what we thought our future would be like with him.

We have a hole in our heart that goes deep into our spirit. We feel like a lost soul swimming around in a sea of pain and death because the beloved is still living but in his own world and not letting us in.

We want to know what's wrong with us. Aren't we good enough for them? Didn't you love me once? What really happened? All these questions go through our mind and it really does not matter because it's over. Usually when it's gone and over nothing can bring it back, unless two adult people want their love and are willing to reach an understanding with each other through the heart. We have to learn to compromise with each other. When people are in pain they shut off their own healing energy and at this time should seek some form of help.

Grace came every week, for well over a year. I could see a true healing taken place in her mind, body and spirit. She wanted to be completely healed, accepting that her relationship was over. It also had to do with letting go of an over-responsible life. She learned to trust more in God and herself and to be calm in times of trouble.

Grace had a piece of property that had been up for sale for three years and she asked me for spiritual help to sell her property and farm house. I told her to visualize it being sold. One afternoon on my healing table I had a vision for Grace because of the energy of White Feather. White Feather told her that a family would come from the South and purchase her property.

"Oh, Jean, I can hardly believe this," Grace said.

"Do not change my vision. Words have great power," I told her.

"See your property being sold in your mind. This will happen within a month. Pray for everyone involved," I said and she agreed to do this. One night I received a phone call from her, she was very happy.

"Jean, the property is in escrow, and it happened just like you predicted. Thank you from the bottom of my heart."

On an emotional level, I spent several healing massages reassuring her. White Feather asked me to talk to her about meditation. I wanted her to practice everyday. White Feather felt that meditation would help balance her life. She encouraged Grace to meditate as she felt this would help with her depression, her feelings of aloneness.

During several of her first massage sessions, White Feather was filling Grace's body with gold and green light which was opening her seventh (top) charka to white light.

Grace recovered from her heartache. She was able to detach from her beloved and they've become friends. White Feather encouraged Grace to meditate. In another session of healing White Feather told Grace,

"The highest form of love is giving, not taking, taking is lust not love."

Grace gives too much of herself to her beloved and her friends. Sometimes she doesn't have enough love left for herself.

"There is a balance, and you, Grace, must find your own level of balance," I told her in one session.

Eventually Grace freed her spirit to love again. This is the affirmation from White Feather that gave her the courage to set herself free: *I am free, and my spirit is free to love again. I give myself permission to move on with my life I let go of all past attacemnts. I look toward my future with hope.*

"Remember, Grace, White Feather is working for your highest good," I said. I suggested in meditation she mentally say: *I clear my mind; I want to hear my inner guidance guide me today. I give myself permission to be loved and lovable, to achieve a goal today, to attract the right mate, to be healed and well.*

Through the years White Feather has given Grace many ideas for a business venture or however she wants to use the energy to create whatever her heart wants. It's up to her to carry out those ideas if she wants too.

I have had many visions for Grace while she was on White Feather's table. The vision that stands out and uplifted her is when I saw a room with blue wallpaper with beige stripes. In between the stripes were pink rose buds. I was in a Victorian house and as I looked around I saw Grace sitting down looking in a round mirror. Her head was bent and a sequined-lined white veil held her silver hair. The veil hung down to her shoulders as she was looking at me with a magical smile on her stunning face. I looked at her with love in my heart and smiled back.

My vision was quickly gone, but I told Grace,

"This should give you hope and it is out in the universe for you if you want to make it come true. It's entirely up to you." I have not heard of Grace getting married but we never know when or if this will happen. In our world nothing will change unless we go for our highest level of love to find our true beloved.

"There are only two ways to live your life. One is as though nothing is a miracle. The other is as though everything is a miracle."

—Albert Einstein

Chapter Thirty-Three

Michael and Sylvia

"There is nothing but divine movement in this world."

—Hafiz

These are healings based on faith and there is nothing to dispute or evaluate, except that the client was healed. Here are a few examples of compassionate healings.

A woman came to me for a healing after she had exhausted every other avenue of getting well. She told me she had no energy left to go on living. It was obvious to me she was suffering from depression and a new disease that had just been diagnosed as, 'Chronic Fatigue Syndrome.' This disease has become widespread in the United States.

Her symptoms associated with this disease were present in her muscles and joints; she had anxiety, depression, difficulty concentrating, fever, headaches, irritability, loss of appetite, sensitivity to light and sleep disturbances, and extreme and often disabling fatigue. I told Danielle what I felt it was, 'Chronic Fatigue Syndrome.' and that she needed a lot of time on White Feathers table to heal.

She was silent for a long moment before she spoke.

"Jean, I think you are exactly right. Please thank White Feather for me and let's get started today," she said.

I gave her a hug, urging her to,

"Please visualize that task of bringing new energy, and see yourself and your intentions rebuilding your new life."

She came to White Feather for almost a year but her symptoms slowly disappeared and she started to have more energy and vitality than she had before in her life. White Feather had done her work through unplugging her energy circuits. She took the action and drew on her inner source and White Feather transferred pure white light to heal her.

She was healed and accepted her new lease on life.

A client of mine named Anna came as a result of a recommendation from her son. She could hardly walk from warts on both of her feet.

"I am in so much pain I can hardly walk," she told me.

"Do you believe in faith healing?" I asked her.

"Yes, I do. I believe in the power of faith healing," she said.

"Well, it will take some time because you need your circulation to be stronger in your body," I told her. My angel, White Feather, can help you heal.

"Yes, my son told me you would help me heal," she said.

"I just know that you can get rid of all these warts," I told her. Anna came to me for over a year every week and her warts were disappearing. She went to her doctor and he asked her what she has been doing differently. Anna told him about her trips to me. He told her to keep doing what you're doing. Anna can walk now without any pain and her lungs had been healed of many, many small bumps. Also she can breathe and take her daily walks of faith.

Anna and I have become very close because she has been coming to see me for years.' We just were having a wonderful conversation about a special tree on a hill by the ocean.

"I used to take my walks by that tree and pray," she confessed,

"Oh, my God, Anna, years ago I would stop by the same tree," We both became quiet for a few minutes and then both of us spoke at the same time.

"Well let's call this tree, The Prayer Tree, we said.

We both laughed and knew we would go back and pray under that same tree because of its power and our connection to the prayer tree. We realized that tree was blessed by God and the angels because it drew people to it.

"Keep moving in the direction of your dreams."

—Thoreau

Chapter Thirty-Four

Magic Starship

"You might as well like yourself. You're going to spend a lot of time together."

—Jerry Lewis—*The Nutty Professor*

A graceful evening sun of deep pinks and lavenders was streaming through the large window of my front room. I was lying on the couch in meditation. I heard the phone ring in the kitchen. I jumped off the couch and walked into the kitchen to answer the telephone. I heard a familiar male voice. It was Charles.

"Do you want to come over for a bowl of chocolate ice cream?" he asked.

I told him I would be over soon.

Charles was waiting for me. He invited me into his living room. We had just sat down when there was a knock at the door. He opened the door and I saw two people, a man and woman he recognized.

"Come in and have some chocolate ice cream with Jean and I," he said.

He introduced me to Star and Paul. Star was a very pretty young woman in her late twenties with blond hair and light blue eyes. Her figure was slender and she was about 5'4". The same height as I am. She reminded me of myself in my earlier years. Paul stood about 5'10" with curly brown hair and a pleasant appearance. Paul looked to be in his early thirties. His dark brown eyes that shown with intelligence.

We sat down and ate our ice cream. There was so much energy that everyone began to talk at once. We talked about almost every subject under the sun. The subject of healing came into the conversation and Star informed me she was a healer. This really held my attention.

"What kind of healing professions are you in?" I asked her.

"Energetic Therapy," she responded.

"What is that?" I asked.

She looked at me with a sunny smile on her face.

"Jean, I take out blockages in the body. I have traveled all over the United States to learn. It takes many, many years to really understand the concept of the work," she said.

"That sounds so interesting," I responded. I then told her about my work and White Feather. Star asked if we could do a trade. I was interested.

"Yes, let's do it." I said.

The couple was at my house the next day at 2:00 P.M. They arrived right on time and we decided that Star would get on the table first. Star climbed on White Feather's table and lay on her stomach. I put a tan sheet over her body. I prayed to the spiritual world for White Feather to direct me. She showed up immediately. I started touching Star through the sheet doing a gentle balance so she could get an idea of how White Feather's hands felt.

\ "Star, White Feather is with us. You are going to get exactly what you need."

Star did not say a word but, I could feel her relax beneath my healing hands. I heard White Feather's soft voice inside myself.

In her Indian dialect, White Feather spoke,

"I am here."

Star was so still and was listening with every sense of her being. I prayed to White Feather to keep me in the light as I worked on you, and to tell me what changes she does need to make in her life to have more abundance.

White Feather told me to tell her,

"Your relationship with Paul is fine right now. It just needs more balancing, to try and have him be more supportive in the relationship. Try and work for a year together and see if this does make you happier in your relationship. If it does not, you might have to move on. I know humans do not want to hear this, but sometimes relationships can go either way depending on your determination to keep the relationship balanced. In your situation there is a choice. Get yourself a part-time job for extra earnings that will help with your financial situation."

As White Feather was talking through me, Star took a deep breath and relaxed even more. In other words she started to trust what White Feather was saying and to enjoy this experience. I did all her acupuncture points and I did a gentle balance of her energy. Then I turned her over on her back.

When the healing massage was complete I asked Star if she wanted to join me in a meditation affirming for our highest good. During the meditation, I heard White Feather's sweet voice, say,

"Both of you will meet again."

"Star, I will always be with you in mind and spirit. Be good to yourself and I will keep you safe on your spiritual path," Then I heard a giggle and she continued,

"I will be there on these bumpy roads to learning. Your car will be safe or anything else you ride in. Go in peace and remember that White Feather loves you." Star

Star had a loving smile on her lovely face.

"Jean, this is a spiritual experience. I love White Feather. I'll never forget her. I am going to take her in my heart always," she said. I almost started crying because she understood the whole principle behind her treatment.

"Star, I appreciate you're kind words. I am almost finished with you" I said.

Star got off the table and then it was Paul's turn.

"Paul, please lay down on your stomach," I said. He climbed on the table. I stood at the end of White Feather's table and put my hands on him. I asked,

"Paul, tell me about your first love," He was very quiet for a few minutes and then he began to talk,

"Jean, this was a long time ago when I was in High School. We were very young and innocent. Of course, at the time, we thought we knew it all. I loved her with all my heart and her name was Debra. She was so funny and pretty. We had a lot of fun together, and it was magical. He took a deep sigh and continued,

"Every thing is magical in our youth, huh, Jean?

He continued,

I just nodded in agreement.

But, Debra didn't love me enough. We broke up and went our separate ways. This just about killed me and I suffered for years. Not any of my relationships were as deep as that first love," he said.

"This is usually the case," I responded.

"You were not mature enough and neither was she to deal with a profoundly deep relationship. When we are young we have such high moral but we don't have past failed relationships to perceive that the relationship could break-up. First love is always fresh and new," I said.

Then I offered White Feathers words,

"Paul, you need to let go of the past and let go of the extra baggage of your past because of Star. Your heart has to be open to receive Stars' love and you need to give her your love and be willing to suffer, and let go of Debra. Please, love Star without reservations. Tell me about your relationship with Star," I asked.

"Jean, I do love Star, but we have to work at it all the time. It doesn't seem to come natural, like my first love."

I took a deep breath because I understood what he was saying because of all the lumps and bumps of my last potholes relationships.

"Paul, all relationships are not made in Heaven. There are hard lessons and you are being guided to learn here. Please, pay attention,"

I continued,

"It takes determination and giving of yourself with an open heart all the time, not just when you feel like it or want something. It won't work if anyone is selfish in the union because before long it will break' up. Communication is very important, sprinkled with love, without talking to each other you can fall into a dark hole," I said. He seemed to recognize the truth in what I was saying.

"Paul, both of you will have to put your whole heart into the relationship and work on it every day. A relationship is one of the hardest things to accomplish because you can't hold back love. You have to put Star first in the relationship and yourself second. It is compromise, compromise and more compromise. Give Star as much help as you can. She is doing healing work and it's very important in the scheme of things," I said.

As I was talking to Paul I was doing a healing massage. He began to relax, as I balanced his energy.

Then White Feather told me to tell him to give this his best shot, in his relationship with Star,

"Okay, I will and wow, I feel so much better," he replied.

I know he was aware of the balance I gave him and I stood at the end of her table and translated in White Feather's Indian dialect,

"Paul, be in harmony with Star and help her as much as you can. Shower her with you're love and support. She is performing healing work that is very important.

White Feather continued,

"I will be with you on your trip back home," she said.

Then she was gone. Paul got up from her table and stretched out his legs.

He thanked White Feather and me with heartfelt sincerity. He then opened the front door and called for Star to come in. Star came back in and this time I climbed on the table.

"Jean, I going to put this roll energy magnet tool on your body. I am going to roll your whole body with this tool," Star said. She rolled my whole body front and back, and then announced,

"I am calling on my angels to come for your healing," She lifted her hands and began calling them;

"Angels come forth!" she said. Then she looked at me and said,

"Jean, I never know what will transpire, it is always different in every treatment."

I understood this because that was the way it was with White Feathers treatments.

"I want you to clear your mind and go outside of your body to get to the truth. I will help you."

Star started talking in a language I had never before heard. I closed my eyes after that I could not move or open my eyes again until the session was over. I knew White Feather was with me. While Star was still vocalizing in her unusual language, I saw a magical swirling spaceship with many, many colored lights whirling with little portholes flashing underside. It was round and looked silvery with shinny blinking colored lights under its body.

"Jean, tell me what you see," Star asked.

"I see two white scrolls with nothing on them. They are just floating around in space on the outside of the spaceship,"

"Put the names of the people you know on the scrolls," she said as she was guiding me. Also whatever you want to happen for your life. Take your time, there is no hurry," she said.

I was surprised that I listed 'Marks' name first. I asked that he would quit drinking, smoking, and all his other terrible habits. I realized I listed him first because he needed the most spiritual work and he was still in my heart. Next I listed my clients on the golden trimmed scrolls. Who do you want to put on the scroll?" Star asked.

She then told me to write his name down and all my clients' names and anyone else's name that I wanted good things to happen. I filled these scrolls to capacity. She asked me to include myself and write everything you want to have happen now and in your future.

While the scrolls were still floating around in space I had a vision of a group of women traveling together. The group was called, *Circle of Spirit*, I do not know exactly why I saw them, but I felt I would meet them later as I traveled with White Feathers book and her healing efforts. These women had unique powers and gifts in the healing world. They were different ages and I was one of the three women. I felt I was going to meet them in my future and I would recognize the other two women. Even though it was a vision, never once doubt it.

.I realized my true healing happened by putting Marks name on the scroll. Finally I was about to release it. It made me see all his habits and what he would have to do to change. This gave me a chance to for release because I was out of my body on this high level and looking from this spiritual depth. I felt my healing and my mental blockages gone.

Star removed my mental blockages. She then told me,

"That I would have angels with me for three days to help keep me safe and continue the work she had done." I was overwhelmed with emotions. It seemed like my experience went on for a long time but I really don't know. Then the scrolls rolled up and slowly disappeared. If were if I was in another world and I was.

I still had my eyes closed and I tried to open them, but they seemed to be glued shut and I could not get off the table. It was as if magic held me down. The more I tried, the tighter I was held.

I heard a strange voice say,

"We are not finished with you. When we are done you may get up, but not yet." he said.

I could hardly believe that I had been out in space spinning in a multi-colored spaceship. I believed with all my heart and mind that I had seen that ship. My own healings on many levels had been completed. I whirled and whirled out in space. I wanted to understand the spiritual connections with the spaceship. Those connections with the 'circle of woman,' and the clients I had put on those scrolls. Slowly, I came back to reality and opened my eyes. I could hear Stars' voice, lovely and gentle, telling me to relax as I came back to earth.

"All your blocks about your life have been removed. The people you put on these white scrolls will have their own experiences. I am proud of you. This takes a lot of courage!" Star told me with a gentle look in her eyes.

As I slowly got off White Feather's table it was hard to come back to reality.

I knew the angels and White Feather were with me, and I felt safe.

"I really feel my life will improve much faster because of my blockages being removed and letting go of a lot of my painful past with my boyfriend and the wolf. I did not want the wolf to chase me down in order to bring me back into submission," I said.

"No, I guess not. You have completed you're work with me," Star said.

"I had unlocked and pry things open to see what is inside. I had to use my wits to keep sane. I had fought tooth and nail to get my peace of mind and I had a right to kept it. I had been careless with my deep feelings and I was with people who were antagonistic and aggressive, I had become a "Tigress." In clearing my psyche and my heart. I had cleansed my life of negativity. Knowing that to have a higher consciousness is the way out of the trap of a wolf and the way out of the torture.

"Star, thank you for this healing experience," I said.

"I am glad you understand and accept this healing," Star responded. We hugged each other and both of us had tears gently rolling down our faces. She opened my front door and called to Paul.

"Please, come in and help me pack," Star said. Paul came in my front door and had a loving look on his face. Star and Paul did not live in my town so we told each other our good-byes. We all hugged each other and they both turned and walked out my front door. I stood in my door way and we all waved good-bye. Tears of sadness ran down my face as I closed the front door because I knew I would miss both of then.

"When we receive intuitive "hits" we find ourselves at an important choice part about whether we are going to trust our intuition or dismiss it."

—Sage Bennet—*Science of Mind Magazine*

Chapter Thirty-Five

Psychic Realm

"I wish I could say I could recapture that feeling now at will, but it's not true. However, just the memory of it gave me strength. It's as if I got to "peek" at the next world."

—Joyce Slates *Dallas, Texas*

All the junk is in the psychic, realm but you also have to be gifted with second sight. If you are psychic, it is up to you learn how to fish out the good and come up with a terrific reading. It takes training, to learn how to do this. You need to study and train your third eye in order to become visually intuitive. In going through the levels of the universe an excellent psychic, has to get above, "time" and that is a third-dimensional construct which they get past, all a psychic, has to do is tune into vibrations.

Some of the junk as I call it hides in the realm of the universe and when the energy and vibrations are right, I can bypass the junk and read the highest source or vibration. This power is within each and everyone of us but you need to be careful because there are phonys that want only your money. Be cautious and you can ask for references or some of their history. The rag magazines sometimes have gypsies that advertise that they have power but really do not. They will tell you anything that you want to hear for your money.

I fell into it because of the healing work that I do with White Feather. It is not something I looked for or wanted. It just happened. White Feather told me I do not need to do it all the time because that is where the junk is, but she said sometimes I receive the information because I'm on a higher level and you can cast a line out for a right thought. Psychic, ability can be learned as I mentioned before, if you understand that everything from a thought, to an event, is made of vibrations. So the best clairvoyants, fish the best channels by clearing their own mind of outside activity. I know everything is out there in the psychic, realm and can be known with the right training.

The first time I was aware I could find a missing child was when I was watching the news and learned that an eight year old girl was missing. I prayed for her and then kept following the story. Then, one night I was praying for her and this thought came to my head that I knew where the perpetrator was. I didn't necessarily know where the child was, but I knew where the predator was.

I had an odd feeling and asked White Feather what she wanted me to know. She told me that the predator's door could be seen from the house where the little girl lived. I did not no one what to do with this information. I felt like I could not do anything about it because perhaps I was wrong and I was afraid of being wrong. Also, I was an unknown person in this field. So know one would have listened to me anyway or maybe they would have. I did not have enough faith in my ability.

A few days later the police investigator announced that they had found the molester living about forty feet from the little girl's house and had found her in the closet dead. I felt guilty to the core for doubting White Feather and not taking the risk to help this girl.

This has happened a few other times. Now, I send anonymous e-mails to the parties involved. I just feel this is not my work, but to be with White Feather and do healing is my mission. There are so many psychics out there today that its overwhelming. Some are really good and some are not.

A study I read from the Stanford University showed that even the best psychic are right only eighty-five percent of the time. Most psychics are off in their timing. If you're psychic it is important to stay tuned to your own *intuition*. Do not let yourself be led like a puppy dog. We have our own ability to be insightful and more if we develop our abilities. We all have the ability to be clairvoyants, but it is harder to be objective. I can read someone else, but have difficulty reading myself, there I cannot be objective. Sometimes when I am in meditation I can get something for my future, but not very often. This makes it hard, but now I just say if I am to know, it will be given to me.

I have had people ask me to do readings for them. One time when I called a psychic she asked me if I would like to work for her company. She knew I had developed my third eye. I knew then I did not make up my abilities in the psychic realm, but I could reach in if I wanted to.

When a client is on White Feather's healing table, I often see spirit images or hear information that come to me and she has always been right. For example, I know when my friend was going to meet her husband when he was coming down her path. I even knew his name and about month later she met him. Now they're married.

White Feather also lets me see what a person's condition is and what can happen if they don't take care of it. For example, if Steven, whom I wrote about in my Illusion Chapter, had not stopped smoking I knew he was playing with fire. I am so thankful he listened to White Feather.

Sometimes, I see things that happen that are a bit awkward for me to know. A client of mine was dating and they were planning to get more involved with each other. I had a dream and when I woke up White Feather let me know that this man had herpes and she insisted on me telling my client. I hesitated, but finally told her. When she confronted him he admitted he had herpes and it was true. I am grateful that I embrace the psychic gift, White Feather has given me, but I do not use this gift unless she tells me it is the right timing.

"God moves in a mysterious way
His wonders to perform;
He plants His footsteps in the sea
and rides upon the storm."

—William Cowper

Chapter Thirty-Six

A World Champion

"The outside of a horse is good for the inside of a man."

—*General (name unknown)*

My favorite race horse, Barbaro, died on Monday January 29, 2007 after an eight-month fight to save him from injuries. On May 20th he suffered a life threatening injury at the Preakness in Baltimore. I happened to be watching the race when he stumbled and the jockey Edgar Prado stopped immediately because he felt him wobble and heard his back leg break. He jumped off him and held

Barbaro back until the veterinarian and ambulance could get to him.

Once they arrived, they found he had broken his right hind leg in three places. I just sat in my front room and prayed my heart out to White Feather for her to help him recover. Barbaro had many surgeries and special slings for his leg, but there were complications. The left hind leg, which had not shattered at the Preakness, became implicated.

These were life-threatening injuries. Eight months Barbaro survived. He fought for his life even if he didn't know he was fighting for his life. His great heart and courage inspired people who were not even racing fans. It was like losing a member of the family. My heart and soul went out to Barbaro. What a champion!

I could see his love and innocence and he loved everyone but he just could not stay any longer with us. If it was not for the owners who wanted to gave Barbaro a chance he would have been put down at the race track. People loved Barbaro. People wanted to know how he was doing if he had a good day or a bad one. I prayed everyday for him. People sent flowers and cards to show how much they loved and cared for him. I sent a card of hope from White Feather. People also became more knowledgeable about horses and how fragile thoroughbreds really are.

Barbaro never got better; he just remained the same. The owners gave Barbaro every chance. They gave him eight months of quality life. When it was clear he would not get better they had no choice but to free him of his pain. The struggle ended, as the Kentucky Derby champion from Maryland was put to sleep at the New Bolton Center veterinary hospital.

Barbaro's surgeon, Dr. Dean Richardson, said that in the end, Barbaro's discomfort was too great.

"It was more than we wanted to put him through," Richardson said in a news conference at New Bolton.

"We intensified all pain medication and continued to through this morning, but we couldn't succeed. We were all there. He knew us," Richardson said.

"He was in the sling," he added.

"He was comfortable. He ate his grass. He was alert and aware. It couldn't have been anymore peaceful."

Monday morning there was a sign of laminitis in Barbaro's two front legs.

"We had no other choice, it was a difficult decision to make," Richardson said,

"But it was about his quality of life and whether we had any reasonable expectation of saving him," he said.

"It might be the end of a champion's struggle but for us we have to move forward. In some ways Barbaro was good for the sport country. Of course we wanted him to make it but something good will come out of this because this lifted the consciousness of people who are in the horse world and people who are not."

Barbaro was a very impressive looking horse and his disposition and composure were second to none. He is a champion and a 'star' that will always shine in our hearts. I visualized him running around kicking up his heels and saying,

"I am free at last."

He will miss all of the special people who loved and helped me.

Gretchen Jackson said,

"Grief is the price we all pay for love. I'd like all of us to say a prayer for Barbaro, and I hope we can turn our love into and energy to help all horses throughout the world. I hope each of us will find a path to support the horse."

No location has been decided on for Barbaro's resting place. It could be just a few hundred yards from the scene of his greatest triumph in the Kentucky Derby. Officials at the Kentucky Derby Museum, located on the grounds of Churchill Downs, said,

"We'd be honored if Barbaro were buried in a garden along with four other Derby winners."

I feel the lessons are many. One of the great things that Barbaro did, was he did not give up, but gave it all he had. He did not complain or become embittered. He had too much love in his heart. He loved everyone and loved life. He had a heart full of love and courage. He was a champion of champions.

We will remember Barbaro for his courage and his strength. That is what we can learn from this race horse's short life, to give it our all and be the best we can be. The horse's courageous fight will give us the valor to go on no matter what we are struggling with in our life. God and thousands of people loved Barbaro a champion among champions. We give thanks to Barbaro's courage and his great heart of giving. Barbaro must know that we will never forget him. He made a big impression in our hearts and soul. He's at peace now, frolicking in Heaven with no pain and he must know how much he is loved and missed. Barbaro is a 'star' among all horses shining brilliantly in the Heavens.

"Life tests the deepest qualities within the human personality,
qualities that emerge in heroic combat not merely with others
but also with oneself and with the powers of the universe."

—Thomas Berry

Chapter Thirty-Seven

The Last Encounter

"Winning isn't everything—but wanting to win is."

—Vince Lombardi

After the many, many years of court battles I had gone through now I was going to get my past alimony. My attorney, Adam, did not think so. He informed me that we'll have to use a stronger strategy. He asked me to make an appointment with him which I did. A couple of days later I went to see him.

At the meeting he told me,

"I am going to make a guaranty agreement contract and dot all the I's and cross all the T's. Then I'm going to add the wolf's son to the contract because they are in business together. I'll make sure they cannot back out of the contract. If they try I'll take them to the cleaners and attach the houses they have and also attach the wolf's bank account," he said.

I just sat there in total shock. Adam explained the contract would be expensive but worth it. I trust him completely.

"Go ahead and do it," I said.

"I am calling the wolf's attorney and I am will make sure the attorneys and you, and the wolf and his son all sign. Adam smiled a slow shy smile,

"The wolf secrets his money with a cunning that Jack Benny would envy," Adam said. And then he looked up and our eyes met, I was surprised by the kindness I saw there. Adam looked so gentle, so concerned, I knew I could absolutely trust him. I looked at Adam and a slow smile came across both our faces,

"I'll give you a call when I have the contract completed," he said.

In leaving his office I turned around,

"I have no doubt that you will do this guaranty agreement right. Thank you," I said as I closed the door behind me. Arriving home I called my friend Joy and told her what my attorney was working on.

"Well you have the right spirit and I have seen you in the past get help from above because of your faith," she said.

"Joy, please do not doubt that I will win. See me getting the check and it's in my hands. Please be positive," I said.

"Right now it's not easy for me," she said.

"Well maybe this is why I am asking you because of your situation with your daughter. I remember what your daughter had gone through with her job and I think its' made you nervous. But please don't bring it into our conversation,

"Maybe that's what wrong with me," she admitted,

"All right, for your sake I'll try and be more positive."

"It wasn't like you to be negative, so I picked up on your attitude. I'm glad I called you and now we understand where you were coming from. I know you'll support my attorney while he doing my guaranty agreement. And please, please, pray that I receive the funding," I said.

"I will. It will be just fine. You have a powerful attorney who's backing you," she said.

"Thank you. I knew you would support me. I'll talk to you later." hanging up the telephone. I thought about our telephone call. Yes, it's easy to have doubts but everyone has to fight their demons, yet I had to be stronger and more determined. I got down and prayed to God and White Feather out loud.

"Please do not let me doubt my own faith, knowing that my faith is stronger than my fears," I prayed.

When I went to bed that night, I remembered the torture from the wolf's words,

"You may end up in an alley with your throat slit!" It was hours before I could fall asleep.

"The whole point of being alive is to evolve into the complete person you were intended to be."

—*Oprah Winfrey*

Chapter Thirty-Eight

Great Faith

"Step out in faith and you will reach your dreams."

—White Feather

I would have never been able to get through these last seven years of going through the court system if it had not been for my faith in God. My faith has lifted and sustained me in the times of my great misery. This could have overwhelmed my spirit and feeling sorry for myself could have been the results. Instead the struggles strengthened me. I had faith and a strong well to overcome all difficulties. Through belief in prayer and meditation I received guidance and help from the Heavenly realms. To live my life with purpose I had to be courageous enough to have great faith.

I had confidence in my prayers and through faith prayers are answered. I had a legitimate desire and I knew that my prayer would be fulfilled. I was praying continuously and felt a great joy in my heart. I know my need would be met. God and White Feather were working toward my highest good to be served.

To change your life completely is like going into the unknown darkness but with faith I carried a brightness of my belief in God and White Feather. I am a woman, who has suffered a great deal, but at the same time I have learned my spiritual lessons through grief and great effort. This was a test of life, a trial to have and opportunity to improve myself. I had emotional wounds that were weeping with poison. I had to pray and become peaceful, wise and full of wisdom. I prepared for the worst and expected the best. Suffering is a good teacher of self-discovery.

My life was a series of moments and I could make them magical. I had to take charge of my emotions and through my faith things would turn out for the best. I knew in my heart that God and White Feather were looking out for my highest good to be served. Once my faith was working, my suffering lifted and was replaced with love. One of the greatest books to read is, "The Experience of a Sigh." It is about Karma and I read this passage.

"Life as it is experienced in the present is the result of the accumulated force of all past actions."

The Buddha who was teaching went on to explain what kinds of actions produced which particular results.

"He said that beings who take the lives of others live just a short time. Beings who refrain from killing, experience a long life span. People who cause harm, cause pain to other living things, experience a lot of disease and sickness. Those who practice harmlessness towards others, non-violence, experience good health. While those who are greedy, miserly, experience great poverty. Those who practice generosity, sharing, and open-handedness, experience abundance."

This is the law of cause and effect. Each action produces a certain results. I had to look inside my heart and let go of all attachments and my faith would help me accomplish this. All things are possible with God. White Feather reminded me that she was lifting me with her wings.

Going into my stretching, and reaching mode I protected myself with soul coverage. Faith would win because faith is just as powerful as love. Just because you cannot see faith does not mean it's not there. You cannot see the wind either and it's there so faith is the same way. It touches you like the wind, a gentle breeze across my face. Go by faith not by sight and that is what I was doing even if I had to grit my teeth and hang on for dear life. Sometimes there are many tests that God gave us like he did Job. Maybe this was my greatest test.

In no longer sabotaging myself I deserve love and happiness. From this moment on, all my struggles in life, those which make my life difficult are leaving me because faith had moved my mountain.

I am giving thanks to God for this experience. White Feather would get me through the tough times. My Tigress was alive and well and I had a big roar that could come out any minute if someone tried to take advantage of me. No one better pull this Tigress by the tail. You cannot go through the wringer and not come out a stronger and better person and my awareness was at its peak. I was counting on my angel White Feather and a Bible verse, *"Now, faith is the assurance of things hoped for, the conviction of things not seen."* From Hebrews 11:01.

This was my favorite verse and it helped me during these troublesome times. Just because we cannot see faith it is still working for us and giving us courage to carry on plus never under-estimated the power of prayer.

To consider how I had to go through the tough times and my court cases I could see light at the end of the tunnel. In fighting for my settlement all the good, bad, and ugly came out. I have a great attorney whom I located through prayer and faith. Since my ex-husband fought so hard against our case we had a judgment for a lot of money. He had been found in contempt of court many times and had racked up a lot of court fees with interest and is indebted to me, the court, and my attorney for a lot of money. I was praying for fairness.

Later when I walked into my attorney's office he gave reassurance,

"I am working on the guaranty agreement and it would cost more money but I will see to it the parties could not back out once the guaranty agreement was signed." he said.

In the agreement my attorney, myself, my ex, and his son, and his attorney had to sign the agreement. Well everyone signed the guaranty agreement and they had a year to get the settlement together and it had to be in my hands by January 7, 2006. I was praying with confidence that this was going to happen. My attorney and I had made a great effort. It has been seven years that this financial merry-go-around with my ex-husband had been going on. Now it was time for action.

Finally, I had a settlement offer and this court battle was coming to an end. At my last court meeting my attorney said,

"You have to get that man out of your life."

What the heck did he think I was trying to do? I had to put my past behind me before I could move forward into my future. You can't use the past to fill in what's missing in the present. I knew my best revenge was to burn my ex-husband by looking hot and living well. I was really not into revenge but after all the heartache and court procedures I might as well let my tigress smell the triumphant.

During 2006 I had no alimony coming so I just had to wait for my settlement. I was working on my manuscript the entire time. I was putting my expectations into my book and it was on the stove of hope. My book was my big investment into my future. This was learning to draw on my spiritual bank account. Everything I had was an expression of Spirit and was manifesting according to God. I would get through this and come out a winner, and I just knew in my heart that prayers are heard and answered.

I wanted to make a difference. I had battled for my freedom thru the court system and now my faith would put me out in front. I had already fought for my freedom and paid the price.

On January 6, 2006 a friend of mine, Karen, called me and asked,

"Did you get your settlement? I have been praying for you," she said.

"No, not yet," I said. It was raining cats and dogs outside. We were talking and she asked,

"May we pray now?"

"Yes, let's pray," she said.

As we were praying I heard a knock at my door.

"Someone's at my door. I'll be right back." I put the telephone down on my bed and walked to my front door. I opened my door and standing there all wet with rain drops dripping from his post office hat was my mailman.

"I have a registered letter that you have to sign for," he said as he handed me the document. He had a pen with him. I signed the card. I walked back into my bedroom and picked up my telephone.

"That was the postman," I told her. I noticed in the corner was the wolf's son's name.

"Could it be my settlement?" I asked nervously and started praying.

"Open the letter," she said excitedly.

I opened the letter and when I saw what it said, the letter almost flew out of my hands. Inside was a check for the full amount of my settlement.

"Oh, my God I got my settlement," I shriek, by then I was shaking with enthusiasm.

"That is wonderful. I am so glad for you," she ecstatically told me.

"I' am overwhelmed and I thank God, White Feather and my attorney and all my friends for praying for me. That's the reason I received my settlement," I shouted.

"This is going to make a difference in my life and help finish White Feather's book. It's very expensive to get a book on the market," I said.

"Well I am so glad this is over and now you can go on with you life," she said.

"Yes," I am so happy and I feel a big load has been lifted from my shoulders," I said.

"Well it has and good luck," she told me.

We said our good-byes on the telephone and we both hung up. I just sat there on my bed with a big smile on my face thanked God and White Feather and then I called my wonderful attorney and told him of the good news.

"They better have sent your settlement check," was what he said to me.

"Thank you for everything," I told him. Tears were stinging my eyes. I knew that my life was in a transformation and that I had planted seeds of faith. Now I could go out and serve God with White Feather guidance.

My new life was just beginning, and receiving my guaranty agreement check I had no more threats from the Hungry Wolf. Winning the guaranty agreement felt great. I knew that my faith, God and White Feather had seen me through this turbulent time. The tigress came out and leaped on the wolf, and she had dinner. I would never again pick a wolf for my partner. Lifting up the guaranty agreement check in my hot little hands I thanked everyone involved. My prayers had been answered and faith had seen me through.

"Where there is no vision the people perish."

—Proverbs 29:18

Chapter Thirty-Nine

The Vision

"My future is firmly in front of me."

—Author and White Feather

To the many deserving citizens, physically challenged public, and youth of the Mendocino Coast, I dedicate this vision of a healing ranch and health resort. Through God's guidance I feel a compelling need to share my personal dream and vision with a very select group of dedicated people moved by the same spirit that is moving me, those willing to step forward and work together with me in transforming this dream into a well-structured reality.

When I took my first pony ride as a small child the feeling was so extraordinary I knew that it would remain with me the rest of my life. My interest in animals of the four legged kind has occupied an important niche in my life ever since those early childhood years.

My dream of owning a horse came true; Misty Moonlight was with me for many years. She was a striking mare and I was not informed at the time of purchase that she had hardly any training. Thus, out of necessity, the two of us became acquainted as trainer and pupil. Over the past several years my wonderful mare and I have shared many exciting experiences together. We progressed through the horse shows placing from sixth to first place. Through the mutual effort of private lessons and hard work, a good portion of my initial desire has been fulfilled. Yet, White Feather continues to encourage me to keep going and believe in the vision that was given to me.

It was a sunny day and soft billowing clouds were in the sky. On top of the clouds I saw this vision of a healing ranch that would bring healings and happiness to the community. It was real and powerful and I knew in God's time it would come true.

I began to steer my thoughts toward disabled children and youth who needed guidance in their life. I began to feel an over powering urge to introduce the disabled to the world of horsemanship and horse therapy. Any youth that is lost in spirit can have a rewarding healing through animals, especially horses.

'The outside of a horse is good for the inside of a man.' These words were written by a General during World War II. I want to be able to share my deep feelings for horses and give the handicapped child a glimpse of the world from a different perspective—to give that young person a new incentive that will encourage personal growth and establish confidence and be an inspiration to accept the challenges as they progress along the road of life.

Many years ago I recall reading an article in the newspaper about a handicapped girl confined to a wheel chair who was taking riding lessons. One day upon arriving for her lesson she was informed by her instructor that there would be no lesson today because her pony was sick. This was a very special child who never had communicated through the spoken word before. The little girl was visibly upset and determined to visit her sick pony. She hurriedly struggled her way to the barn where the pony was kept. She wheeled herself into her pony's stall, lifted herself out of her wheel chair and threw her arms around the pony's neck and spoke her first words ever, "My pony, my pony." The mystical connection between the love of child for a horse and the horses returned love is an entity that the human mind struggles to comprehend.

"The Law of Attraction is always in action."

—Science of Mind

Chapter Forty

Angel Ranch and Health Center

"One of life's most fulfilling moments occurs in that split-second when the familiar is suddenly trans-formed into the dazzling aura of the profoundly new."

—Edward B. Lindaman
—*Thinking in the Future Tense*

The growing need for a holistic ranch with hypnotherapy for physically challenged people is a facility that the city community of the Mendocino Coast, will embrace. Over the past many years I have been continually inspired by my mounting vision of this facility and where it will be located.

The vision I had in the early summer of the late 1980 I will never forget. As I looked into the blue clouds above my head they were bursting with vision. At first I could not believe what I was seeing at that time then I got into the spirit of the apparition. According to my vision and understanding, this will, be a very unique place, an inland coastal setting, with redwoods, huckleberry, rhododendrons, protected from the chilling coastal winds, and just beyond the fog belt—a warn and nurturing place where growth and understanding thrive.

Through my mind's eye, I see the structures as rustic in nature, focusing on a central lodge with a massive native stone fireplace, which would be an assembly point with an "A" frame profile. There

290   The Hungry Heart

will be several neat rustic cabins in a wooded setting. Nearby will be a series of hookups for RVs to accommodate those who bring their own camping set-ups.

There will be two, possibly three arenas for training, warming up and riding with special features to facilitate the needs of the physically challenged and children who need to be spiritually lifted. The horse facilities will continue the rustic wood theme and will be constructed to utilize the best of the natural features of the terrain and specifically for the convenience and welfare of the student rider. This will probably be the first ride of most students. Their spirits will be uplifted and the healing will have begun through the students' love of the horse and the admiration of both.

The people involved, instructors, management, students and guests, will find this a place of great inspiration and personal growth. As this project unfolds, I see it evolving in three-phases.

PHASE I: The genesis phase: getting the project in motion, securing the proper site, construction of basic facilities, training personnel, securing the right horses, adequately insuring the facility, generating sufficient starting capital, and of most importance, bringing horse and rider together to initiate therapy. This will expand as the years go by.

PHASE 2: First growth phase, expansion. Develop riding trails according to the needs of the riders, confidence builders; each trail will be distinctive in that it will place special emphasis on certain muscle groups and types of body motion. This phase will seek out more community involvement, such as Boy and Girl Scouts, 4-H Club participation, other youth groups as well as schools and senior citizens. The beginning of our holistic health dream will get under way. Organic fruits and vegetables will be grown for and by the physically challenged or anyone interested in this activity. Contact with farm animals will be emphasized as part of the therapy process. At this state I would like to see a non-denominational Chapel constructed as a place for prayer and contemplation where God and man can find the quiet to communicate.

PHASE 3: In this phase I hope to see an on-site physical therapist and a clinic for volunteers from the medical community who would apply their talents to the holistic health approach. Included in this medical team should be an acupuncturist, acupressure, healing massage therapist, specialist, herbalist and a chiropractor—all who champion the belief in evaluation and treating internal and external medical problems in terms of the whole functioning being.

I would like to see this ranch become a beacon for the physically challenged and youth who have been spiritually damaged where hope never dies, and where determination and belief in self reach new heights in mind, body, and spirit. With Gods' help and White Feathers guidance I hope to see the day when this facility will become training, center for the Special Olympics and the opportunity for the youth to be healed and receive a new image of who they really are.

At this very moment I know that this ranch is White Feathers' dream of a richer tomorrow for humans. I know that she is a real gift that has been given to me and I intend to enjoy her and help others know about her and learn to trust her. I know White Feather is real and has a heart as big as the universe. I am continuing to work with her and I know within, nothing is more important.

White Feather's guidance is showing me the way to true fulfillment of the heart and the success will follow. The ranch will be real and no longer a dream. Dreams do come true. All things are possible with God. I salute her with my heart and soul. Thank you White Feather I want to express my love and loyalty. I never will take you for granted. I knew White Feathers' wings were supporting my every achievement because without her I would not be able to do her healing work. I am blessed for knowing her because her spirit soars with the eagles. White Feather is the wind beneath my wings.

◆   ◆   ◆

We have come to the end of this journey together. I seek to make this world a better place. I want to make a difference in the needed areas of your life, in finding purpose, growing spiritually, or finding faith, for the first time.

Together, we can be a powerful driving force that will transform the world and ultimately heal the planet. Please take the first baby step and I'll see you in the light. If you like to order my book at $19.95 US plus shipping and handling. My CD is $7.00 plus shipping handling of $1.11. Not including book.

Mail the money order (no personal checks) for your C.D to: Jean R. Cane, Post Office Box 356, Fort Bragg, California 95437 My C.D. is inspiring and will help people meditate and relax.

Postal envelope is $1.09. Please include your pacific prayer request or how the book has helped you.

Also there is a website for abused animals from the ASPCA which is: www.myaspca.org and their phone number is: 1-888-776-0111 for $18.00 dollars a month you can save an abused animal. It's wonderful what the ASPCA is doing for our beloved animals. It is up to us to save the animals on this planet including the endangered species. We must live our life by faith not by sight.

Thank you,

Jean Cane/author

◆   ◆   ◆

Dear Friend,

If you are interested in helping fund my vision and become a partner, I invite you to join me as a spiritual partner in the vision of the Angel Ranch, a holistic center, and an equine therapy facility. This will be a new kind of nonprofit organization with programs which are designed to help heal and give anyone a fresh start in life. We are all each others angels and must act accordingly to help each other. If you'd like to become a partner in the Angel Ranch Foundation (write me @ post office box 356, Fort Bragg, Ca.95437) we are looking for major investors. I am praying for two major partners. Please contact me through our web site at http://www.Angel-Ranch.org (pending but will be done soon) or if you want to buy my book, "*The Hungry Heart*," and get your song of White Feathers Heart CD for $7.00 plus shipping and handling, it is available. Thank you.

I look forward to hearing from you. I believe that my vision will come true.

Blessings,

Jean R. Cane

About the Author

Jean Cane is a person who truly believes in her healing ability through White Feather her spiritual guide. She met White Feather in a dream in 1992 from there her life changed completely because of her healing massage through White Feather.

Prior to meeting White Feather, Jean worked in the health industry for many years as a Licensed Vocational nurse. Then, following her desire to teach, she attended classes at the College of the Redwoods receiving her associate degree in teaching in 1991. Jean studied metaphysics through Church of Religious Science from 1992–2005. She has combined her love of teaching and her strong grasp of metaphysical concepts to create a series of inspiring lectures on personal growth, which she offers to community clubs and organizations. She self-published her first book, *The Hungry Heart*, in 2007. She is currently working on her second book in this series—*Reflections of the Heart*.